D0369015

ROMANS

Books in the PREACHING THE WORD Series:

MARK, VOLUME ONE:
Jesus, Servant and Savior

MARK, VOLUME TWO:
Jesus, Servant and Savior

COLOSSIANS AND PHILEMON:
The Supremacy of Christ

EPHESIANS:
The Mystery of the Body of Christ

ROMANS
Righteousness from Heaven

P R E A C H I N G   T H E   W O R D

ROMANS

Righteousness from Heaven

R. Kent Hughes

CROSSWAY BOOKS • WHEATON, ILLINOIS
A DIVISION OF GOOD NEWS PUBLISHERS

Romans.

Copyright © 1991 by R. Kent Hughes.

Published by Crossway Books, a division of
Good News Publishers, Wheaton, Illinois 60187.

Cover banner: Marge Gieser

Photo of author taken by Paul Toht

First printing, 1991

Printed in the United States of America

Unless otherwise noted, all Bible quotations are taken from *Holy Bible: New
International Version*, copyright © 1978 by the New York International Bible Society.
Used by permission of Zondervan Bible Publishers.

Library of Congress Cataloging-in-Publication Data
Hughes, R. Kent.
   Romans : righteousness from heaven / R. Kent Hughes
      p.   cm. — (Preaching the word)
   Includes bibliographical references and indexes.
   1. Bible. N.T. Romans—Commentaries. 2. Bible. N.T.
Romans—Meditations. I. Title. II. Title: Romans, righteousness
from heaven. III. Series: Huges, R. Kent. Preaching the word.
BS2665.3H78 1991   227'.107—dc20   90-49412
ISBN 0-89107-524-0

99		98		97		96										
15	14	13	12	11	10	9	8	7	6	5	4	3	2			

To
Robert "Romans" Seelye

For in the gospel
a righteousness from God is revealed,
a righteousness that is by faith from first to last,
just as it is written,
"The righteous will live by faith."

(Romans 1:17)

Table of Contents

Acknowledgments

I must express appreciation to my secretary, Mrs. Sharon Fritz, for her patience and care in typing the manuscript of these studies; also to Mrs. Peggy Wick for her careful typing of the manuscript onto computer, Mr. Herbert Carlburg for his cheerful, weekly proofreading, Mr. Brian Hoch for bibliographical research, and Rev. Jeff Buikema, pastor of Covenant Presbyterian Church, LaCrosse, Wisconsin, for his reading of the manuscript and helpful suggestions. Lastly, special thanks to Mr. Ted Griffin, Managing Editor of Crossway Books, for his expertise and repeated kindnesses.

A Word to Those Who
Preach the Word

There are times when I am preaching that I have especially sensed the pleasure of God. I usually become aware of it through the unnatural silence. The ever-present coughing ceases and the pews stop creaking, bringing an almost physical quiet to the sanctuary — through which my words sail like arrows. I experience a heightened eloquence, so that the cadence and volume of my voice intensify the truth I am preaching.

There is nothing quite like it — the Holy Spirit filling one's sails, the sense of his pleasure, and the awareness that something is happening among one's hearers. This experience is, of course, not unique, for thousands of preachers have similar experiences, even greater ones.

What has happened when this takes place? How do we account for this sense of his smile? The answer for me has come from the ancient rhetorical categories of *logos, ethos,* and *pathos.*

The first reason for his smile is the *logos* — in terms of preaching, God's Word. This means that as we stand before God's people to proclaim his Word, we have done our homework. We have exegeted the passage, mined the significance of its words in their context, and applied sound hermeneutical principles in interpreting the text so that we understand what its words meant to its hearers. And it means that we have labored long until we can express in a sentence what the theme of the text is — so that our outline springs from the text. Then our preparation will be such that as we preach, we will not be preaching our own thoughts about God's Word, but God's actual Word, his *logos.* This is fundamental to pleasing him in preaching.

The second element in knowing God's smile in preaching is *ethos* — what you are as a person. There is a danger endemic to preaching, which is having your hands and heart cauterized by holy things. Phillips Brooks illustrated it by the analogy of a train conductor who comes to believe that he has been to the places he announces because of his long and loud heralding of them. And that is why Brooks insisted that preaching must be "the bringing of truth through personality." Though we can never *perfectly* embody the truth we preach, we must be subject to it, long for it, and make it as much a part of our ethos as possible. As the Puritan William Ames said, "Next to the Scriptures, nothing makes a sermon more to pierce, than when it comes out of the inward affection of the heart without any affectation." When a preacher's ethos backs up his *logos*, there will be the pleasure of God.

Last, there is *pathos* — personal passion and conviction. David Hume, the Scottish philosopher and skeptic, was once challenged as he was seen going to hear George Whitefield preach: "I thought you do not believe in the gospel." Hume replied, "I don't, but *he does*." Just so! When a preacher believes what he preaches, there will be passion. And this belief and requisite passion will know the smile of God.

The pleasure of God is a matter of *logos* (the Word), *ethos* (what you are), and *pathos* (your passion). As you *preach the Word* may you experience his smile — the Holy Spirit in your sails!

R. Kent Hughes
Wheaton, Illinois

ROMANS

Paul, a servant of Christ Jesus, called to be an apostle and set apart for the gospel of God — the gospel he promised beforehand through his prophets in the Holy Scriptures regarding his Son, who as to his human nature was a descendant of David, and who through the Spirit of holiness was declared with power to be the Son of God by his resurrection from the dead: Jesus Christ our Lord. Through him and for his name's sake, we received grace and apostleship to call people from among all the Gentiles to the obedience that comes from faith. And you also are among those who are called to belong to Jesus Christ. To all in Rome who are loved by God and called to be saints: Grace and peace to you from God our Father and from the Lord Jesus Christ. (1:1-7)

1
Introducing Paul to Rome

ROMANS 1:1-7

No reasonable person would dispute that the book of Romans is one of the most powerful and influential books ever written. The epistle of Paul to the Romans has been the written force behind some of the most significant conversions of church history. St. Augustine, the most brilliant theologian of the early centuries, came to conviction of sin and salvation after reading some verses from the thirteenth chapter. Martin Luther recovered the doctrine of salvation by faith from his study of Romans 1:17 and went on to lead the Protestant Reformation. While listening to the reading of Luther's preface to the book of Romans, John Wesley felt his heart "strangely warmed" in conversion and became the catalyst of the great evangelical revival of the eighteenth century. John Bunyan was so inspired as he studied the great themes of Romans in the Bedford jail that he wrote the immortal *Pilgrim's Progress*. In our own century, while we may not always agree with his theology, Karl Barth's arguments from the book of Romans devastated liberal Christianity.

There is no doubt about the power of the book of Romans. The study of it produces genuine excitement and genuine trepidation — excitement because of the possibilities the life-changing themes of Romans bring to us, and trepidation at reasonably expounding their massiveness. I would invite each reader to offer the following prayer as we begin the study of this great book.

Father, I know that a humble spirit is indispensable to learning. And
I pray that as I now consider the themes of Romans — so great, so

history-changing, and sometimes so familiar — that through the
study of them you will give me a spirit of humility, that I will be con-
stantly learning even from the familiar. I pray that the power that
was exhibited in the lives of Augustine, Luther, Wesley, and so many
others — that power which comes from understanding the funda-
mental doctrines of the faith and appropriating them in life — will
be seen in me. Give me a continued spirit of humility. May I continue
in prayer throughout this study. May your blessing rest upon my life.
I pray this in Jesus' name, Amen.

Paul begins his letter with an introduction which is longer than
usual. It is also more theological and personal than any of his other epis-
tles' introductions. The apostle is tremendously concerned that the
Roman people receive what he has to say — that they not "turn him off"
before they have read his arguments. Thus, he reveals himself and his theology, hoping that if they understand something of who he is and what
he believes, they will give him a hearing.

The importance of this for us comes from the well-known fact that
how a person perceives himself determines largely how he or she will act.
A healthy self-perception tends to produce a healthy approach to life. I
recently read of a second-grader in Tennessee who submitted an essay
entitled "My Face" to his teacher. It read: "My face has two brown eyes.
It has a nose and two cheeks. And two ears and a mouth. I like my face.
I'm glad my face is just like it is. It is not bad, it is not good, but just
right." That is terrific! Now Paul introduces us to his own healthy,
dynamic life view which, if appropriated, can produce power in us. As
we go through his introduction in verses 1-7, we are going to see:

    I. Paul's view of himself (v. 1)
    II. Paul's view of preaching (vv. 2-4)
    III. Paul's view of his commission (v. 5)
    IV. Paul's view of the Roman believers (and us) (vv. 6, 7)

Paul's introduction introduces us to deeper and more productive
levels of spiritual life.

PAUL'S VIEW OF HIMSELF (v. 1)

First, in verse 1 Paul describes himself as "Paul, a servant of Christ Jesus,
called to be an apostle and set apart for the gospel of God." In just one sentence he capsulizes his self-perception to his Roman hearers. That he intro-

duces himself as a "servant" (*doulos*) is very significant. He could have introduced himself as "Paul, an eminent theologian, master of the Old Testament Scriptures, front-line warrior, brilliant of intellect," but he chooses *doulos*. Paul was well aware that to the Romans this was an abject, servile term. However, he also knew that the Jews viewed it as a title of great honor when attached to God. Paul has both views in mind — and both were glorious to him. Elsewhere (1 Corinthians 4:1) he refers to his slavery with another word, one used of the lowest galley slave.

So we see that the key to Paul's self-image is servanthood. At the root of his psyche this incredibly productive man views himself primarily as a slave of Christ. No matter who we are — pastor, teacher, office worker, corporation president — if we are to be productive for God, we must be servants—"For even the Son of Man did not come to be served, but to serve" (Mark 10:45).

The next facet of his self-perception is that he sees himself as "called to be an apostle." In Galatians 1:15-17 Paul describes how he persecuted the Church before he was a Christian, and then says,

> But when God, who set me apart from birth and called me by his grace, was pleased to reveal his Son in me so that I might preach him among the Gentiles . . . I went. . . .

Paul was not self-appointed! God called him! How essential this was to Paul's ongoing service. Whenever things got rough, he could always reflect upon the evidence of his election: God had summoned him. Therefore, he understood that difficult circumstances did not come because he had wrongly appointed himself as an apostle, but because God had appointed him and he was being faithful. At the base of Paul's self-perception was the fact that his lifework was God's doing. What a comfort — what a motivation!

Closely following, and completing, his self-concept is the final phrase, "set apart for the gospel of God." The word translated "set apart" has the same root as the word "Pharisee." In fact, the Greek sounds very much the same. A Pharisee set himself apart for the Law, but God set Paul apart for the gospel. He was a Pharisee of the highest order. "Fashioned of the same stuff as all other men, a stone differing in no way from other stones, yet in his relation to God — and in this only — he is unique."[1] Paul saw himself as uniquely separated for the preaching of the Good News.

How would Paul answer the question, who are you? "I am Paul, a bond-servant of Christ, called as an apostle, set apart for the gospel of God

— that is who I am." Sometimes pandemonium broke loose around him, and he could have easily felt like a speck of flotsam on the tide — but he did not! He was sustained by his call as an apostle. He was set apart for the Good News. Above all, he was a *doulos*. He knew who he was!

Next, how did Paul view his task of preaching the gospel?

PAUL'S VIEW OF PREACHING (vv. 2-4)

Verses 1 and 2, taken together, reveal that Paul saw his preaching as being an extension of the ancient Old Testament message:

> Paul, a servant of Christ Jesus, called to be an apostle and set apart
> for the gospel of God — the gospel he promised beforehand through
> his prophets in the Holy Scriptures.

His task was not to proclaim a theological novelty. The gospel was in the Old Testament Scriptures. Paul longed to announce "that Christ died for our sins according to the [Old Testament] Scriptures" (1 Corinthians 15:3). So much of Messiah was revealed in the Old Testament. Who would Jesus' mother be? A virgin. Of what house was he to be? Of David. Where would he be born? Bethlehem. What name would he be given? Immanuel. What death would be his? The cross — piercing the body without breaking his bones. Where? At Jerusalem, outside the city.[2] Paul's task was rooted as far back as the Garden of Eden, the patriarchs, and the prophets.

According to verses 3 and 4 his task was to preach that Christ was both *human* and *divine*. Verse 3 stresses Christ's humanity by avowing that: "as to his human nature [he] was a descendant of David." The Greek here is *ek spermatos*, from the very seed of David — thus emphasizing his intense humanity. Jesus was a man. He was not play-acting.

Verse 4 equally stresses his divinity by saying, "and who through the Spirit [or his *spirit*] of holiness was declared with power to be the Son of God by his resurrection from the dead."

The story is told that a certain M. Lepeau complained to Talleyrand that a new religion of his — one he considered a great improvement over Christianity — had failed to catch on with the people. He asked Talleyrand for some suggestions. Talleyrand dryly said, "M. Lepeau, to insure success for your new religion, all you need do is have yourself crucified and then rise from the dead on the third day!" The resurrection "declared" that Jesus was the Son of God. The Greek word is very helpful in getting the force of the idea because it is related to our English word *horizon*, "the boundary between heaven and earth." God's mighty deed in raising Jesus from the dead "horizoned" him — that is, it clearly marked out Jesus as the divine Son. Paul's entire view was dominated by Christ as the Son of God.[3]

But it must also be noted in verse 4 that Paul says it was not only the Resurection which declared Christ's divinity, but it was also substantiated "Through the Spirit [or, his *spirit*] of holiness" — that is, the holiness of his human nature. James Denny put it this way: ". . . the sonship, which was declared by the resurrection, corresponded to . . . the spirit of holiness which was the deepest reality in the Person and life of Jesus."[4] The Resurrection verified with power that Christ's perfect life came from his being divine. Paul wanted the Romans to know that his task in sharing the Good News was to preach that Jesus, in accord with the ancient Scriptures, was the resurrected human/divine Savior.

Here Paul's life and task come together. He is appointed by God, he is divinely set apart, he is above all a servant — and his message is "horizoned" before him by the resurrection of Jesus who was both human and divine. The entire sky is filled with this reality. It is this vision which drives Paul to such supreme heights of service.

We have seen Paul's view of himself in verse 1, then his view of his task in verses 2-4, and now we come to his view of his power and commission in verses 5, 6.

PAUL'S VIEW OF HIS COMMISSION (v. 5)

How does Paul perceive his commission? Largely as a matter of *grace*. He says in verse 5: "Through him and for his name's sake, we received grace and apostleship to call people from among all the Gentiles to the obedience that comes from faith." Here Paul means grace in the widest sense of God's favor — that is, salvation, guidance, wisdom, illumination, and power to serve. Grace is always an amazing thing to Paul, as we see later in Romans: "where sin increased, grace increased all the more" (5:20). The grace of God is infinite and eternal. It has no beginning and no end. Karl Barth said, "Only when grace is recognized to be incomprehensible is it grace."[5] If we think we understand God's love and grace, we are probably without it. Paul views his apostleship and ministry to the Gentiles as the overflow of God's mysterious grace to him.

Everything came from God! "*I the brook, thou the spring.*"[6]

Paul has told the Romans what he wants them to know about himself. He is a servant. He is God-appointed, not self-appointed. He is separated out for the gospel. His entire horizon, the very atmosphere of his life, is dominated with the resurrected human-superhuman Christ. And finally he sees his commission and apostolic power in terms of incomprehensible grace.

Paul's view of himself made all the difference in the world. In fact, it has been making a difference in the world for 2,000 years. What would we be like if we saw ourselves as God-owned, our task as preaching the resurrected Christ, and everything in life as a matter of grace?

OUR VIEW OF OURSELVES (vv. 6, 7)

So much for Paul's self-concept and divine commission. Now, as he closes his introduction in verses 6, 7, he gives his view of the believers in Rome, which suggests how they should regard themselves and how we should regard ourselves. "And you also are among those who are called to belong to Jesus Christ. To all in Rome who are loved by God and called to be saints: Grace and peace to you from God our Father and from the Lord Jesus Christ." There are three applications of this verse to us. First, we are "loved by God." Paul does not mention the believer's love for God, but rather that which is far more fundamental — God's love for the believer.

Sometimes I like to recount how much I am loved by thinking of John 3:16 (KJV) in this way:

> *For God* — The greatest Lover
> *so loved*— The greatest degree
> *the world,* — The greatest company
> *that he gave* — The greatest act
> *his only begotten Son,* — The greatest gift
> *that whosoever* — The greatest opportunity
> *believeth* — The greatest simplicity
> *in him* — The greatest attraction
> *should not perish,* — The greatest promise
> *but* — The greatest difference
> *have* — The greatest certainty
> *everlasting life* — The greatest possession.

Fellow believers, we are loved by God! We need to get used to this, but we should never get over it.

Second, we are "called to be saints." How is this possible? We are not

20

called because we are saints, but we are saints because we are called. And as saints we are set apart for holiness. Thus, we are in continuity with the saints of all the centuries and are in continuity and unity with each other.

Lastly, we are recipients of "grace" and "peace." Paul says, "Grace and peace to you from God our Father and from the Lord Jesus Christ." This greeting bears the poetry of redemption, for the regular Greek greeting was "Rejoice!" (*chaire*), and the regular Jewish greeting was "Peace" (Hebrew *shalom,* Greek *eiriene*). But here Paul combines the two, and then replaces rejoice (*chaire*) with the similar sounding but far richer *charis*—"grace." He in effect combines the greetings of the Eastern and Western worlds, then modifies the Western and gives the whole world the sublime Christian greeting, "Grace and peace." The two combine naturally and beautifully in cause and effect, because when God's grace comes upon us, taking away our sins and making us objects of his favor, his peace floods our being.

We have seen how Paul's self-perception — his image of himself, his task, and his commission and power — made the difference in how he lived his life. Would to God that we would have this same self-perception and know the same fire.

But whether we ascend to his level or not, there is a self-view that all believers of all ages have embraced and which we joyously embrace:

> *We are loved of God,*
> *We are saints,*
> *We are objects of his grace and unending favor,*
> *His peace is ours*
> *Forever.*

First, I thank my God through Jesus Christ for all of you, because your faith is being reported all over the world. God, whom I serve with my whole heart in preaching the gospel of his Son, is my witness how constantly I remember you in my prayers at all times; and I pray that now at last by God's will the way may be opened for me to come to you. I long to see you so that I may impart to you some spiritual gift to make you strong — that is, that you and I may be mutually encouraged by each other's faith. I do not want you to be unaware, brothers, that I planned many times to come to you (but have been prevented from doing so until now) in order that I might have a harvest among you, just as I have had among the other Gentiles. I am obligated both to Greeks and non-Greeks, both to the wise and the foolish. That is why I am so eager to preach the gospel also to you who are at Rome. I am not ashamed of the gospel, because it is the power of God for the salvation of everyone who believes: first for the Jew, then for the Gentile. For in the gospel a righteousness from God is revealed, a righteousness that is by faith from first to last, just as it is written: "The righteous will live by faith." (1:8-17)

2

Paul's Motivation
for Ministry

ROMANS 1:8-17

Whard hen my family visited Park Street
Church recently, I made it a point to look for a bronze plaque bearing the
inscription, "Joseph S. Olzewski S.K. 2/c U.S.C. Lost February 3, 1943
North Atlantic." I did this because of a remarkable personal experience that
Allan Emery relates in his book *A Turtle on a Fencepost*. The day after
Pearl Harbor, Emery, like thousands of others, enlisted — his choice being
the Coast Guard. He was immediately put to work in his hometown,
Boston, as a quartermaster, and he was given the Friday night duty of
guarding one of the wharfs. On one particular Friday he had wisely decided
to get some sleep before duty and was in his bunk resting when one of his
new acquaintances, Joseph Olzewski, came by in immaculate dress blues
— his hat squared, piping on his snow-white cuffs, his shoes spit-shined.
He gave his biggest smile and asked Emery how he looked. Emery replied
that he looked great and asked what the big event was. Joe excitedly
explained that at the USO the previous night a wealthy girl had invited him
to spend the weekend at her apartment on Beacon Hill. She was going to
take him to the opera that night and had plenty of records and alcohol. He
didn't have to be back until 0700 Monday morning. He ended the story by
saying, "This is going to be the greatest time of my life." Emery replied that
he would be praying for him. His friend walked out but immediately reen-
tered asking, "What did you say?"

"I said I'd be praying for you," replied Emery.

"Why will you be praying for me when I'm going to have the first great weekend in my life?"

"Because, Joe, Monday morning you'll be back aboard ship and you will not be the same person you are tonight. Sin leaves its mark."

Joe swore at Emery and went out into the night.

Emery prayed for Joe as he prepared for guard duty. And he was startled when an unsmiling and agitated Joe suddenly reappeared in the guard post floodlights.

"How can you have a good time when someone's praying for you?" he said. "You've ruined my weekend. I stood up my date, and I've been waiting until you came on duty. Now tell me how to find God."

That night Joseph S. Olzewski heard for the very first time in his life the promises of God — and he believed. The change was immediate. He joined Park Street Church, spent his free time on the Common inviting other servicemen to services, prayed with his buddies at St. Paul's Cathedral which was always open, and grew in his knowledge of the Scriptures under Dr. Harold Ockenga. Then on February 1, 1943 he volunteered for sea duty on a mine sweeper headed for Iceland, and just a few days out of New York a torpedo found its mark.[1]

Stories like this motivate me! They have a way of clearing the fog away and allowing those things which are truly important to appear. My feelings are something like Snoopy in a Peanuts cartoon. Linus had just thrown a stick for Snoopy to retrieve. His first instinct was to chase the stick. But he paused a few moments and decided against it. "I want people to have more to say about me after I'm gone than 'He was a nice guy . . . he chased sticks.'" When I am reminded of the gospel's power to change lives, I am motivated to stop "chasing sticks" and get back to what is really important.

That is how the concluding verses (8-17) of Paul's introduction to the book of Romans affect me, because in them he describes what is behind his own burning motivation to minister at Rome. They encourage us to "go for it."

In verses 8-10 Paul writes that he had heard of the Romans' faith and its widespread fame. This prompted him to make unceasing requests to visit the Christians in Rome. In verses 11-17 he gets down to the specifics of his motivation. First (in verses 11-13), there is the motivation which springs from the prospect of mutual encouragement. Second, in verses 14 and 15 there is the motivation which comes from a sense of obligation. Third (vv. 16, 17), there is the motivation which grows from his confidence in the power of the gospel. As we examine these, we will see that they intensify so that the final motivation (his confidence in the gospel's power) is by far the supreme driving force behind his ministry. As we examine this text, we need to keep in the back of our minds that everyone can enlarge his or her spiritual vision by internalizing the elements of Paul's motivation to minister to Rome.

PAUL'S FIRST MINISTRY MOTIVATION: MUTUAL ENCOURAGEMENT (vv. 11, 12)

To begin with, as verse 11 indicates, Paul simply wants to help them: "I long to see you so that I may impart to you some spiritual gift to make you strong." Paul is not sure what gift or gifts he might impart because he has not been to Rome. He simply wishes to enhance their spirituality. Paul said almost the same thing to the church in Corinth: "what I want is not your possessions but you" (2 Corinthians 12:14). He is not in it for what he could do for himself, but what he could do for them.

Paul's spirit was for all practical purposes duplicated in the life of General Booth, founder of the Salvation Army. Once when General Booth stood before Queen Victoria and she asked what she might do for him, the rugged old man replied, "Your Majesty, some people's passion is money, and some people's passion is fame, but my passion has been men."

However, Paul also knows that the benefit would be mutual, as he goes on to say in verse 12, "that is, that you and I may be mutually encouraged by each other's faith." The apostle claims that the faith of these beginners will encourage him! The Apostle John experienced the same thing:

> We proclaim to you what we have seen and heard, so that you also may have fellowship with us. And our fellowship is with the Father and with his Son, Jesus Christ. We write this to make our joy complete. (1 John 1:3, 4)

Had someone other than a humble and experienced John or Paul written this, they would have said, "And these things we write, so that *your* joy may be made complete." But John and Paul knew that very few things will strengthen an older believer's faith more than the vibrant faith of a new believer. On the flipside, there is little that will benefit a new believer more than exposure to the mature faith of a more experienced brother or sister in Christ.

What an example this first element of mutual encouragement is to us! I am sure that when Allan Emery and Joseph Olzewski parted, the older could have written what Paul wrote in verses 11, 12:

I long to see you so that I may impart to you some spiritual gift to make you strong — that is, that you and I may be mutually encouraged by each other's faith.

This mutuality is always one of the grand underlying motivations for ministry. When you experience it, you long for more. *Paul could not get enough!*

PAUL'S SECOND MINISTRY MOTIVATION: A SENSE OF OBLIGATION (vv. 14, 15)

Paul describes his sense of obligation in verses 14 and 15:

I am obligated both to Greeks and non-Greeks, both to the wise and the foolish. That is why I am so eager to preach the gospel also to you who are at Rome.

The apostle says he must pay a gospel-debt to all Gentiles. He uses two phrases to describe the entire Gentile population of the world. When he says, "Greeks and non-Greeks" he means those under Greco-Roman culture and those outside it — everyone! "Wise and foolish" means those who have intelligence and those who do not — everyone! Paul sees himself as a man who cannot rest until every gospel cent is paid to every Gentile creditor. That is why he wants to go to Spain after ministering in Rome (cf. 15:23, 24).

We must note that his debt is to God, but the payment is to men. The great nineteenth-century missionary to China, Hudson Taylor, realized this, as was seen when it was suggested by someone that he had given his life to the Orient because he loved the Chinese. To this he shook his head and answered thoughtfully, "No, not because I loved the Chinese, but because I loved God."

What a freshness would come to our motivation if we saw ourselves as great debtors to our neighbors, our community, our city — to the poor as well as the rich. This kind of indebtedness might even make us run the risk of appearing a fool by telling a deluded sinner we will pray for him.

PAUL'S THIRD MINISTRY MOTIVATION: CONFIDENCE IN THE POWER OF THE GOSPEL (vv. 16, 17)

Paul's confidence in the power of the gospel, a massive theme of the book of Romans, is revealed here in two of the most powerful verses in all of the Bible. Here we have in summary the entire argument of the book of Romans and the very heart of Paul's motivation. If he had been wearing a three-piece suit, Paul might well have burst the buttons as he gathered his breath to say:

> I am not ashamed of the gospel, because it is the power of God for the salvation of everyone who believes: first for the Jew, then for the Gentile. (v. 16)

Rome was *the* city of the world. Her law was the foundation for all that followed, her art was borrowed but appreciated, her military system was the wonder of the world. Yet:

> How pitiless she was! . . . Amid all the ruins of her cities we find none of a hospital, none . . . of an orphan school in an age that made many orphans. The pious aspirations and efforts of individuals never seem to have touched the conscience of the people. Rome had no conscience; she was a lustful, devouring beast, made more bestial by her intelligence and splendor.[2]

When Paul preached at Jerusalem, the religious center of the world, he was mobbed. When he preached at Athens, the intellectual center of the world, he was called a "seed-picker." When he preached at Rome, the legislative center, he was masterful. He was always ready. He was not ashamed.

Why? ". . . because it [*the gospel*] is the power of God for the salvation of everyone who believes: first for the Jew, then for the Gentile" (v. 16b). Anyone who has sat for very long under the preaching of the Word has heard many times that the Greek word translated "power" is *dunamis*, the word from which we get *dynamite*. The gospel indeed has incredible power. But because TNT has a negative connotation, it may be better to use the word *dynamic* for the gospel.

"Gospel" means "good news." There was good news long before the coming of Christ. Whenever a baby was born, it was gospel, "good news." Paul is not ashamed of this Good News because it is the dynamic, unharnessable power of God to effect salvation and all its temporal and eternal benefits for everyone who believes.

We must never be ashamed! Paul said this because he knew of the human proclivity to be embarrassed or to deny what we know to be true. The wonder is that God is not ashamed of us.

How does belief in the gospel of Christ bring salvation? The answer, in verse 17, is one of the most important statements in Scripture: "For in the gospel a righteousness from God is revealed, a righteousness that is by faith from first to last, just as it is written: 'The righteous will live by faith.'" First, the gospel reveals what this "righteousness from God" is— that it is a radical, heavenly righteousness. Philippians 3:9 speaks of a "righteousness . . . which is through faith in Christ — the righteousness that comes *from God* and is by faith." Second Corinthians 5:21 refers to this God-given righteousness also: "*God* made him who had no sin to be sin for us, so that in him we might become the righteousness of God." Romans 5:17 calls it "the gift of righteousness." It is not human righteousness but "the righteousness of God." Anders Nygren says, ". . . 'the righteousness of God' is a righteousness originating in God, prepared by God, revealed in the gospel and therein offered to us."[3] It is an alien righteousness—righteousness from Heaven.

Second, the gospel is revealed through Christ, who suffered in our place because our human righteousness was not good enough. Through the Resurrection he offers his righteousness to us. So we see God's righteousness in the gospel. But specifically we understand this by faith: "a righteousness that is by faith from first to last" (v. 17), an intensified phrase which means "entirely of faith" (Cranfield, Nygren, Hodge).[4]

Paul concludes with a quotation from Habakkuk 2:4 — "'The righteous will live by faith.'" Understanding this makes an eternity of difference for those seeking Christ. When Martin Luther was searching for God, for a long time he thought that "the righteousness of God" was a condemning righteousness. And seeing the righteousness of God as God's standard of judgment sometimes drove him to despair. However, little by little he began to understand, and finally the day came when he saw that *God gives his own righteousness to make man righteous through faith*—"This righteousness from God comes through faith in Jesus Christ to all who believe" (3:22)— and Luther's life was turned upside down. In the library of Rudolstadt, Germany, a glass case holds a letter written by Luther's youngest son, Dr. Paul Luther. It reads:

> In the year 1544, my dearest father, in the presence of us all, narrated the whole story of his journey to Rome. He acknowledged with great joy that in that city, through the Spirit of Jesus Christ, he had come to the knowledge of the truth of the everlasting gospel. It happened this way. As he repeated his prayers on the Lateran staircase, the words of the Prophet Habakkuk came suddenly to his mind: "The just shall live by faith." Thereupon he ceased his prayers, returned to Wittenberg, and took this as his chief foundation of all his doctrine.[5]

With this understanding, Luther went on to withstand the entire world!

Think of how the righteousness revealed in Christ motivated Paul! It is possible for men and women to stand sinless before God. It is possible to know that one has eternal life. It is possible to be free from the frustration of trying to earn righteousness and Heaven. The sole requirement is faith. Here is the greatest news ever proclaimed!

Now let us put the puzzle together. First Paul was motivated by the prospect of mutual encouragement. The prospect of ministry was pleasant to Paul, because everyone would benefit. Next he was motivated by a sense of debt. God had given him so much, he could never pay it back. Lastly, and most of all, he was motivated by his confidence in the gospel. He confidently proclaimed, "I am not ashamed of the gospel, because it is the power of God for the salvation of everyone who believes" (v. 16).

Some of us who know Christ are busy chasing sticks when we should have as our goal something far greater — the ministry of the gospel wherever God has placed us. If we are "chasing sticks," and if we continue as we are, we will be remembered for that alone. How much better to internalize the motivating elements of Paul's life!

Some do not understand what it means to have the righteousness of God. Unlike Joseph Olzewski, they have never known what it is to be free from their sins — to be righteous before God — to have Christ in their life. The Bible has never been alive to them. They have not experienced the joy of being encouraged in the faith.

Christ can change all that. It is so simple. The gospel is "the power of God for the salvation of everyone who believes." It is all a matter of faith.

Do you believe?

The wrath of God is being revealed from heaven against all the godlessness and wickedness of men who suppress the truth by their wickedness, since what may be known about God is plain to them, because God has made it plain to them. For since the creation of the world God's invisible qualities — his eternal power and divine nature — have been clearly seen, being understood from what has been made, so that men are without excuse. For although they knew God, they neither glorified him as God nor gave thanks to him, but their thinking became futile and their foolish hearts were darkened. Although they claimed to be wise, they became fools and exchanged the glory of the immortal God for images made to look like mortal man and birds and animals and reptiles. Therefore God gave them over in the sinful desires of their hearts to sexual impurity for the degrading of their bodies with one another. They exchanged the truth of God for a lie, and worshiped and served created things rather than the Creator — who is forever praised. Amen. (1:18-25)

3

Understanding Unbelief (I)

ROMANS 1:18-25

Harry Emerson Fosdick, the leading voice of Modernist Christianity during the twenties and thirties, expressed some very unorthodox thoughts in the opening chapter of his famous book *A Guide to the Understanding of the Bible*.[1] To summarize his views: Primitive man had a devilish concept of God. Noah's God destroyed the earth with a flood. Abraham's God was a bloodthirsty God who wanted a human sacrifice. The God of Moses was the horrible God of volcanic fire, speaking to him from Sinai. Little by little man has advanced as the centuries rolled on. David began to have high ethical thoughts of God, but they were mixed with the terrible imprecatory Psalms that call down wrath upon the enemy. By the time of the prophets, God was really improving. He now hated unrighteousness and spoke out against the crimes committed by men. And when Jesus came along, the idea of God took on the marvelous concepts of fatherhood and brotherhood, the greatest idea up to that time. But Jesus also had the repugnant idea of Hell. This, Fosdick argued, must be abandoned in order to continue the upward curve of development.

Fosdick was, of course, reflecting much of the thinking of modern man, whether religious or secular: a loving God cannot be a God of judgment or Hell — enlightened man is progressively shedding such backward ideas.

Lord Bertrand Russell said essentially the same thing in his *Why I Am Not a Christian*:

31

There is one very serious defect to my mind in Christ's moral character, and that is that He believed in hell. I do not myself feel that any person who is really profoundly humane can believe in everlasting punishment. Christ certainly as depicted in the Gospels did believe in everlasting punishment, and one does find repeatedly a vindictive fury against those people who would not listen to His preaching. . . . You do not, for instance, find that attitude in Socrates. You find him quite bland and urbane toward the people who would not listen to him, and it is, to my mind, far more worthy of a sage to take that line than to take the line of indignation.[2]

The idea of a God of wrath and judgment is offensive to modern man's sensibilities.

Any who are sympathetic to some of the thinking just expressed do not like what is stated in the text we will now study. The only salve I can offer is that this is not my message — it is the Spirit's message given through the Apostle Paul to the church at Rome (and to us).

Paul begins his negative thought (the first negative used in the book) by saying in verse 18: "The wrath of God is being revealed from heaven against all the godlessness and wickedness of men. . . ." God is a God of "*wrath*," or as some translations have it, "anger." It is important that we understand exactly what this means or the rest of the passage will be confusing. First, it does not mean that God is given to a capricious, uncontrolled anger. There are two basic words in the Greek language used to express anger. From *thumos* we get our words *thermometer* and *thermos*. This is red-hot anger — the kind that overcomes people when they lose control and smack someone on the nose. It is impulsive and passionate. That is not the word used in our text. The word here is *orge*, which signifies a settled and abiding condition. It is controlled. "The wrath of God" is not human wrath, which at its best is only a distorted reflection of God's wrath because it is always compromised by the presence of sin. "The wrath of God" is perfect, settled, controlled.

Second, this wrath of God is parallel to the righteousness of God. You will notice that the opening line of verse 17 contains the phrase, "a righteousness from God is revealed," and the opening of verse 18 says, "The wrath of God is being revealed." The wrath of God is a counterpart to the righteousness of God.

Third, God's wrath is not directed against goodness, but against "all the godlessness and wickedness of men." "The wrath of God" does not portray a Deity who "flies off the handle" and indiscriminately thumps anybody who happens to be at hand. God's wrath is perfect as to its quality and its object. That is the general concept we must keep in mind as we go through our passage.

As Paul continues, he gets very specific as to why the ungodly and unrighteous are under God's wrath, and in doing so he gives us somewhat of an anatomy of unbelief. This passage can help the unbeliever come to belief and can help the believer grasp the distinctives of unbelief and become better equipped to live out Christianity in an unbelieving world.

THE FIRST DISTINCTIVE OF UNBELIEF: THE SUPPRESSION OF TRUTH (vv. 18-20)

We see the first specific reason for the wrath of God when we read the whole of verse 18:

> The wrath of God is being revealed from heaven against all the godlessness and wickedness of men who *suppress the truth* by their wickedness.

This suppression of the truth is not passive. It carries the idea of holding something down. This is much like the little boy who smuggled his dog into his room to spend the night. When he heard his parents coming, he put the dog in his toybox and sat on the lid, then tried to talk to his parents while ignoring the repeated thump of his poor pet. The idea of suppression here is, *continual and aggressive striving against the truth.* Paul opens our eyes to the fact that all who are without Christ are in the constant process of holding down the truth and therefore are subject to God's abiding anger. There are no exceptions! This is as true in the darkest Pacific jungle as in our concrete forests!

What do unbelievers suppress? Verses 19 and 20 tell us. This is again one of the key theological statements in the Holy Scriptures.

> . . . since what may be known about God is plain to them, because God has made it plain to them. For since the creation of the world God's invisible qualities — his eternal power and divine nature — have been clearly seen, being understood from what has been made, so that men are without excuse.

What mankind holds down is the basic knowledge of the majestic transcending power of God as Creator and Sustainer. I cannot agree with those who think that this verse teaches a full-blown natural theology wherein all the attributes of God are easily discernible to the observer of nature, so that by watching the universe they come to the explicit conclusion of God's existence and the need for the sacrifice of Christ. Our text is very clear that "God's invisible qualities" are "his eternal power and divine nature" (v. 20), and that is what Nature reveals. Along with this, man sees by implication his own finiteness — the great gulf between himself and God.

One summer one of my associate pastors and I were walking home together on a particularly clear night. We looked at the North Star, the Big Dipper, the Pleiades. My fellow minister identified the Dog Star (Sirius), the brightest in both hemispheres. Then we began to joke about how all this happened "by chance." The vastness and precision of our cosmos declares the necessity of a magnificent God!

The argument from order is overwhelming. If I put ten pennies in my pocket and number them 1 to 10, then put my hand back in my pocket, my chances of pulling out the number 1 penny would be one in ten. If I place the number 1 penny back in my pocket and mix all the pennies again, the chances of pulling out penny number 2 would be one in a hundred. The chances of repeating the same procedure and coming up with penny number 3 would be one in a thousand. To do so with all of them (1 through 10 in order) would be one in ten billion! Noting the order and design of our universe, Kepler — founder of modern astronomy, discoverer of the "Three Planetary Laws of Motion," and originator of the term *satellite* — said, "The undevout astronomer is mad." David sang:

The heavens declare the glory of God; the skies proclaim the work of his hands. Day after day they pour forth speech; night after night they display knowledge. (Psalm 19:1, 2)

And he wandered away and away
With Nature, the dear old nurse,
Who sang to him night and day
The rhymes of the universe.[3]

Creation reveals the existence of a God who presides in majestic, transcendent, sustaining power. It also reveals the infinite distance between us (creatures) and him (the Creator).

Verse 19 says, "since what may be known about God is plain to them, because God has made it plain to them." The word "plain" means manifest. This is not a secret, covert revelation. There is no need for a Diogenes with his lamp. You do not have to be an intellectual. All can understand as much as they need to know.

Paul concludes in verse 20, "men are without excuse." Bertrand Russell, who dismisses "The Argument from Design" in three paragraphs, is without excuse. So is the cabbie who has never read a book in his life. The truth is, it takes a concerted act of the will to deny that a vastly powerful God made and sustains the Creation. If one is not at least searching after God, he or she is suppressing the truth.

The first distinctive of the anatomy of unbelief, then, is the suppression of the truth. The second is a perversion of the truth.

THE SECOND DISTINCTIVE OF UNBELIEF: THE PERVERSION OF THE TRUTH (vv. 21-23)

> For although they knew God, they neither glorified him as God nor gave thanks to him, but their thinking became futile and their foolish hearts were darkened. Although they claimed to be wise, they became fools and exchanged the glory of the immortal God for images made to look like mortal man and birds and animals and reptiles. (vv. 21-23)

The opening phrase of verse 21 tells how perversion to idolatry initially came about. "For although they knew God, they neither glorified him as God . . ." means there was a time when idolaters saw God as majestic, transcendent, all-powerful, infinitely greater than themselves. However, though they understood this, they did not honor him, but instead worshiped images like themselves. They refused to worship God for who he is and rather reduced him to their own level through idolatry. They minimized the vast chasm between the creature and the Creator.

This resulted in a progressively degenerating idolatry. In verse 21b Paul says, "their foolish hearts were darkened." This is significant because "heart" is a comprehensive term for all man's faculties. Not only was their moral judgment darkened, but their intellect and reasoning power suffered also. The magnificent idea of God as revealed in Nature was lost to them. The tragedy of idolatry is that it falls infinitely short of giving its people any idea of what God is really like! Verse 22 says, "Although they claimed to be wise, they became fools." The root word for "fools" is the same root from which we derive our word *moron*. This is an ugly term which refers not so much to one's intellect as to his moral condition.

Verse 23 portrays the progressive degeneration that the perversion of idolatry brings. First they worshiped an image of a man, second birds, then quadrupeds, and ultimately reptiles — crawling things. You cannot go any lower than this.

So we see that first man suppresses the truth about the greatness of God, and then he perverts it by worshiping insulting images. In essence, having gotten rid of the true knowledge of God, he worships images with which he is comfortable. *The ungodly man worships himself.*

We must ever keep before us the "eternal power and divine nature" of God as revealed in creation! We must always consciously strive to remember his majestic transcendence and his "otherness" or we will fall into idolatry. Quite frankly, even those of us in the evangelical tradition, with its valid and needed emphasis on the availability of God in Christ, are in danger of this form of idolatry. Very often we hear God addressed in casual terms that would scandalize some of our earthly employers. Sometimes we hear music that so sentimentalizes Christ that he is emptied of his divinity. We need to be careful! We must never address God with anything but the most humble attitude. We must never jest about him or about divine things. We must keep our own creatureliness and his supremacy before us.

THE THIRD DISTINCTIVE OF UNBELIEF: THE PERVERSION OF LIFE (vv. 24, 25)

The final distinctive of unbelief is the perversion of life itself.

> Therefore God gave them over in the sinful desires of their hearts to sexual impurity for the degrading of their bodies with one another. They exchanged the truth of God for a lie, and worshiped and served created things rather than the Creator — who is forever praised. Amen. (vv. 24, 25)

The logic here is so clear: first a suppression of the majestic revelation of God, then a perversion to man-centered idolatry, and finally a perversion of man himself. "In the end their humanism (man-centeredness) resulted in the dehumanization of each other."[4] In the end, man lowers himself to a condition below God's created purpose. As we will see in our next study, man, having rejected the witness of God in creation, goes on to live contrary to the very order of creation.

We have seen something of the "why" of the wrath of God, but our text also tells us something of the "how" of God's wrath: "God gave them over." This horrible phrase is repeated three times before chapter 1 closes. God avenges himself by allowing the decline of evil men and women. That is what we see today all around us — men and women slipped to such depths that it would disgrace animals to have such conduct among them. God's wrath is all around us, and it seems that more wrath (God's giving people over to sin) is falling daily.

Of course, we also know that God's wrath is not yet completely worked out. I am reminded of the story of a farmer who was an unbeliever and antagonistic to the gospel. He owned a piece of land contiguous to the local church. On the Lord's Day he got great joy out of running his tractor back and forth beside the church. Spring came, and his corn sprouted. It was more than knee-high by the Fourth of July, and in the fall there was a tremendous harvest. He had the greatest satisfaction in this, so he wrote a letter to the pastor of the church. In it he said that obviously God did not exist because the farmer had consciously gone against what the Christians felt were the structures of God, and yet look how he was blessed. The pastor wrote just one line back to him: "God doesn't settle his accounts in October."

There is one other aspect of the "wrath of God" which is demanded by the parallelism with "the righteousness from God" in verse 17. Just as "the righteousness from God" was best revealed in Christ's death on the cross, so too is the wrath of God. We understand from the Gospels that after Jesus gave his mother to John, darkness fell upon the land from the sixth hour until the ninth hour. Was this darkness sent to hide the hideous physical sufferings of God's Son? No. It was to hide the agony of his Son as he became a curse for us. In Jewish thinking, to be cursed was to be separated from God. Jesus had never known anything but face-to-face fellowship with the Father. They had worked together in the creation of the universe. They were one another's delight. Now, as Jesus bore our sins, he became a curse. "Christ redeemed us from the curse of the law by becoming a curse for us, for it is written: 'Cursed is everyone who is hung on a tree'" (Galatians 3:13).

At this moment of separation, the pain from the nails was nothing to Jesus. Neither was the flayed back or the uneven stake. There is no experience so painful as separation from God. Jesus cried, "My God, my God, why have you forsaken me?" (Psalm 22:1). The wrath of God against our sin was seen when Christ suffered alone for our sins.

If a man is not a Christian, it is because he is suppressing the truth about God, pushing down God's own revelation of who he is. Further, he is not a Christian because he is given to idolatry. Martin Luther said, "Whatever your heart clings to and relies on is your god." An unbeliever has his own "self-created gods." Finally, he is under God's wrath when he fails to acknowledge in his heart of hearts the extent of his sin. And if he dies without Christ he will go to Hell. Jesus said, "Whosoever believes in the Son has eternal life, but whoever rejects the Son will not see life, for God's wrath remains on him" (John 3:36).

Consider the two revelations: the revelation of the wrath of God justly coming upon all mankind because man suppresses the truth, perverts the truth, and perverts life, and secondly the revelation of the righteousness of God from faith to faith, righteousness he gives us so we can stand righteous before him. If one does not have the righteousness of God, he or she has the wrath of God. Those are the two revelations and the two choices. Are you under the wrath of God today? Or do you cling to the righteousness of God which has been revealed to you?

Therefore God gave them over in the sinful desires of their hearts to sexual impurity for the degrading of their bodies with one another. They exchanged the truth of God for a lie, and worshiped and served created things rather than the Creator — who is forever praised. Amen. Because of this, God gave them over to shameful lusts. Even their women exchanged natural relations for unnatural ones. In the same way the men also abandoned natural relations with women and were inflamed with lust for one another. Men committed indecent acts with other men, and received in themselves the due penalty for their perversion. Furthermore, since they did not think it worthwhile to retain the knowledge of God, he gave them over to a depraved mind, to do what ought not to be done. They have become filled with every kind of wickedness, evil, greed and depravity. They are full of envy, murder, strife, deceit and malice. They are gossips, slanderers, God-haters, insolent, arrogant and boastful; they invent ways of doing evil; they disobey their parents; they are senseless, faithless, heartless, ruthless. Although they know God's righteous decree that those who do such things deserve death, they not only continue to do these very things but also approve of those who practice them. (1:24-32)

4

Understanding Unbelief (II)

ROMANS 1:24-32

Several years ago when I was study-ing the opening chapters of Romans, I took a few minutes to scribble a positive alternative rendering of Romans 1:24-32. This is what I wrote:

> Therefore, God *gave them over* in their hearts to self-control and purity, that their bodies might be honored among them. For they kept and cherished the truth of God and worshiped and served the Creator, who is blessed forever, rather than the creature. Amen.
>
> For this reason God *gave them over* to pure and wholesome lives, lived with carefree ease even in the most intimate relations so that all received in their own persons the due reward of their fidelity.
>
> And just as they saw fit to acknowledge God in all things, God *gave them over* to a sound mind, to do those things which are proper, being filled with all righteousness, goodness, generosity, kindness; full of selflessness, life, healing, openness, kindliness; they are gen-tle in speech, always building others up, lovers of God, respectful, humble, self-effacing, inventors of good, obedient to parents, under-standing, trustworthy, loving, merciful; and as they know the ordi-nance of God, that those who practice such things are possessors of life, they do the same, and give hearty approval to those who do like-wise.

By reversing Paul's thoughts, one of the most terrible portions of Scripture becomes sublime. God's grace brings freedom from bondage, light from darkness, life from death. I would like to suggest that we keep this in mind as we tunnel through the final verses of Romans 1 because it is a dark journey. To be frank, these verses leave little about which to smile. At the same time, the truth they hold is needed today as much as at any other time in history — especially in the history of our nation.

This dark passage can bring grace to those without Christ, just as it did to a brilliant physician in one of Richard Halverson's Bible studies on Romans who said, "I don't ever remember reading the Bible, but tonight I have seen myself in Romans 1; now what do I do about it?"[1]

As we have seen, the background of the passage consists of this: All unbelievers suppress the truth of God's "eternal power and divine nature." As they refuse to honor him and exchange the great truth for a lie, they bring about an idol-making perversion of the truth. Finally their suppression and perversion of the truth culminates in a perversion of life, until God gives them over to their sin.

God allows men and women to go as far down as they desire. His wrath is shown in the removal of his restraining power. What we have in verses 24-32 are the dimensions of the depravity to which unbelieving men and women will go in working out God's wrath on themselves. I have titled these verses, "The Dimensions of Depravity." It is good for us to consider all this because any Christian who truly grasps mankind's depravity will be more effective in living for Christ in this fallen world. There are three aspects to man's fallenness:

I. The Sensual Dimension (vv. 24-27)
II. The Mental Dimension (vv. 28-31)
III. The Ultimate Dimension (v. 32)

As we discuss the sensual dimension, we will do our best to stay within the bounds of propriety. At the same time we must speak frankly about what our text says.

THE SENSUAL DIMENSION OF DEPRAVITY (vv. 24-27)

Therefore God gave them over in the sinful desires of their hearts to sexual impurity for the degrading of their bodies with one another. They exchanged the truth of God for a lie, and worshiped and served created things rather than the Creator — who is forever praised. Amen.

Because of this, God gave them over to shameful lusts. Even their women exchanged natural relations for unnatural ones. In the same way the men also abandoned natural relations with women and were inflamed with lust for one another. Men committed indecent acts with other men, and received in themselves the due penalty for their perversion. (vv. 24-27)

In plain language Paul was referring to sexual perversion, both heterosexual (v. 24) and homosexual inversion (vv. 26, 27). While both are in view, the emphasis is upon homosexual inversion as an illustration of the extremity of mankind's depravity. The text is even more explicit in the original than in our English translations. The words used for "men" and "women" are literally "male" and "female," so that verses 26 and 27 really read like this:

> . . . for their females exchanged the natural function for that which is unnatural and in the same way the males abandoned the natural function of the female and burned in their desire toward one another, males with males committing indecent acts [or, as Dr. Robertson suggests, "deformities"[2]] and receiving in their own persons the due penalty of their error.

There is no doubt as to what the apostle is speaking about. Why does Paul, in describing the depth of mankind's depravity, turn first to sexual sin — especially homosexuality? There are other sins which are just as bad. As C. S. Lewis wrote:

> If anyone thinks that Christians regard unchastity as the supreme vice, he is quite wrong. The sins of the flesh are bad, but they are the least bad of all sins. All the worst pleasures are purely spiritual. The pleasure of putting other people in the wrong, of bossing and patronizing and spoiling sport, and backbiting; the pleasure of power, of hatred. For there are two things inside me competing with the human self which I must try to become: they are the animal self, and the diabolical self: and the diabolical self is the worst of the two. That is why a cold, self-righteous prig, who goes regularly to church, may be far nearer to hell than a prostitute. But of course, it's better to be neither.[3]

Why does Paul single out homosexuality then? Because it is so obviously unnatural, and therefore automatically underlines the extent to which sin takes mankind. Other sins are just as evil, but they are naturally evil. God has emphasized the sin of inversion to show us that inside the unbelieving man is a running sore which indicates a far deeper dimension of the wounds of sinful society. (We should note that chapter 1 ends with the sins of the mind and spirit, of which all sinners are guilty.)

I would also offer a brief word to those who are involved in homosexual inversion. It is not a sickness, but a sin,[4] and that ought to be encouraging because there is a remedy for sin, whereas many sicknesses have no cure. The Scriptures indicate that homosexuality is a sin from which one can recover.

> Do you not know that the wicked will not inherit the kingdom of God? Do not be deceived: Neither the sexually immoral nor idolaters nor adulterers nor male prostitutes nor homosexual offenders nor thieves nor the greedy nor drunkards nor slanderers nor swindlers will inherit the kingdom of God. And that is what some of you were. But you were washed, you were sanctified, you were justified in the name of our Lord Jesus Christ and by the Spirit of our God. (1 Corinthians 6:9-11)

Some of the Corinthians were previously homosexuals, drunkards, thieves, but they were "washed" — *cleansed.*

Paul also emphasized this sin because it was all around him. He was writing from Corinth, the sin capital of Asia. Greek culture taught that homosexual love was the purest and highest of loves. Many highborn Greeks maintained male lovers along with their wives. It was no different in Rome. Fourteen of the first fifteen emperors were homosexuals. Sounds like today, does it not? Romans 1 describes any major city in the world today: Hong Kong, San Francisco, Vienna, Zagreb, Berlin, New York, Tokyo, Chicago.

Dr. R. H. Graves, who once ministered in Canton, said that a man he met declared Paul could not have written this chapter, but only a modern missionary who had been in China. Romans is for today! Romans is relevant! A recent issue of *Time* magazine indicated that homosexuals make up 15 to 20 percent of the population of San Francisco and that the City Council passed, by an 8-3 vote,

> . . . new rules which require the city to treat all qualifying [i.e., *homosexual*] live-in partners as if they were spouses. For instance, they will have the same visitation rights at local jails and hospitals, and city workers would get a day off to attend a mate's funeral. But what backers were most eager to win was low-cost ($50 a month)

health benefits, which city employees will pay for at the same rate as they do for a husband or wife.[5]

A mainline denomination's magazine carried an admonishment that said essentially this: Homosexuality should be accepted as a variant lifestyle — the homosexual relationship is neither unnatural, sinful, nor sick. In this article practicing homosexuals were portrayed as whole, healthy, appealing persons. In the Chicago area, where I minister, this sin is rampant. I talked to one physician who says he treats two or three people a week who are diseased or fearful of disease because of homosexuality. He said, "The average person in this town thinks that our city is relatively free of homosexuality — that those with such problems live outside its borders. That just isn't true." Paul describes the running sores of a depraved society which has suppressed the truth of God — and it turns out that he is describing *our* country, *our* town, *our* neighborhood. Where these things exist, so do all the elements of depravity.

At the end of verse 27 Paul completes his thoughts on this subject with an ominous statement, "and received in themselves the due penalty for their perversion." Anyone who has counseled those in bondage to this sin know what Paul is talking about — a loss of personal identity, an uncertainty as to one's role and place in life. Yet, there is another element to this which is substantiated by the statement's parallelism with verse 24 ("the degrading of their bodies"). God's wrath falls as a penalty on their very bodies.

The "Great Pox" of Columbus' sailors introduced a virulent strain of syphilis which spread to the rest of the world in less than 100 years. The disease existed from far more distant times, but never like this. A 1972 issue of *Time* said:

> After the ordinary cold, syphilis and gonorrhea are the most common infectious diseases among young people, outranking all cases of hepatitis, measles, mumps, scarlet fever, strep throat and tuberculosis put together.[6]

That was 1972. Who knows what the statistics are today.

The sexually-transmitted herpes virus infection can also be dated to ancient times, but today it is epidemic. A 1982 *Time* cover story, "The New Scarlet Letter," revealed that an estimated 20,000,000 Americans now have sexually-communicated herpes. Worse, it is completely incurable. As *Time* said, "It won't kill you, but you won't kill it either." The reason for the virus's exponential increase, according to *Time*, has been the escalation of sexual license.[7]

By far the most terrifying event to those involved in sexual perversion is the occurrence, largely in the gay community, of AIDS (Acquired Immunodeficiency Syndrome), from which the victims lose their immunities to disease and eventually die of pneumocisitis pneumonia or a cancer called Kaposis sarcoma.

This receiving "in themselves the due penalty for their perversion" is an outworking of the wrath of God because of the suppression of the truth. But it is also a sign of the grace of God, for a couple of reasons.

First, the fear of contracting a sexually-transmitted disease is a great inducement to refrain from sexual license. Married and unmarried philanderers have become extremely wary. Monogamy and fidelity are on the upswing.

But there is a second element of God's grace — and that is that some people, through the pain of disease and personal fragmentation, have come to the end of themselves and have become finally ready for a massive dose of God's grace. It is their only hope.

As we have seen, sexual license — especially inversion — reveals to us the dimensions of a society's depravity. According to Biblical revelation, what we see around us means that our particular culture is on the skids. If we are believers, this encourages us to draw close to Christ so that we are really living what we say we believe. If we are unbelievers, it is meant to drive us (as it did the brilliant physician we mentioned) to faith.

Most of us are not caught in the sins of perversion and inversion. Perhaps we could congratulate ourselves (God help us!) on not having committed those sins. But none of us, whether as nonbelievers or even as believers, can truly deny experiencing most of the dimensions of mental depravity.

THE MENTAL DIMENSION OF DEPRAVITY (vv. 28-31)

Paul says that unbelieving minds become depraved minds.

> Furthermore, since they did not think it worthwhile to retain the knowledge of God, he gave them over to a depraved mind, to do what ought not to be done. (v. 28)

Literally, they were given over to a "rejected mind." They rejected God, and God rejected their mental attitude. Cranfield says that such a mind is "so debilitated and corrupted as to be a quite untrustworthy guide in moral decision."[8] This does not mean that man is as bad as he could be, for there is always room for "deprovement."

Paul then gives, in verses 29-31, the specific dimensions of a depraved mind. It would be easy to imagine that these are the exaggerations of an hysterical moralist, but the Greek and Roman writers said the same things themselves — and sometimes more.

> They have become filled with every kind of wickedness, evil, greed and depravity. They are full of envy, murder, strife, deceit and malice. (v. 29a)
>> They are gossips, slanderers, God-haters, insolent, arrogant and boastful; they invent ways of doing evil; they disobey their parents . . . (vv. 29b, 30)
>>> . . . they are senseless, faithless, heartless, ruthless. (v. 31)

These are the dimensions of the "depraved [or rejected] mind." Not all those who are without Christ have done all these things, but these kinds of things come most naturally to them. The tendency is for deeper and deeper decline.

THE ULTIMATE DIMENSION OF DEPRAVITY (v. 32)

Verse 32, which gives the ultimate dimension of the sinful mind, neatly frames this terrible picture:

> Although they know God's righteous decree that those who do such things deserve death, they not only continue to do these very things but also approve of those who practice them.

Man reaches the nadir of depravity when he heartily applauds those who give themselves to sin. To delight in those who do evil is a sure way to become even more degraded than the sinners one observes. This, I think, was one of the supreme horrors of the Roman Colosseum. Those committing the mayhem were supremely guilty, but those watching and applauding were perhaps even more wretched.

What a telling application this has on our media-captivated society. Millions sit in their living rooms watching debauchery, violence, deceit and many other vices — and applaud what they see! It makes little difference whether the vices are real or portrayed, the effect is much the same — an increasingly depraved mind on the part of the viewer.

Approving another's sin or encouraging another's sin is a sign that life has reached its lowest dimension.

We Christians are not exempt from this. Satan knows that if he can get us to laugh at things we believe we would never do, our defenses will fall. Maybe someday our unwitting approval will give way to action. We need to be careful what we watch and applaud.

As Thomas Aquinas pointed out, according to Psalm 8 man is made a little lower than the angels. This suggests that man is in a position somewhere between the angels above and the beasts below. Angels are spirits without bodies. (Sometimes they take on bodies, but they are spirit beings.) Animals are bodies without spirits. Man is in between because he is body and spirit. This puts man in a mediating position. It has always been man's prerogative to move upward toward the spiritual or downward toward the animal, and we become like that upon which we focus. This is why we cannot sin "a little bit." All sin moves us downhill individually, nationally, and culturally.

As our society has moved downward toward the beast, no one seems able to say, "This far and no further." No one can put a limit on sensuality. Incest is even being promoted by some. Our culture has been unable to draw the line on pornography. Such are the dimensions of depravity.

What is the answer? Why does God give a civilization over to this kind of thing? He does it because when darkness prevails, and despair and violence are widespread, men and women are most ready to come to the light. He gives mankind up so that in their despair they might give themselves to his grace. Do you remember Isaiah's prediction?

> The people walking in darkness have seen a great light; on those living in the land of the shadow of death a light has dawned. (Isaiah 9:2)

In the first century mankind was sunk in the darkness of despair. Idolatry had penetrated the whole world. Men had turned from the true God, whom they could have known. In that hour, in the darkness of the night, over the skies of Bethlehem the angels broke through, and a great light of hope shone forth. From that hope all light streams. The angels' message was the coming of the Lord Jesus, the availability of the gift of "righteousness from God" (cf. 1:17).

Against the growing darkness of our own time we need to make this message as clear as we possibly can — by our testimony, by our lives, by the joy and peace of Heaven in our hearts. God has found a way to break through human weakness, arrogance, despair, and sinfulness to give us peace, joy and gladness. Just as Jesus was born in Bethlehem so long ago, so he can be born in any person's heart now. This is the good news of the gospel. In this decaying world in which we live, we can see again the glory of this truth as it delivers people from their sins. "You are to give him the name Jesus, because he will save his people from their sins" (Matthew 1:21).[9]

In Ephesians 2, Paul again paints a similar picture of the dimensions of man's depravity, concluding in verse 3 with: "we were by nature objects of wrath." However, he does not stop there but continues:

> But because of his great love for us, God, who is rich in mercy, made us alive with Christ even when we were dead in transgressions — it is by grace you have been saved. And God raised us up with Christ and seated us with him in the heavenly realms in Christ Jesus, in order that in the coming ages he might show the incomparable riches of his grace, expressed in his kindness to us in Christ Jesus. For it is by grace you have been saved, through faith — and this not from yourselves, it is the gift of God. . . . (vv. 4-8)

Christ came in the darkest night, and he can meet us even in the midnight of our souls.

You, therefore, have no excuse, you who pass judgment on someone else, for at whatever point you judge the other, you are condemning yourself, because you who pass judgment do the same things. Now we know that God's judgment against those who do such things is based on truth. So when you, a mere man, pass judgment on them and yet do the same things, do you think you will escape God's judgment? Or do you show contempt for the riches of his kindness, tolerance and patience, not realizing that God's kindness leads you toward repentance? But because of your stubbornness and your unrepentant heart, you are storing up wrath against yourself for the day of God's wrath, when his righteous judgment will be revealed. God "will give to each person according to what he has done." To those who by persistence in doing good seek glory, honor and immortality, he will give eternal life. But for those who are self-seeking and who reject the truth and follow evil, there will be wrath and anger. There will be trouble and distress for every human being who does evil: first for the Jew, then for the Gentile; but glory, honor and peace for everyone who does good: first for the Jew, then for the Gentile. For God does not show favoritism. All who sin apart from the law will also perish apart from the law, and all who sin under the law will be judged by the law. For it is not those who hear the law who are righteous in God's sight, but it is those who obey the law who will be declared righteous. (Indeed, when Gentiles, who do not have the law, do by nature things required by the law, they are a law for themselves, even though they do not have the law, since they show that the requirements of the law are written on their hearts, their consciences also bearing witness, and their thoughts now accusing, now even defending them.) This will take place on the day when God will judge men's secrets through Jesus Christ, as my gospel declares. (2:1-16)

5

God's Perfect Judgment

ROMANS 2:1-16

As we begin our study of Romans 2, we need to focus on this thought: mankind does not accept God's assessment of human sin and the imperative of divine judgment. This is not to say that men will not admit they are sinners. It is very easy to get a non-Christian to agree that he is a sinner ("nobody's perfect"), but it is almost impossible to get him to realize the gravity of his sin. Typically he has no trouble agreeing that those who are guilty of "big sins" like murder and rape and treason deserve judgment — even death. However, that God's wrath should fall on those guilty of such "lesser sins" as envy or arrogance does not seem quite right to them.

Most people do not take God's word about sin and judgment seriously, but rather reject it and replace it with their own *ad hominem* reasoning. By way of illustration, when our school-age children want to justify participation in an activity of which we do not approve, their most common reasoning is, "But everybody's doing it." (That is the answer we parents used to use too — and still do.) "Nobody's perfect!" "To err is human, to forgive is divine." Or as the philosopher Heine said in a moment of now-famous cynicism, "God will forgive . . . it is his trade." Such thinking suggests that since we are human we are under moral obligation to sin, and that God is under moral obligation to forgive us.

Inherent in the common thinking that because everyone is doing it, it is not so bad — as long as we do not commit the "biggies" we will be okay — is the assumption that God does not mean what he says or say what he means.

This problem is twofold: first, man does not understand God's holiness, and, second, he does not understand his own sinfulness. As to God's holiness, sinful man's idolatrous mind fails to see God as the transcendent, wholly-other, perfect God who is infinitely above him, but rather imagines that he is like himself. As to sin, man forgets that he is made in the image of God and that every sin communicates a distortion of the image of God to the rest of creation. It is through such ignorance that the world suggests that if God does judge as he says, he insults his own integrity, holiness, and justice.

The eternal fact is, God means what he says and says what he means. Moreover, his judgment, despite moralisms to the contrary, is *perfect*. That is what 2:1-16 is all about. As we come to understand (or reaffirm our understanding) of the perfection of God's judgment, we will bring health to our souls. For those of us who are believers, this will drive us toward a greater authenticity in life — and thus spiritual power. For the non-Christian, there will be strong encouragement to face fundamental issues about oneself and God.

THE PERFECTION OF GOD'S JUDGMENT: RELIGIOUS PEOPLE (vv. 1-4)

There are three major points in this section, and the first, covered in verses 1-4, is this: We see the perfection of God's judgment in that even the most religious people do not fool him. Just as millions of religious moralizers today think they are going to get by because they are good people and God must certainly forgive them, thousands in the Jewish nation in Christ's time thought the same way.

But they took it one step further. They believed everyone else would be judged except the Jewish race! A common tradition claimed that Abraham himself sat at the gate of Hell to keep all Jews out, regardless of their deeds. Trypho the Jew is alleged to have said, "They who are the seed of Abraham according to the flesh shall in any case, even if they be sinners and unbelieving and disobedient towards God, share in the eternal Kingdom."[1] The apocryphal Wisdom of Solomon, written in the first century, bears this and many similar statements: "So while chastening us thou scourgest our enemies ten thousand times more. . . ." (12:22). Many Jews believed they were immune from God's wrath simply because they were Jews. So we can well imagine how a moralizing Jew would read the condemnation of the pagan world in Romans 1. "Go get 'em, God! Amen!" The self-righteous Jew never dreamed that he was under the same condemnation. He was blind to his actual condition.

However, God was, and is, under no such delusion. Good religious moralizers do not fool him. So in the opening four verses of chapter 2 Paul states that they too are under judgment, and then reveals that God perfectly understands the psychology of these people.

> You, therefore, have no excuse, you who pass judgment on some-one else, for at whatever point you judge the other, you are con-demning yourself, because you who pass judgment do the same things. Now we know that God's judgment against those who do such things is based on truth. So when you, a mere man, pass judg-ment on them and yet do the same things, do you think you will escape God's judgment? Or do you show contempt for the riches of his kindness, tolerance and patience, not realizing that God's kind-ness leads you toward repentance? (vv. 1-4)

The reason these religious moralizers stand condemned is that they prac-tice the same things as unbelieving pagans. God sees sin in their hearts that they do not see — and condemns them.

Here we discern some divine insights into the psychology of reli-gious moralizers then and today. We also get some insight into our own hearts because vestiges of these sins are common to all believers' hearts. The first insight into the minds of self-righteous moralizers is that they do not understand the nature and extent of sin. They imagine that because they have not actually committed one of the principal sins they are beyond judgment. The truth is, they may not have overtly committed adultery, but it has happened in their heads. They did not overtly steal, but their minds have robbed even their loved ones. They have not overtly committed murder, but numerous times the mental knife has plunged. God sees all this! He is not deceived by our indulging in self-righteous delusion by renaming our personal sins. Others lie and cheat — we sim-ply stretch the truth. Others betray — we protect our rights. Others steal — we borrow. Others are prejudiced — we have convictions.[2]

The second insight, related to the first, is that the self-righteous have an intrinsic blindness to their own faults. They do not see they are doing the same things for which they condemn others. An example of this psy-chology is found in the life of David after he had committed adultery with Bathsheba and had Uriah her husband murdered. Nathan the prophet came and told the king the tale of a rich man who took a poor man's sheep which the poor man loved and slaughtered it to feed his guests. David was horrified and responded,

"As surely as the Lord lives, the man who did this deserves to die!
He must pay for that lamb four times over, because he did such a
thing and had no pity." Then Nathan said to David, "You are the
man!" (2 Samuel 12:5-7)

David, though immensely guilty of a similar and far greater sin, was blind
to his own condition even while enraged at the similar sin of another. The
religiously self-righteous easily forgets his own wrongs and feels that others' sins are worse than his own.

Next, the self-righteous moralizer is not only blind but judgmental
to the extreme. There is no one more censorious than such a person —
no one! Hell will be full of judgmental, goodie-goodie people.
Unfortunately, such thinking is not confined to the damned. It is also the
favorite "indoor sport" of many Christians. It is the sin with which I am
constantly assailed and to which I often personally succumb. However, I
am never more miserable than when I am judging another person.

There is nothing more destructive to the spread of the Good News
than this. It is a fact that if you have a censorious, self-righteous spirit,
others will sense it without your saying a word. The set of your jaw, the
moisture in your eye, the flush of your countenance, the tone of your
voice will give you away — and you will bring, not life, but death to others!

There is yet another facet of the psyche of the self-righteous reli-
gionist — he wrongly thinks he will escape judgment by taking God's
side in condemning the unrighteous. He whispers in his prayers the sins
of others: "Lord, how terrible that was. Lord, they are sinning. Lord,
thank you that I am not like them." But God is not swayed by the accusations of the self-righteous.

The last characteristic of the religious moralizer is that he actually
thinks the "kindness, tolerance and patience" of God in his life is a kind
of divine OK on the course he has chosen, rather than seeing it as a chance
for repentance.

Or do you show contempt for the riches of his kindness, tolerance
and patience, not realizing that God's kindness leads you toward
repentance? (v. 4)

Sometimes God brings people to himself through difficulties as they
come to the end of themselves and cast their lives upon him. But he also
draws people to repentance through "kindness, tolerance and patience."
No one should assume he is all right with God just because life is easy

for him at a given time. God calls people through sunshine as well as through rain.

So we see the psychology of the self-righteous: their ignorance of the nature and extent of sin, blindness to their own sins, extreme judgmentalism, siding with God against others' sins, interpreting God's kindness as approval. God understands those who are truly self-righteous. He is never fooled. That is why his judgment will be rendered with unerring, terrible perfection. *He sees all.* In Psalm 139:4 David says, "Before a word is on my tongue you know it completely, O Lord." God knows the real intention behind every spoken word. God knows instantly and effortlessly everything about us. A man may be a "good" person — upright, outwardly moral, sure of his goodness. But if he dies without Christ, Christ will say to him, "You, therefore, have no excuse" (v. 1). And his judgment will be perfect.

So we see, first, that God's judgment is perfect because even the most religious people cannot fool him. Next, in verses 5-11 we see the perfection of God's judgment because he judges everyone with absolute impartiality.

THE PERFECTION OF GOD'S JUDGMENT: ABSOLUTE IMPARTIALITY (vv. 5-11)

Read verses 5-11, keeping God's impartiality in mind.

> But because of your stubbornness and your unrepentant heart, you are storing up wrath against yourself for the day of God's wrath, when his righteous judgment will be revealed. God "will give to each person according to what he has done." To those who by persistence in doing good seek glory, honor and immortality, he will give eternal life. But for those who are self-seeking and who reject the truth and follow evil, there will be wrath and anger. There will be trouble and distress for every human being who does evil: first for the Jew, then for the Gentile; but glory, honor and peace for everyone who does good: first for the Jew, then for the Gentile. For God does not show favoritism.

It is absolutely clear that God is perfectly impartial in his judgment. The word for "favoritism" suggests in its original form that he is not swayed by a person's face. We may imagine there is something about us that will persuade God to make an exception — our intelligence, our position, our many acts of kindness — but apart from the blood of Christ, he will not be moved.

The basis of God's judgment of us will be our works. This does not mean some will be saved by works. Rather, believers will give an account of their works, and nonbelievers will be judged according to their works. The standard of judgment for those with a religious heritage will be the same as those who have none: works. In an eternally real sense, unrepentant man is making deposits in a bank account from which he will one day collect to his unending woe. God cannot be fooled. He is absolutely impartial. Such defenses as "My mother sang in the choir," "I'm a church member," "My grandfather was a preacher" will never meet the righteous standards of a holy God.

THE PERFECTION OF GOD'S JUDGMENT: FAULTLESS DISCRIMINATION (vv. 12-16)

Lastly, in verses 12-16 we see the perfection of God's judgment because he judges everyone with faultless discrimination. Again our text stresses that whether a person has access to God's Word or not, he will be judged by his deeds, and when he falls short he will indeed be lost.

> All who sin apart from the law will also perish apart from the law, and all who sin under the law will be judged by the law. For it is not those who hear the law who are righteous in God's sight, but it is those who obey the law who will be declared righteous. (vv. 12, 13)

Paul anticipates that some may think this is unfair because the Jews have had the advantage of God's written Word. So he explains how perfectly discriminating God is in applying his judgment:

> (Indeed, when Gentiles, who do not have the law, do by nature things required by the law, they are a law for themselves, even though they do not have the law, since they show that the requirements of the law are written on their hearts, their consciences also bearing witness, and their thoughts now accusing, now even defending them.) (vv. 14, 15)

Paul says that while the Gentiles do not have the Law written in their hearts, not even the Ten Commandments, nevertheless "the requirements of the law are written on their hearts." That is, they know the moral standard of God.

With incredible discrimination God judges those lacking God's Word by how well they live according to the sense of right and wrong in their hearts. Sweden's great theologian Anders Nygren states this very exactly: "The heathen's conscience stands as an objective witness . . . showing that he actually knew what he did wrong."[3] God's judgment is so perfect that he takes into account one's moral perception in rendering judgment. To be sure, no one escapes condemnation. All fall short. None measure up to their own moral perceptions of right or wrong, let alone God's Law. No one will ever be able to rise before God and declare that he has been unfair. His judgment is so precise that he takes into account the delicate moral perceptions of each person.

THE PERFECTION OF GOD'S JUDGMENT: CONCLUSION

What does all this teaching regarding the perfection of the judgment of God mean to those who believe and to those who do not believe?

To Christians it means that God knows everything and that one day we will stand before him to give account of our lives. He knows what has gone on in our hearts. Alva McAllaster suggested something of this when she wrote:

> Envy went to church this morning. Being legion he sat in every pew. Envy fingered wool and silk fabrics, hung price tags on suits and neckties. Envy paced through the parking lot scrutinizing chrome and paint. Envy marched to the chancel with the choir during the processional. Envy prodded plain Jane wives, and bright wives . . . and kind men . . . envy stared.[4]

The truth is, envy is not the only thing that goes to church. So do sensuality and pride and malice and judgmentalism and many others. And God knows it all.

We should pursue a profound honesty before God, for he knows everything. We need to admit our inner spiritual sins (even the "really bad" sins) and ask for his help. We must reject worldly rationalizing and moralizing, for in these ways the sickness and impotence of the Church is perpetuated. Furthermore, we need to pray specifically and honestly for deliverance and for grace. "Blessed are those who hunger and thirst for righteousness, for they will be filled" (Matthew 5:6).

Those who are not believers must realize that if they do not have the righteousness of Christ through faith, their sins are yet upon them, and

God will judge them with perfect judgment. Handy moralizations — "Everybody's doing it," "To err is human, to forgive is divine," "Nobody's perfect" — will not suffice. In verse 16 Paul refers to "the day when God will judge men's secrets through Jesus Christ, as my gospel declares." The day of judgment is coming, and men and women need to "settle out of court" while they can. Jesus said, "If you do not believe that I am the one I claim to be, you will indeed die in your sins" (John 8:24). However, the Scriptures also tell us, "Yet to all who received him, to those who believed in his name, he gave the right to become children of God" (John 1:12). Peter wrote:

> He himself bore our sins in his body on the tree, so that we might die to sins and live for righteousness; by his wounds you have been healed. (1 Peter 2:24)

What a challenge the perfection of the judgment of God brings to all of us! Believers should strive for a profound inward righteousness. Nonbelievers should seek the righteousness that comes from God by faith.

Now you, if you call yourself a Jew; if you rely on the law and brag about your relationship to God; if you know his will and approve of what is superior because you are instructed by the law; if you are convinced that you are a guide for the blind, a light for those who are in the dark, an instructor of the foolish, a teacher of infants, because you have in the law the embodiment of knowledge and truth — you, then, who teach others, do you not teach yourself? You who preach against stealing, do you steal? You who say that people should not commit adultery, do you commit adultery? You who abhor idols, do you rob temples? You who brag about the law, do you dishonor God by breaking the law? As it is written: "God's name is blasphemed among the Gentiles because of you." Circumcision has value if you observe the law, but if you break the law, you have become as though you had not been circumcised. If those who are circumcised keep the law's requirements, will they not be regarded as though they were circumcised? The one who is not circumcised physically and yet obeys the law will condemn you who, even though you have the written code and circumcision, are a lawbreaker. A man is not a Jew if he is only one outwardly, nor is circumcision merely outward and physical. No, a man is a Jew if he is one inwardly; and circumcision is circumcision of the heart, by the Spirit, not by the written code. Such a man's praise is not from men, but from God. (2:17-29)

6

The Heart of the Matter

ROMANS 2:17-29

A passage in the *The Great Divorce* perfectly portrays a characteristic which I believe is common to people who reject Christ and are lost — a misleading religious confidence. Lewis makes this point in a fanciful conversation between a resident of Hell (who apparently does not know he is in Hell) and an old acquaintance who is visiting from Heaven.

After some typically British opening comments, the resident of Hell remarks that as he remembered, his old friend had gotten rather narrow-minded towards the end of his life — believing in a literal Heaven and Hell. At length the visitor from Heaven interjects,

"Is it possible you don't know where you've been?"

"Now that you mention it, I don't think we ever do give it a name. What do you call it?"

"We call it Hell."

"There is no need to be profane, my dear boy. I may not be very orthodox in your sense of that word, but I do feel that these matters ought to be discussed *simply*, and *seriously*, and *reverently*."

"Discuss Hell *reverently*? I meant what I said. You have been to Hell."

"Go on, my dear boy, go on. That is so like you. No doubt you'll tell me why, in your view, I was sent there. I'm not angry."

"But don't you know? You went there because you are an apostate."

"Are you serious, Dick?"

"Perfectly!"

"This is worse than I expected. Do you really think people are penalised for their honest opinions? Even assuming, for the sake of arguement, that those opinions were mistaken."[1]

Although Lewis knew from the Scriptures that no one will be in Hell without knowing he is there, this fanciful conversation perfectly captures the misleading religious confidence of the damned.

Someday untold numbers, both the small and the great, will stand before the Great White Throne, at first disbelieving they are really there. Jesus himself made this clear in Matthew 7:22, 23:

"Many will say to me on that day, 'Lord, Lord, did we not prophesy in your name, and in your name drive out demons and perform many miracles?' Then I will tell them plainly, 'I never knew you. Away from me, you evildoers!'"

It is difficult to conceive that earnest, sincere religious people will be lost, but this and other Scriptures indicate this is indeed so. Moreover, some who will be judged come from among orthodox people who subscribe to the Apostle's Creed and can repeat the Nicene Creed:

I Believe in the Lord Jesus Christ
The Only Begotten Son of God
Begotten of Him before all ages
God of God, Light of Light
Very God of Very God. . . .

Some who believe in the inerrancy of the original autographs of Scripture — some who would fight to the last for the veracity of the Bible — will be lost! Why? Because they have been lulled by a false religious security which has prevented them from getting to the heart of the matter. Perhaps some of these will even read these words.

We have the antidote to such self-deception in 2:17-29, where Paul warns religious people like us to guard ourselves from the dangers of a false religious confidence.

Paul underlines two principal dangers here. The first is the danger of thinking we are okay because we possess the truth.

PAUL'S WARNING ABOUT OVERCONFIDENCE (VV. 17-24)

This, of course, was the great danger for the religious-minded Jew of Bible times. Every Jew realized that in respect to the truth he was privileged far above the rest of the people on the earth. Paul insightfully describes this sense of privilege in verses 17, 18:

> Now you, if you call yourself a Jew; if you rely on the law and brag about your relationship to God; if you know his will and approve of what is superior because you are instructed by the law . . .

In this one sentence the apostle notes that their sense of privilege had six aspects. First, *they were called Jews*, which means "praise to Jehovah." So proud were they of this name that many of the Jews living in Gentile cities used it as a surname. *Kent Hughes, Jew.*

Second, they relied upon *the possession of the Law* (the Torah) as giving them a unique standing before God. The thought here is not that they saw their special status coming from living by the Torah, but simply from possessing it.

Third, *they bragged regarding God.* Boasting in God can be good if it is for the right reason, but they were boasting because of their being God's favorites, the true people of God.

Fourth, *they prided themselves on knowing his revealed will*, derived from the Ten Commandments and other Old Covenant Scriptures.

Fifth, *they discerned the things that were essential.* That is, they prided themselves on being able to make superior moral judgments. They were far beyond the ignorant Gentiles!

Sixth, *they were instructed from the Law.* The Law was a light to their feet.

These six things were wonderful privileges. But as wonderful as they were, they had a deluding effect on the Jews. When they compared their enlightenment with the abysmal theological ignorance of the Gentiles they looked very good. Of course they were acceptable to God!

We today recognize their spiritual blindness. But the blade cuts both ways, does it not? The sword that pierces the heart of the religious Jew also pierces ours. It is easy to imagine we are okay because we know so much more about the Bible than the average person on the street, especially in this day of Biblical illiteracy. We can read the Bible in twenty-five versions if we want. Some of us carry around Bibles that have as many as eight parallel translations. It is a great temptation for the pastor to imagine that, as he struts to the pulpit carrying his Hebrew Bible in one hand and the Greek in the other, he is okay, when in fact he may have a heart of stone.

We know God's revealed will (the Bible) so well. We can find a verse for everything. Ultimately, it can become very natural to imagine as we look at the dark world all around us that we have a patent on the truth of God — we are okay! May God open our eyes as often as they need to be opened.

Finally, this delusion from privilege can lead to the deadly pride of arrogant presumption. Paul describes this in verses 19, 20:

> . . . you are convinced that you are a guide for the blind, a light for those who are in the dark, an instructor of the foolish, a teacher of infants, because you have in the law the embodiment of knowledge and truth . . .

Such pride and presumption can make one insufferable. That is what it did to the Jews. They fancied themselves guides — lights — correctors — teachers — and so looked down with condescension and scorn on the unwashed. The Gentiles sensed this and resented it. Tacitus said, "Among themselves their honesty is inflexible, their compassion quick to move, but to all other persons they show the hatred of antagonism." In Alexandria the Jews allegedly took an oath never to show kindness to a Gentile.[2] The very privileges which should have produced saints produced arrogant, loveless egotists instead!

Again, the sword cuts both ways because those who hold the truth of the gospel often become this way as well. Prideful presumption upon religious privilege can breed a self-righteous, self-centered, self-deceived stuffed shirt.

> To some who were confident of their own righteousness and looked down on everybody else, Jesus told this parable:

> "Two men went up to the temple to pray, one a Pharisee and the other a tax collector. The Pharisee stood up and prayed about himself; 'God, I thank you that I am not like all other men — robbers, evildoers, adulterers — or even like this tax collector. I fast twice a week and give a tenth of all I get.' But the tax collector stood at a distance. He would not even look up to heaven, but beat his breast and said, 'God, have mercy on me, a sinner.'" (Luke 18:9-13

Whenever a follower of Christ feels superior, he should beware, for such an attitude is not a sign of God's grace. To come into a position of spiritual privilege only to succumb to self-righteous arrogance indicates that one's soul is in great danger. Our familiarity with holy things must never give way to spiritual presumption.

I heard someone who had come to know Christ just a few weeks earlier excitedly tell another Christian, "I have found the most wonderful verse in all the Bible. It's John 3:16 — 'For God so loved the world . . .'" That is the way it ought to be with each one of us! There is ever danger for those of us who take for granted the oracles of God.

To those who have succumbed to the pride of privilege and presumption, Paul asks some penetrating but healing questions. These are good therapy for all of us. Because they were meant to humble his hearers, they were asked in such a way that they demanded agreement.

> . . . you, then, who teach others, do you not teach yourself? You who preach against stealing, do you steal? You who say that people should not commit adultery, do you commit adultery? You who abhor idols, do you rob temples? You who brag about the law, do you dishonor God by breaking the law? (vv. 21-23)

Many of the Jewish teachers and leaders were guilty of these offenses — and it was common knowledge. Everyone knew of cases where the most orthodox had left loopholes in their business dealings for a little "refined stealing." The Talmud itself charged three of its most illustrious rabbis with adultery.[3] And while they abhorred idolatry and the dishonor of God, they had robbed God's Temple by profaning sacred things, committing, as Cranfield says, "subtle forms of sacrilege."[4] Even if they had not done these things overtly, spiritually they were guilty! Thus, in just a few sentences Paul does away with the false security which they could derive from having the truth. They were not okay. Their lives did not measure up to the truth they possessed.

Paul ends his cross-examination with a burst of accusation: "As it is written: 'God's name is blasphemed among the Gentiles because of you'" (v. 24). Not only do they not measure up to their privilege and presumption in having the truth, but they disgrace it! The sacred name of God which none of these religious Jews would ever repeat with his lips was because of them actually blasphemed by the Gentiles with whom they associated. Similarly, Nathan solemnly told David, ". . . by doing this you have made the enemies of the Lord show utter contempt" (2 Samuel 12:14). Abraham experienced essentially the same thing when he told

Pharaoh that Sarah was his sister and Pharaoh took her into his harem. After the discovery Abraham and Sarah went away, and Abraham had no more testimony for God before the Egyptians.

Stuart Briscoe tells about having to deal with a fellow employee who had embezzled a large sum of money from the bank for which they both worked. The reason the man embezzled was that he had two wives and families to support. When he was apprehended and fired, he stunned everyone by saying, "I am very sorry for what I have done, and I need to know whether I should fulfill my preaching commitments on Sunday in our local church." Briscoe says that in the following weeks he spent a great part of his time mending the damage done by that man's blatant inconsistency. To his chagrin, he found that his fellow workers not only despised the man, but ". . . were quick to dismiss the church he belonged to as a 'bunch of hypocrites,' the gospel he professed to believe as a 'lot of hogwash,' and the God he claimed to serve as 'nonexistent.'"[5]

We have all, unfortunately, heard the name of God blasphemed by unbelievers because of immoral actions by those who claim to be believers. We may assume that because we have the truth we are okay, but this is a dangerous presumption. God is not impressed by our claims of orthodoxy, and neither is the world. What *does* impress God and the world is an orthodoxy which produces a new life — an orthodoxy of action.

PAUL'S WARNING ABOUT FALSE SECURITY IN ASSOCIATION (vv. 25-27)

There is another danger, a natural twin to the danger of thinking we are acceptable to God because we have the truth: namely, thinking we are right before the Lord because we are affiliated with his people. The Jews supposed they were secure because they were part of God's chosen people through circumcision. They believed circumcision somehow secured salvation. Rabbi Menachem, in his commentary on the Book of Moses, wrote, "Our Rabbis have said that no circumcised man will see Hell."[6] Another said, "Circumcision saves from Hell." The midrash Tillim says, "God swore to Abraham that no one who was circumcised should be sent to Hell."[7]

The rite of circumcision was a beautiful thing. When originally given to Abraham, it was a public demonstration or testimony of his commitment to God. Paul says in 4:11 that "he [Abraham] received the sign of circumcision, a seal of the righteousness that he had by faith while he was still uncircumcised." This signified that all of his life was God's and was meant to signify this among his descendants. It was something like a wedding ring between God and his people. Yet, Paul says that circumcision will *not* justify a man before God.

> Circumcision has value if you observe the law, but if you break the law, you have become as though you had not been circumcised. (v. 25)

Circumcision was of great value if one understood and lived its intended significance. However, if its meaning was disregarded, it was as meaningless as a wedding ring on an adulterer's finger. Faith and performance gave circumcision its reality.

Paul continues by logically turning to the other side of the coin:

> If those who are not circumcised keep the law's requirements, will they not be regarded as though they were circumcised? The one who is not circumcised physically and yet obeys the law will condemn you who, even though you have the written code and circumcision, are a lawbreaker. (vv. 26, 27)

Paul is not exactly saying that uncircumcised Gentiles can keep the Law, but rather that if they do they will be reckoned as circumcised. Moreover, they then could be called to bear witness in judgment against the circumcised who have transgressed the Law. Paul's argument was devastating! One of the greatest insults in Judaism was to call another Jew "an uncircumcised one," and this is what Paul had done in no uncertain terms. Circumcision alone does not justify a man. His actions must be consonant with his profession of faith.

In applying this to ourselves, all we have to do is substitute for the word "circumcision" any of the following: Church membership — baptism — confirmation — Methodist — Baptist — Presbyterian — and so on. The great mistake of Catholics, Protestants, and Jews when asked about their relationship to God is to cite their religious affiliation as evidence of their relationship.

"Are you a believer?" "Of course. I've been a member of First Church for twenty-five years."

"Are you a believer?" "I'm a Catholic! Does that answer your question?"

"Are you a believer?" "Why yes, I was baptized right here in Christian Church."

There are as many answers as there are affiliations and rites, but none will convince God — they are all outward circumcisions.

PAUL'S ASSURANCE IN A RIGHT HEART (vv. 28, 29)

In conclusion Paul takes us to the very heart of the matter.

> A man is not a Jew if he is only one outwardly, nor is circumcision merely outward and physical. No, a man is a Jew if he is one inwardly; and circumcision is circumcision of the heart, by the Spirit, not by the written code. Such a man's praise is not from men, but from God. (vv. 28, 29)

I like Dr. Barnhouse's rendering:

> For he is not a Christian who is one outwardly, nor is that "church membership" which is outward in the flesh; but he is a Christian who is one inwardly; and "church membership" is that of the heart, in the Spirit, not in the letter, whose praise is not of men, but of God.[8]

It is so easy to be self-deceived by our familiarity with the truth and/or our religious affiliations. But God is not fooled at all. A passage in the prophecy of Ezekiel (33:30-32) amazingly describes the self-deception and hypocrisy of religious people. I use the word *amazingly* because this Old Testament text is so contemporary. In these verses God addresses Ezekiel the preacher:

> "As for you, son of man, your countrymen are talking together about you by the walls and at the doors of the houses, saying to each other, 'Come and hear the message that has come from the Lord.'"

The people's talk about going to hear the preaching of the Word uses conventional terms of religious piety. However, verse 31 indicates the true state of their hearts:

> "My people come to you, as they usually do, and sit before you to listen to your words, but they do not put them into practice. With their mouths they express devotion, but their hearts are greedy for unjust gain."

They sit in the congregation and look like the real thing, but their hearts are set on making money. Ultimately, according to verse 32, nothing happens.

"Indeed, to them you are nothing more than one who sings love songs with a beautiful voice and plays an instrument well, for they hear your words but do not put them into practice."

God is never fooled. The truth is, earnest, confident, religious people will ultimately be lost. Some who believe the creeds implicitly and mouth untarnished orthodoxy will be told, "Depart from me, I never knew you."

We all need to go to the heart of the matter. The Old Testament recognized that circumcision was a matter of the heart. Moses said to his people,

"The Lord your God will circumcise your hearts and the hearts of your descendants, so that you may love him with all your heart and with all your soul, and live." (Deuteronomy 30:6)

Jeremiah exhorted his people to deal with their hearts saying, "Circumcise yourselves to the Lord, circumcise your hearts" (Jeremiah 4:4a). The New Testament also describes a true believer in terms of inner circumcision:

For in Christ all the fulness of the Deity lives in bodily form, and you have been given fullness in Christ, who is the head over every power and authority. In him you were also circumcised, in the putting off of the sinful nature, not with a circumcision done by the hands of men but with the circumcision done by Christ. (Colossians 2:9-11)

We must each consider the question, Where does our confidence lie? Does it rest either on our knowledge of God's Word or our religious affiliation? If so, we are deluded.

True salvation is a matter of the heart.

... That if you confess with your mouth, "Jesus is Lord," and believe in your heart that God raised him from the dead, you will be saved. For it is with your heart that you believe and are justified, and it is with your mouth that you confess and are saved. (Romans 10:9, 10)

There are people who can quote most of the verses I quote (maybe more) and who have as good a knowledge of the English Bible as I have. But they do not have Christ. I have even seen such people come to Christ.

God's Word is surgical. It is meant to pierce hearts. If God has spoken to you and revealed your need and your heart is troubled, there is hope for you.

What advantage, then, is there in being a Jew, or what value is there in circumcision? Much in every way! First of all, they have been entrusted with the very words of God. What if some did not have faith? Will their lack of faith nullify God's faithfulness? Not at all! Let God be true, and every man a liar. As it is written: "So that you may be proved right in your words and prevail in your judging." But if our unrighteousness brings out God's righteousness more clearly, what shall we say? That God is unjust in bringing his wrath on us? (I am using a human argument.) Certainly not! If that were so, how could God judge the world? Someone might argue, "If my falsehood enhances God's truthfulness and so increases his glory, why am I still condemned as a sinner?" Why not say — as we are being slanderously reported as saying and as some claim that we say — "Let us do evil that good may result"? Their condemnation is deserved. What shall we conclude then? Are we any better? Not at all! We have already made the charge that Jews and Gentiles alike are all under sin. As it is written: "There is no one righteous, not even one; there is no one who understands, no one who seeks God. All have turned away, they have together become worthless; there is no one who does good, not even one." "Their throats are open graves; their tongues practice deceit." "The poison of vipers is on their lips." "Their mouths are full of cursing and bitterness." "Their feet are swift to shed blood; ruin and misery mark their ways, and the way of peace they do not know." "There is no fear of God before their eyes." Now we know that whatever the law says, it says to those who are under the law, so that every mouth may be silenced and the whole world held accountable to God. Therefore no one will be declared righteous in his sight by observing the law; rather, through the law we become conscious of sin. (3:1-20)

7

The Religious Advantage

ROMANS 3:1-20

Hans Christian Andersen's story of *The Emperor's New Clothes* is among everyone's favorites because of its humor and because of the point it so aptly makes. We probably all know the story: A certain emperor was very fond of appearances and clothing. So when certain clever philosophers (actually they were con men) offered to weave him a rare and costly garment, he was quite receptive. He especially liked their promise that the garment would be invisible to all but the wise and pure in heart. The delighted emperor commissioned his new clothing at great cost, and the con men sat before the empty looms and pretended to be weaving.

Soon the emperor's curiosity became such that he sent his chief minister to see how things were going. Seeing no cloth on the busy looms, and not wanting to be thought unwise and impure in heart, the official returned with a report about the fabulous beauty of the cloth. After a time the weavers asked for more money. Again the emperor became impatient, sending his second chief minister, who returned with an even more enthusiastic report. Next the emperor went himself. Though he too saw nothing, he did not want to appear stupid, so he proclaimed the clothing excellent and beautiful. He even gave the weavers medals.

Finally, on the day set for the grand parade, the con men dressed the emperor in his nakedness and then skipped town. As the emperor paraded before his people *au naturel*, the whole populace joined in praising his beautiful new clothing, lest they be thought of as fools and knaves. Thus the absurd parade continued — until in a moment of quietness a child was heard to say, "The emperor has no clothes!" At once everyone knew the

71

truth, including the emperor. One innocent but honest remark by a small child who did not know enough to keep his mouth shut stripped away the hypocritical pretense of the entire nation.

The Emperor's New Clothes is such a great story that we use the term proverbially to describe a common tendency: We remain quiet while a fallacy is being promoted to which everyone is subscribing, because we do not want to be thought of as fools.

As we approach the third chapter of Romans, we must keep in mind that it well describes the condition of the Jews whom Paul has just been addressing. The Jews imagined themselves to be clothed with a righteousness that was actually nonexistent. They were duped by a misleading religious confidence. So Paul, like the little boy, stripped away their layers of delusion. They believed that because they possessed the Word of God they were safe. They saw themselves as guides to the blind, correctors of the foolish, teachers of the immature. But Paul undressed them, proving that having God's Word is no guarantee of life. Paul also stripped away their errant confidence in circumcision, showing that their religious affiliation would not save them.

As he undressed his fellow Jews, he also undresses us, stripping away our misleading confidence in having God's Word and our "right" affiliations. For all mankind, Jew and Gentile alike, true righteousness is a matter of the heart! ". . . a man is a Jew if he is one inwardly; and circumcision is circumcision of the heart, by the Spirit, not by the written code" (2:29).

Paul argument was devastating! It really did leave his religious kinsmen naked. And Paul, who was widely experienced in this particular debate, anticipated the reader's reaction, which he voiced for them in the first verse of chapter 3: "What advantage, then, is there in being a Jew, or what value is there in circumcision?" This was not a frivolous objection. Today we would phrase the question differently: "If being affiliated with God's people through such things as baptism and church membership will not save us, and if having the Word of God is not enough to ensure our salvation or holiness, what is the advantage of being under the umbrella of the Church and Christianity?" I think this is a fair question, especially for those of us who have not benefited from being raised in a church. As we will now see in verses 1-20, there were substantial advantages in being raised a Jew, and there are likewise solid advantages in being raised under the teaching of the Church today.

Paul addresses this matter of advantage from three perspectives. The first is in verses 1, 2, the second is in verses 3-8, and the third — which is where we will focus most of our attention — is in verses 9-20.

THE JEWISH ADVANTAGE:
THE WORD OF GOD (vv. 1, 2)

Even as Paul voiced the anticipated question of his readers in verse 1 by saying, "What advantage, then, is there in being a Jew, or what value is there in circumcision?" he was ready with an answer in verse 2: "Much in every way! First of all, they have been entrusted with the very words of God." Specifically, he meant that their primary advantage was that they had the entire Old Testament revelation of God, the *logia* of God.

Having the written self-revelation of God was an immense advantage to the Jew, and it remains so for us today. First, because we have *the written description of God's eternal nature*. God's Word teaches us that God is the all-powerful Creator and completely sustains the universe. It reveals that he is perfect in holiness, in righteousness, in love, in justice. We learn from this that there is an infinite gulf between us and him. The God of the Scriptures is majestic, transcendent, beyond total human comprehension. Having this disclosure from God is an immense help because this is not how the natural mind thinks of God, no matter how intellectual or intelligent it is. The unbeliever always wrongly closes the gap between God and man — either by bringing God down or by raising man up. There is therefore a huge advantage for those who have the written Word of God.

The second advantage of having the oracles of God is that we have a written description of *the nature and purpose of man*. This is closely tied in with the revelation of God because if we see the majesty of God, we are able to see ourselves as we truly are. Human beings who respect God the Creator can begin to understand the mystery of their own being. This, coupled with the Scripture's revelation of our radical corruption, allows us to see ourselves as lost sinners, a fact which those without the oracles of God cannot fully see. Our ultimate personal advantage in having God's Word is that we have written directions as to what is required of mankind — that we are to love God with all our being (Mark 12:30, 31).

The advantage of being among God's people, then, as an initiated Jew and today as a churchgoer is tremendous. We have God's Word. We know what God is like. We know what we are like. And we know what he requires for salvation.

What Paul is saying in his imaginary dialogue is powerful stuff, and he knew it! He had suffered violence in other places for saying the same thing. He knew his hearers' minds were flying to irrational objections because he had heard them all before in many heated conversations.

THE JEWISH ADVANTAGE:
DESPITE IRRATIONAL OBJECTIONS (vv. 3-8)

In verses 3-8 Paul names the objections and answers them, showing that the advantage of being a Jew still stands. The objections are three. First: "What if some did not have faith? Will their lack of faith nullify God's faithfulness?" (v. 3). This is a strange objection which argues essentially: "Paul, how can you possibly say we Jews have so completely failed in our privileged position and still insist that we are an advantaged people? If we have failed as you insist, God's Word is powerless and he is unfaithful." Paul's answer is found in verse 4:

> Not at all! Let God be true, and every man a liar. As it is written: "So that you may be proved right in your words and prevail in your judging."

God is always true, no matter how much man falls short. The apostle has quoted David's repentant words after his sin with Bathsheba, affirming God's justice and giving proof that God remains faithful and true no matter how individuals may sin. The objection is therefore illogical.

The second objection is in verse 5:

> But if our unrighteousness brings out God's righteousness more clearly, what shall we say? That God is unjust in bringing his wrath on us? (I am using a human argument.)

Here God is accused of using the Jews to his advantage — showing his righteousness by their failure. Therefore he is unrighteous and cannot rightly judge those whom he has so used.

Verse 6 has Paul's answer: "Certainly not! If that were so, how could God judge the world?" That is, "You know better than that — God will judge the world, including you."

The third objection is similar:

> Someone might argue, "If my falsehood enhances God's truthfulness and so increases his glory, why am I still condemned as a sinner?" Why not say — as we are being slanderously reported as saying and as some claim that we say — "Let us do evil that good may result"? (vv. 7, 8)

Here is a base argument: "What you are saying, Paul, is an incentive to

sin. If being bad makes God look good, we will be bad so he looks good."
This ridiculous argument disregarded the difference between good and
evil. Paul does not even answer it, but simply says in verse 8b, "Their
condemnation is deserved."

These were irrational, foolish arguments! Even so, they accurately
represent the thinking of those who had the privilege of having the written Word of God but rejected it. I have heard unbelievers who were raised
under the Word say things that are just as crass.

The truth is, our advantage is great in every way. First and foremost,
we have the written self-revelation of God. We know what God is like —
and the rest of the world does not. We know what we are like as well, but
others without God's Word lack this knowledge. We know what God's
standards are. It is hard for us to imagine what it is like to be without his
Book. We have no idea what it is like to grow up without the Church.
Some of us have great-grandparents, grandparents, parents, brothers and
sisters, and spouses who all know Christ. Our massive advantage is not
a thing to be trifled with. We should thank God every day for our incalculable advantage.

THE JEWISH ADVANTAGE:
DESPITE UNIVERSAL SIN (vv. 9-20)

As Paul comes to a final point, he dramatizes the immensity of the
advantage of the Jew (and us) because all the world is equally under sin.
If this argument does not thrill us, perhaps nothing will. In verse 9 Paul
indicts the entire human race: "What shall we conclude then? Are we
any better? Not at all! We have already made the charge that Jew and
Gentiles alike are all under sin." The force of the language here leaves
no doubt about what is meant. The word is "sin — not "sins" — and
means "the dynamic of sin," and "under" means "under the power or
dominion of." Everyone in the world is under the power of the dynamic
of sin!

What we have in this statement and in the following verses is the most
explicit description of the total depravity of mankind in all of Scripture. This
does not mean man is as depraved as he could be, but that there is always
room for "deprovement" because he is under the power of sin.

Dr. Addison Leitch used to illustrate this by saying that if the color
of sin were blue, every aspect of us would be some shade of blue. The Latin
precursor of our word *radical* is the word *radix*, which means "root." We
are all infected with a radical corruption. We are morally ruined at our very

roots. Jesus said the fruit is corrupt because the tree is radically corrupt (cf Mathew 7:15-20).

Paul charges all humanity, however good some individuals may appear, with this radical corruption. Turgenev, the Russian poet, caught it perfectly when he said, "I don't know what the heart of a bad man is like, but I do know what the heart of a good man is like and it is terrible."

Paul substantiates his charge by stringing a series of Old Testament texts together. This is called a *charaz*, which literally means "stringing pearls."[1] He quotes six Old Testament sources in fourteen sweeping statements with devastating artistry. First he describes mankind's depraved *character* and then his depraved *conduct* and finally the *cause*.

As to our *character*, the apostle says in verse 10, "'There is no one righteous, not even one.'" In case anyone was thinking there 'might be an exception, he does away with that idea once and for all — "'not even one.'" We use relative terms for righteousness in respect to earthly standards, but the standard used here is the righteousness of God which is perfectly manifested in the righteousness of Christ, and none of us comes close to that. Only Jesus Christ kept the great commandment to love God with all his heart, with all his soul, with all his strength, and with all his mind, and his neighbor as himself (Luke 10:27). How many of us have kept this divine requirement perfectly since we got up this morning? "'Not even one.'"

"'There is no one who understands. . . '" (v. 11). Understands what? The depth of the attributes of God. Sin makes this impossible. No matter what level of spiritual life and understanding we reach, there will always be a deficiency in our understanding. Moreover, the more we sin, the less capable of understanding we become. "'. . . no one who seeks God'" (v. 11). That is, no one by nature wants to know God. This is a verse which many Christians simply do not believe. Often we speak of someone we know who is "really seeking after God." That just is not so! The word translated "seek" means "to seek out," implying a determined search.[2] Mankind does not search for God or the truth. Rather, he suppresses it and finally turns to idolatry (1:18-23). There is one exception: if the Holy Spirit is truly working in one's heart, there is an authentic seeking.

Verse 12 goes on, "'All have turned away, they have together become worthless.'" This describes the logical outcome of the preceding statements. Because no one has stayed on the path to God, they have become useless. They cannot fulfill their purpose as creatures made in the image of God. They are like fish that cannot swim or birds that cannot fly. "'There is no one who does good, not even one'" (v. 12b). Obviously men do good things, but they do not do them consistently or profoundly.

A good work must not only conform to the commandments of God, it must come from a heart committed to honoring him, and no one habitually does this. Thus far Paul's *charaz* is devastating. Man's character forms a sad string of "pearls" indeed.

Now Paul turns to man's *conduct*. His emphasis is first on human speech, and he paints a disgusting picture, proceeding from throat to tongue to lips to mouth:

> "Their throats are open graves; their tongues practice deceit." "The poison of vipers is on their lips." "Their mouths are full of cursing and bitterness." (vv. 13, 14)

The speech of those without God is like the odor from an open sepulchre. Sometimes it is filthy, sometimes it is deceiving, sometimes it is as deadly as a cobra's bite.

Paul's final touch as to conduct in verses 15-17 sounds like a condensed history of the world. As we read these verses we must remember that the activity of the feet is a frequent Scriptural metaphor for one's approach to life.

"'Their feet are swift to shed blood; ruin and misery mark their ways, and the way of peace they do not know.'"

Man's depravity is seen in his rush to violence. Will Durant wrote in his *Lessons From History*: "In the last 3,421 years of recorded history only 268 have seen no war."[3] During World War II it was estimated that it took $225,000 to kill one enemy soldier. I wonder how much is being spent by the major nations today. Man loves violence!

Paul describes one final pearl on his *charaz* in verse 18: "'There is no fear of God before their eyes.'" First the *character*, then the *conduct*, and now the *cause*: the fear of God is left out of their thinking.

Paul's charge still stands today. The entire human race — Jews or Gentiles, religious or irreligious, pious or pagans — is utterly depraved. Note the overwhelming force of Paul's conclusion:

> Now we know that whatever the law says, it says to those who are under the law, so that every mouth may be silenced and the whole world held accountable to God. Therefore no one will be declared righteous in his sight by observing the law; rather, through the law we become conscious of sin. (vv. 19, 20)

OUR ADVANTAGE

Some may ask, How can we conclude that those who have the Word, as we do, are advantaged since all are under sin? The answer is seen in the last line of our text: "through the law we become conscious of sin" (v. 20b). "Conscious" is literally "the intimate knowledge [the *epignosis*] of sin." *The first function of the Law is to unmask us and show us we are sinners, and this is our supreme advantage.* We understand at least to some extent our radical corruption.

So God's Word strips away our "emperor's clothing" of self-deceit and reveals our souls' nakedness. The world system proclaims we are robed and well when we are not. God's Word cries above the self-deceived crowd that we are not okay. We say, "I am rich; I have acquired wealth and do not need a thing," but God says, "You are wretched, pitiful, poor, blind and naked" (Revelation 3:17). What advantage does this bring to us? Much in every way!

We must each see our own nakedness. We must make use of our great advantage of truly knowing who we are and who God is, and what he wants of us as declared in his Word:

> I counsel you to buy from me gold refined in the fire, so you can become rich; and white clothes to wear, so you can cover your shameful nakedness; and salve to put on your eyes, so you can see. (Revelation 3:18)

But now a righteousness from God, apart from law, has been made known, to which the Law and the Prophets testify. This righteousness from God comes through faith in Jesus Christ to all who believe. There is no difference, for all have sinned and fall short of the glory of God, and are justified freely by his grace through the redemption that came by Christ Jesus. God presented him as a sacrifice of atonement, through faith in his blood. He did this to demonstrate his justice, because in his forbearance he had left the sins committed beforehand unpunished — he did it to demonstrate his justice at the present time, so as to be just and the one who justifies the man who has faith in Jesus. Where, then, is boasting? It is excluded. On what principle? On that of observing the law? No, but on that of faith. For we maintain that a man is justified by faith apart from observing the law. Is God the God of Jews only? Is he not the God of Gentiles too? Yes, of Gentiles too, since there is only one God, who will justify the circumcised by faith and the uncircumcised through that same faith. Do we, then, nullify the law by this faith? Not at all! Rather, we uphold the law. (3:21-31)

8

The Miracle
of Righteousness

ROMANS 3:21-31

As we have seen, Paul made and sustained the charge that all mankind is under the dynamic of sin and therefore radically corrupt. To do this he employed the rabbinical preaching technique called *charaz*, the stringing together of a number of short Old Testament quotations to drive home his point. Paul thus exposed the devastating *character* of man's depravity:

> "There is no one righteous, not even one; there is no one who understands, no one who seeks God. All have turned away, they have together become worthless; there is no one who does good, not even one." (vv. 10-12)

Paul then described the *conduct* of man's depravity as seen in his words and actions. Lastly, he stated the *cause* of man's depravity by quoting Psalm 36:1 in verse 18: "'There is no fear of God before their eyes.'" In view of all this there could be no conclusion other than that the entire human race suffers from a radical inner corruption. For any honest soul today, Ivan Turgenev's admission ("I do not know what the heart of a bad man is like, but I do know what the heart of a good man is like, and it is terrible") says it all. All mankind is under the dynamic of sin.

This dynamic presents a dilemma for both God and man. From the human point of view, how can we as such profoundly corrupt beings ever be made righteous in the sight of God? Divine justice demands the condemnation of mankind, yet divine love wants to reach out to the guilty human race.

Given this great dilemma, we come to the universally acknowledged great divide of Paul's letter to the Romans: God with his heavenly creativity comes up with what I like to call "The Miracle of Righteousness." God's total answer is sufficient for man's total failure. The great Donald Grey Barnhouse superinscribed a heart over these verses in his Bible because "I am convinced today, after these many years of Bible study, that these verses are the most important in the Bible."[1] These verses are certainly the turning point in Romans, and they could be the turning point for each of us as we study this passage.

What is the miraculous arrangement whereby profoundly corrupt sinners can be made just before a holy God? This is possible for three reasons, stated consecutively in verses 21-26 of our text. The first is in verse 21, where we see that the miracle of justification is possible because a special righteousness exists separate from the works of the Law.

THE MIRACLE OF JUSTIFICATION: RIGHTEOUSNESS APART FROM THE LAW (v. 21)

"But now a righteousness from God, apart from law, has been made known, to which the Law and the Prophets testify" (v. 21). What is this righteousness apart from the works of the Law like? Dr. Barnhouse used to illustrate it by drawing a yardstick which he called the divine measure. At the top he wrote Christ's words from Matthew 5:48 — "Be perfect, therefore, as your heavenly Father is perfect." The apex of the yardstick represented the absolute righteousness of Christ. Then he would draw vertical lines alongside the measure that represented varying degrees of man's righteousness. One line would reach three-quarters up because some people are 75 percent righteous. One would almost touch the top, representing someone who is 98 percent righteous, but never quite makes it because, as Barnhouse wrote on the side, "for all have sinned and fall short of the glory of God" (3:23).

This was a good illustration in many respects, but it also taught something fundamentally wrong. It unwittingly implied that some need 25 percent grace and others 2 percent. While it is indeed true that all "fall short of the glory of God," it is not true that human righteousness ever comes close to this special righteousness apart from the Law. Specifically, this righteousness is not a legal righteousness, but is rather a status of righteousness before God which comes to us as a gift. It is infinitely beyond human righteousness. It is a radical righteousness.

Paul says in verse 21 that it "has been made known, to which the Law and the Prophets testify." The Law pointed to this radical righteousness as mankind kept falling short of the Law's commands. Along with this, the Law's insistence on blood sacrifice reminded mankind that the works of righteousness would never be enough. The Old Testament prophets witnessed to this radical righteousness by direct statement — for example, Isaiah 45:24: "They ["every knee . . . every tongue," v. 23] will say of me, 'In the Lord alone are righteousness and strength.'" The Law and the Prophets bear witness to this righteousness apart from the Law.

The greatest display of this radical righteousness was of course the life of Christ. From a human perspective Jesus Christ achieved eternal life through sheer merit. He is the only man who ever deserved eternal life simply by the way he lived. Jesus is the radical righteousness of God! As Paul says in 1 Corinthians 1:30, "[Christ Jesus] has become for us wisdom from God—that is, our righteousness, holiness and redemption."

What does the existence of this radical righteousness apart from the Law mean to us? Everything! Our radical corruption, so clearly spelled out in Paul's *charaz*, precludes any hope of making it by works. But the existence of a righteousness apart from works gives hope to us. Moreover, the hope is equally offered to everyone because we are all on the same level, whether we are 80 percent or 20 percent righteous. The miracle of justification is possible because a special righteousness exists separate from works, a righteousness which comes to us through Jesus Christ. That is my hope, and I trust it is yours.

THE MIRACLE OF JUSTIFICATION: RIGHTEOUSNESS BY FAITH (vv. 22, 23)

> This righteousness from God comes through faith in Jesus Christ to all who believe. There is no difference, for all have sinned and fall short of the glory of God. (vv. 22, 23)

Paul's forthright statement here underlines what we have been saying. Human righteousness is of great importance in human relations and should not be practically minimized, but it does not produce God's salvation. The ethical moralist and the sexual voyeur both fall short. Paul reduces the best that any man can do to zero. There is no distinction.

The key to having the righteousness of God is *faith*. The redundancy of the opening line of verse 22 emphasizes this: "This righteousness from God comes through faith in Jesus Christ to all who believe."

Elsewhere (Philippians 3:9) Paul calls this "the righteousness that comes from God and is by faith." Verse 28 of our text says it with great clarity: "For we maintain that a man is justified by faith apart from observing the law." When Martin Luther translated this verse into German he felt the sense of it so strongly that he added the word "alone" — "by faith alone!" *Sola fide.*

What does this mean to us? Again the answer is, *everything!* As radically corrupt sinners, we rise from helplessness to hope when we see that a righteousness exists apart from the Law. And our hope skyrockets when we see that our righteousness comes through faith. Everyone who believes will have it!

The miracle of justification is possible because God's special righteousness comes through faith. Considering the depths of our sin, there is no other way any of us could make it!

THE MIRACLE OF JUSTIFICATION: RIGHTEOUSNESS FROM CHRIST'S WORK (vv. 24-26)

> ... and are justified freely by his grace through the redemption that came by Christ Jesus. God presented him as a sacrifice of atonement, through faith in his blood. (vv. 24, 25a)

A key to God's making this righteousness possible is found in the term "sacrifice of atonement" (literally "propitiation"). F. F. Bruce, one of the most prominent New Testament scholars of our time, points out that the same word is used twenty times in the Greek Old Testament to denote the golden cover of the Ark of the Covenant, the so-called mercy seat, the place where the priest sprinkled the blood of sacrifice to assuage God's just wrath on sin.[2] Similarly, Anders Nygren argues that verse 25 should read, "whom God displayed publicly as a mercy seat in His blood."[3]

In using this symbol Paul had several things in mind. He remembered that the mercy seat was the place where God manifested his *presence* in Israel. God said to Moses:

> "There, above the cover between the two cherubim that are over the ark of the Testimony, I will meet with you and give you all my commands for the Israelites." (Exodus 25:22)

Paul also knew that God manifested his *glory* at the mercy seat. On the Day of Atonement when the priest entered the Holy of Holies, it was necessary that a cloud of incense cover the mercy seat so he would not die (Leviticus 16:13).

Most of all, the apostle remembered that the priest had to sprinkle blood seven times on the mercy seat to make *atonement* for God's people and to turn away God's wrath at their sins (Leviticus 16:14ff.). The Ark contained the Law of the Ten Commandments, and the ceremony portrayed the fact that a broken Law stood between a holy God and mankind. But through the shedding of blood this place of judgment became the place of reconciliation. In Christ's death the demands of God for justice against a sinful race are fully met, leaving him free to be merciful to those who formerly merited only judgment. Christ is our mercy seat, and he has been displayed by God as such (v. 25).

We have considered how Christ made possible our righteousness. Why he did it is outlined in the remainder of verses 25 and 26:

> He did this to demonstrate his justice, because in his forbearance he had left the sins committed beforehand unpunished—he did it to demonstrate his justice at the present time, so as to be just and the one who justifies the man who has faith in Jesus.

Simply put, in the past God did not pour out his full wrath on men for their sins. He was patient and merciful. Some might question his righteousness in doing this. However, in Jesus' death he demonstrated his wrath against sin. It is here — in Christ being the mercy seat — that we see the miraculous love and creativity of God. God found a way to forgive us and yet maintain his moral integrity. He forgave us without condoning our sin. How? By directing toward himself, in the person of his Son, the full weight of the wrath we deserved. Thus God's holy character is not compromised.

The amazing genius of God is further seen in that his plan also preserved the dignity of mankind. God does not act as if our sin does not matter. C.E.B. Cranfield explains it this way:

> The purpose of Christ's being . . . (*hilasterion*, mercy seat) . . . was to achieve a divine forgiveness which is worthy of God, consonant with His righteousness, in that it does not insult God's creature man by any suggestion that he is after all of but small consequence.[4]

Lastly, God demonstrates through Jesus' death that his hatred of man's evil is as real as his forgiveness of man's sin. God did not spare his

Son one iota of the wrath we deserve. The only way God could save us consistent with his own justice was the way he did — and it cost him everything!

We are loved! This is so wonderful that perhaps we should lie flat on our faces, struck dumb before God — or perhaps on our backs laughing. So phenomenal is his love that both responses would be proper.

It is good to often reflect on this miracle of justification. First, the miracle was made possible because a special radical righteousness exists apart from the Law. This is immensely encouraging because in our radical corruption we could never become acceptable to God. Next, the miracle comes through faith, not works. Everyone can make it in Christ if they want to. Lastly, the miracle of justification is possible because of the genius of God who made his Son a mercy seat, receiving our just judgment and giving us life. There is a double transfer — all that we are and have done becomes Christ's, and all that he is and has done becomes ours. Second Corinthians 5:21 tells us, "God made him who had no sin to be sin for us, so that in him we might become the righteousness of God." Praise God!

What does this radical righteousness mean practically? It means there is to be no boasting:

> Where, then, is boasting? It is excluded. On what principle? On that
> of observing the law? No, but on that of faith. For we maintain that
> a man is justified by faith apart from observing the law. (vv. 27, 28)

When it comes to salvation, boasting is unthinkable. Everything is of God. This is a call for humility, and humility paves the way for the exhilarating, infinite grace of God to deluge our bankrupt human hearts and bring us life. This is where all who are without Christ must begin. They must put down their pride and boasting and come with empty hands that they might receive this radical, true righteousness.

What else does this righteousness through faith mean? It means we are all on equal footing.

> Is God the God of Jews only? Is he not the God of Gentiles too? Yes,
> of Gentiles too, since there is only one God, who will justify the cir-
> cumcised by faith and the uncircumcised through that same faith.
> (vv. 29-30)

Since there is only one God, salvation is the same for everyone. When we get to heaven some of us will be surprised at who is there. And some people will be surprised when they see us there!

Justification is indeed a miracle. If you have not received his radical righteousness, do so right now. If you are ready for new life, acknowledge your radical sinfulness to God. Agree with him that "There is no one righteous, not even one," that "All have turned away," that "there is no one who does good, not even one!" Trust God's promise that there is a righteousness apart from the works of the Law. Tell God you are solely resting your faith on Christ who died for your sins, so you could become the righteousness of God. Thank him for cleansing you.

Or if you have already taken this step of faith into new life in Christ, tell someone else who does not yet know him about this miracle of justification.

What then shall we say that Abraham, our forefather, discovered in this matter? If, in fact, Abraham was justified by works, he had something to boast about — but not before God. What does the Scripture say? "Abraham believed God, and it was credited to him as righteousness." Now when a man works, his wages are not credited to him as a gift, but as an obligation. However, to the man who does not work but trusts God who justifies the wicked, his faith is credited as righteousness. David says the same thing when we speaks of the blessedness of the man to whom God credits righteousness apart from works: "Blessed are they whose transgressions are forgiven, whose sins are covered. Blessed is the man whose sin the Lord will never count against him." Is this blessedness only for the circumcised, or also for the uncircumcised? We have been saying that Abraham's faith was credited to him as righteousness. Under what circumstances was it credited? Was it after he was circumcised, or before? It was not after, but before! And he received the sign of circumcision, a seal of the righteousness that he had by faith while he was still uncircumcised. So then, he is the father of all who believe but have not been circumcised, in order that righteousness might be credited to them. And he is also the father of the circumcised who not only are circumcised but who also walk in the footsteps of the faith that our father Abraham had before he was circumcised. It was not through law that Abraham and his offspring received the promise that he would be heir of the world, but through the righteousness that comes by faith. For if those who live by law are heirs, faith has no value and the promise is worthless, because law brings wrath. And where there is no law there is no transgression. Therefore, the promise comes by faith, so that it may be by grace and may be guaranteed to all Abraham's offspring — not only to those who are of the law but also to those who are of the faith of Abraham. He is the father of us all. (4:1-16)

9

Sola Fide

ROMANS 4:1-16

A preacher, long-departed from the truth of the gospel, told the following story to summarize the faith he taught. It seems that a frog one day fell into a pail of milk, and though he tried every conceivable way to jump out, he always failed. The sides were too high, and because he was floating in the milk he could not get enough leverage for the needed leap. So he did the only thing he could do. He paddled and paddled and paddled some more. And *oila!* — his paddling had churned a pad of butter from which he was able to launch himself to freedom. The preacher's message was: "Just keep paddling, keep on working, keep on doing your best, and you will make it."

We smile at this exaggerated simplification, but this actually describes our American "man on the street" folk religion quite well. Despite the fact that "Amazing Grace" is our favorite hymn, most people think that if you just do your best you will somehow make it to Heaven. Modern man is, as a matter of fact, deeply hostile to the concept of justification by faith alone through God's grace. He is much more comfortable with the motto: "We get our salvation the old-fashioned way. We earn it!" Justification through the "good life" — that computes.

Such thinking is, of course, nothing new. It is endemic to human nature and has characterized religious thinking from time immemorial. It was the received wisdom, the conventional thinking, of the Jews in the time of Jesus and Paul. For those people then, Abraham was the prime example of a man who was justified by his works, as rabbinic literature eloquently testifies. The Mishnah's third division *Kiddushin* (4.14) makes a specious interpretation of Genesis 26:5, wrongly concluding: "and we find that Abraham our father had performed the whole law before it was given, for it is written, '*Because that Abraham obeyed my voice and kept my charge, my commandments, my statues, and my laws.*'[1] The earlier Book of Jubilees (*circa* B.C. 100) similarly says, "For Abraham was perfect in all his deeds with the Lord, and well-pleasing in righteousness all the days of his life."[2] So perfect was Abraham thought to be that another book, *The Prayer of Manasses*, concluded that Abraham never had need of repentance: "Thou, therefore, O Lord, that art the God of the righteous, hast not appointed repentance unto the righteous, unto Abraham. . . ."[3] What claims! 1) Abraham performed the whole Law before it was written, 2) he was perfect in all his deeds, and 3) he had no need of repentance. Conclusion: Abraham was justified by his works and therefore is an example to follow. Case closed!

Perhaps closed for some, but not for the Apostle Paul, the lawyer of grace. Paul acknowledges that Abraham was righteous, but he denies that the Jews had any right to present him as an example of righteousness by the works of the Law. Here in Romans 4 Paul takes Abraham away from the proponents of works-righteousness and brilliantly sets him forth as an example of those who are saved, not by works, but by faith alone — *sola fide*.

SOLA FIDE FOR ABRAHAM (vv. 1-5)

The apostle begins, "What then shall we say that Abraham, our forefather, discovered in this matter? If, in fact, Abraham was justified by works, he had something to boast about — but not before God. What does the Scripture say?" And here he quotes Genesis 15:6 in answer: "'Abraham believed God, and it was credited to him as righteousness'" (vv. 1-3). Paul's point here is that Abraham was justified by faith *before* he did any of the great works for which he is so famous.

In order to catch the full impact of Abraham's amazing faith we need to frame Genesis 15:6 in its context. Abraham had just come off a great military victory in which he and 318 of his men had rescued Lot, defeating four kings in battle (Genesis 14), and like Elijah after his great victory over the prophets of Baal, Abraham was suffering a post-victory letdown. Perhaps as he drifted off to sleep, he was reflecting with weary negativism on his having been in the land for ten years but still having no heir to carry on the line. But then God spoke to him in a vision: "'Do not be afraid, Abram. I am your shield, your very great reward'" (Genesis 15:1). Rousing words! Nevertheless, Abraham, still discouraged, recited his plight: "'O Sovereign Lord, what can you give me since I remain childless and the one who will inherit my estate is Eliezer of Damascus? . . . You have given me no children'" (Genesis 15:2, 3). It was at this point that the promise of the Lord came to him: "'This man will not be your heir, but a son coming from your own body will be your heir.' He took him outside and said, 'Look at the heavens and count the stars — if indeed you can count them.' Then he said to him, 'So shall your offspring be'" (Genesis 15:4, 5).

We do not know whether Abraham's response was immediate or after some thought, or even whether it was verbal or mental, but we do have this immortal record: "Abram believed the Lord, and he credited it to him as righteousness" (Genesis 15:6). Though Abraham had been childless all his eighty-plus years, though Sarah had been infertile all those years and was well beyond childbearing years, Abraham *truly believed* he would have an heir from his own body. Because of this, before his great works, it was "credited to him as righteousness." God was so pleased with Abraham's faith that he not only credited him with righteousness, but that night appeared as "a smoking fire pot with a blazing torch .º.º. and passed between the pieces" of a sacrifice (Genesis 15:17), thus signifying that the promise he had made to Abraham (children and blessing) was unconditional.

The word "credited," *logizomai*, appears eleven times in Romans 4 and has the idea of crediting to one's account. This is evident despite the various ways different translations render it: *counted, reckoned, considered, imputed, computed*. These all mean that righteousness was credited to Abraham's account because of faith, not because of works!

Paul destroyed the wrongful use of Abraham as an example of the conventional works-salvation view — and he did it using the sacred text of the Genesis Torah. Salvation for Abraham, their model of models, was *sola fide*!

Having established the faith alone principle from Genesis 15:6, the apostle next states the principle in what were startling terms to the traditional Jewish ear: "Now when a man works, his wages are not credited to him as a gift, but as an obligation. However, to the man who does not work, but trusts God who justifies the wicked, his faith is credited as righteousness" (vv. 4, 5). This was shocking indeed, first because Paul discourages working for salvation! To be sure, in other places he encourages good works (cf. Philippians 2:12, 13) but not here where the doctrine of salvation is at stake.

Second, this was shocking because the paradoxical description of God as a "God who justifies the wicked" (literally *the ungodly*) assaulted traditional sensibilities. In the Old Testament the acquittal of the wicked and the condemnation of the innocent is repeatedly denounced. In fact, to discourage such injustice God presented himself as an example saying, "I will not acquit the guilty" (Exodus 23:7). Thus, to say that God justifies the wicked seemed outrageous to the law-abiding Jews. How could this be? The answer lies in the difference between law and grace. God forbids in the Law what in fact he does in the gospel.[4]

Sola fide, the doctrine of faith alone, offends our natural sensibilities. We naturally think justification ought to go to the good, those who are trying to do their best — the paddlers. But not to the ungodly! We can understand how Abraham was justified by faith, because he was a God-fearer. But the wicked? But the truth is, *we are all ungodly/wicked*. None of us are good enough. Salvation will be *sola fide*, or it simply will not be. "You see, at just the right time, when we were still powerless, Christ died for the ungodly" (5:6). Again, grace has power which the Law never had.

SOLA FIDE FOR DAVID (vv. 6-8)

Having established that Abraham was reckoned as righteous by faith *before* his good works, and having memorably stated the *sola fide* principle, Paul presents the experience of another great Old Testament saint — King David. Here he refers to David's blessedness and joyous relief at having his sins against Bathsheba and Uriah forgiven, an *undeserved* righteousness bestowed upon him, as described in Psalm 32:1, 2. Paul explains in verses 6-8:

> David says the same thing when he speaks of the blessedness of the man to whom God credits righteousness apart from works: "Blessed are they whose transgressions are forgiven, whose sins are covered. Blessed is the man whose sin the Lord will never count against him."

Ostensibly, Paul turned to this psalm because of the rabbinical principle of interpretation that when the same word is used in two Biblical passages, each can be used to interpret the other. (Genesis 15:6 and Psalm 32:2 both contain the same word — *logizesthai*, LXX and *hasab*, MT — which the NIV renders "credited" in Genesis 15:6 and "count" in Psalm 32:2.)[5]

But a deeper reason David had unmerited righteousness credited to him is, it was because of faith! David had broken three of the ten Commandments outright as he coveted Bathsheba, committed adultery, and murdered Uriah — and the Old Testament sacrificial system made no provision for such premeditated sin.[6] This is why David cried in Psalm 51:16,17:

> You do not delight in sacrifice, or I would bring it; you do not take pleasure in burnt offerings. The sacrifices of God are a broken spirit; a broken and contrite heart, O God, you will not despise.

David's case was hopeless. There was nothing he could do but cast himself on God's mercy. Regarding this, F. F. Bruce says of Psalm 32:

And if we examine the remainder of the psalm to discover the ground on which he was acquitted, it appears that he simply acknowledged his guilt and cast himself in faith upon the mercy of God.[7]

Paul calls David "blessed," and David twice calls himself "blessed" because when there was no work that could possibly atone for his sins he was forgiven on *sola fide*! So the principle of faith alone was mightily established and illustrated in the life of Israel's greatest king — a "man after [God's] own heart" (1 Samuel 13:14). Nothing you and I can ever do can atone for our sins. Our only hope is "a righteousness from God, apart from law . . . to which the Law and the prophets testify. This righteousness from God comes through faith in Jesus Christ to all who believe" (3:21, 22).

SOLA FIDE FOR GENTILES (vv. 9-12)

The intense Jewishness of Paul's argument could lead some at this point to assume that *sola fide* was for Jews only. After all, Abraham is the Jew of Jews, the grand patriarch. So Paul now asks the question, "Is this blessedness only for the circumcised, or also for the uncircumcised? We have been saying that Abraham's faith was credited to him as righteousness" (v. 9). And he answers his own question in favor of the Gentiles:

> Under what circumstances was it credited? Was it after he was circumcised, or before? It was not after, but before! And he received the sign of circumcision, a seal of the righteousness that he had by faith while he was still uncircumcised. So then, he is the father of all who believe but have not been circumcised, in order that righteousness might be credited to them. And he is also the father of the circumcised who not only are circumcised but who also walk in the footsteps of the faith that our father Abraham had before he was circumcised. (vv. 10-12).

Paul's answer indicates that Abraham was credited as righteous at least fourteen years *before* he was circumcised. Genesis 15:4-6 records the promise to Abraham that he would have an heir. Genesis 16:16 records that he was eighty-six years old when Hagar bore him Ishmael (as a result of his attempting to help God bring about the promise). And Genesis 17:24 indicates that Ishmael was thirteen when he, his ninety-nine-year-old father Abraham, and his whole household were circumcised. Thus, there is a space of some fourteen years, assuming that Hagar became pregnant soon after Abraham's faith in Genesis 15:6. But the time gap may be even greater because traditional Jewish chronology places circumcision twenty-nine years after Genesis 15:6.[8]

The point is, Abraham was declared a righteous man while a Gentile — and remained so for some fourteen to twenty-nine years before he was a Jew! Therefore, *sola fide* was a Gentile principle long before it was Jewish reality. *Sola fide* is for everyone — Jew and Gentile! Abraham is the father of uncircumcised believers and the father of circumcised believers — not on the ground of circumcision but of faith. Through the solidarity of faith, Jews and Gentiles are brothers and sisters in Christ.

SOLA FIDE TRANSCENDS THE LAW (vv. 13-15)

If circumcision and its many blessings had nothing to do with Abraham's justification, the Law had even less to do with it. Paul explains in verse 13, "It was not through the law that Abraham and his offspring received the promise that he would be heir of the world, but through the righteousness that comes by faith." The historical fact is, as Paul has written in Galatians 3:17, the Law came 430 years after Abraham was made heir to the promise by faith — and there is thus no way the Law could invalidate or restrict its scope. To make the promise conditional on obedience to the Law, which was not even hinted at when the promise was given, would nullify the whole promise. Righteousness, and its promised benefits, has always come by faith to those who live by faith!

Pursuing righteousness both by the Law and by faith is impossible, "For if those who live by law are heirs, faith has no value and the promise is worthless, because law brings wrath. And where there is no law there is no transgression" (vv. 14, 15). The Law makes the promise worthless, because if we have to keep the Law to receive the promise, the promise will never be fulfilled. Moreover, the Law promotes transgression and wrath (cf. 5:20; 6:7, 8). No one can keep the Law, so the Law enhances one's sense of transgression and failure and the sense of being under God's wrath. The Law promotes defeat and pessimism, but faith brings joy, assurance of the promise, and thus a life of optimism.

"Don't be fooled," says Paul in effect, "the principle of faith transcends the Law." Abraham was credited as righteous because of his faith. So was David. *Sola fide* preceded the Jews; it preceded the Law; it is for everyone!

SOLA FIDE (v. 16)

Paul draws this magnificent conclusion: "Therefore, the promise comes by faith, so that it may be by grace and may be guaranteed to all Abraham's offspring — not only to those who are of the law but also to those who are of the faith of Abraham. He is the father of us all" (v. 16). The universal principle of grace teaches us that salvation comes by faith alone. Oh, how badly our frog-paddling world needs to know this!

Today it is fashionable to derive our preaching agendas from the "felt needs" of men and women on the street — the homiletics of consensus. But I am convinced that the average person on the street does not know what he needs. What today's person really needs is a clear understanding of the opening chapters of Romans. I am convinced that is what the church needs too, far more than advice on how to raise children or how to handle money (subjects which I do preach on!).

We need to understand just how radically sinful we are — how sin so effects every part of us that we are totally unable to live up to God's standards and effect our own salvation — that we are lost in ourselves.

We need to understand that we are in need of a radical righteousness which comes "from God" alone (1:17) and that "This righteousness from God comes through faith in Jesus Christ to all who believe" (3:22). We need to understand that we must "be found in him, not having a righteousness of my own that comes from the law, but that which is through faith in Christ — the righteousness that comes from God and is by faith" (Philippians 3:9), so that we can say, "he saved us, not because of righteous things we have done, but because of his mercy" (Titus 3:5a).

It was *sola fide* for Abraham—*sola fide* for David—*sola fide* for the Gentiles—*sola fide* before, during, and after the Law—it is always for all *sola fide*.

> *Not what these hands have done*
>   *Can save this guilty soul;*
> *Not what this toiling flesh has borne*
>   *Can make my spirit whole.*
> *Not what I feel or do*
>   *Can give me peace with God,*
> *Not all my prayers and sighs and tears*
>   *Can bear my awful load.*
> *Thy work alone O Christ,*
>   *Can ease this weight of sin;*
> *Thy blood alone, O Lamb of God,*
>   *Can give me peace within.*
> *Thy grace alone, O God,*
>   *To me can pardon speak,*
> *Thy power alone, O Son of God,*
>   *Can this sore bondage break.*
> *I bless the Christ of God;*
>   *I rest on love divine;*
> *And, with unfalt' ring lip and heart,*
>   *I call this Savior mine.*
>
>   (Horatius Bonar, 1861)

As it is written: "I have made you a father of many nations." He [Abraham] is our father in the sight of God, in whom he believed — the God who gives life to the dead and calls things that are not as though they were. Against all hope, Abraham in hope believed and so became the father of many nations, just as it had been said to him, "So shall your offspring be." Without weakening in his faith, he faced the fact that his body was as good as dead — since he was about a hundred years old — and that Sarah's womb was also dead. Yet he did not waver through unbelief regarding the promise of God, but was strengthened in his faith and gave glory to God, being fully persuaded that God had power to do what he had promised. This is why "it was credited to him as righteousness." The words "it was credited to him" were written not for him alone, but also for us, to whom God will credit righteousness — for us who believe in him who raised Jesus our Lord from the dead. He was delivered over to death for our sins and was raised to life for our justification. (4:17-25)

10

The Faith of Abraham

ROMANS 4:17-25

One of the favorite books around our house is the *Guinness Book of World Records*. It has been on our shelf for years. Now and then I see one of my boys reading it to stock up on trivia. How much did the heaviest man weigh? (1,069 pounds.) How tall was the tallest man of modern times? (8'11". He wore a size 37AA shoe.) What is the world's record for bearing children? (Sixty-nine. The record was set by a Russian peasant woman who achieved great honor in her country. She had eight sets of twins, seven sets of triplets, and four sets of quads.) This is terribly important information for the trivia buff, hence our valued dog-eared copy! But, alas, I did find an error in the esteemed *Guinness Book* because it states that the oldest mother on record gave birth in October 1956 at the age of fifty-seven, thus setting the world record. However, this is entirely wrong![1]

The last part of Romans 4 focuses on the events surrounding the true world record for the oldest mother and the world-changing implications of that birth. Paul has stated a masterful argument for justification by faith in Romans 3, culminating in the summary statement in verse 28: "For we maintain that a man is justified by faith apart from observing the law." Justification comes by faith alone, or *sola fide* as Luther translated it. As *The Living Bible* plainly translates verse 28, "we are saved by faith in Christ and not by the good things we do."

Earlier in chapter 4 Paul has sustained the argument that justification comes by faith alone. He turned to the example of the patriarch Abraham and demonstrated that Genesis 15:6 means what it says: "Abram believed the Lord, and he credited it to him as righteousness."

Abraham's righteousness by faith was established some fourteen years before he was circumcised. So Paul's conclusion is that righteousness comes by faith apart from the works of the Law, and that it is equally available to all, whether they be people of the Law or not.

In 4:17-25 Paul explains the nature of true faith by describing what went on inside Abraham relative to the miraculous, world-record-setting birth of Isaac. It is as if Paul was able to unfasten the wing nuts holding down the top of Abraham's head and give us an intimate look at the inner workings of this great man of faith. As we consider the example of Abraham, each of us will come to a better understanding of faith. First, we will see Abraham's perception of the *object* of his faith. Second, we will see Abraham's perception of the *obstacles* of his faith. Third, we will see Abraham's perception of the *objectives* of his faith.

ABRAHAM'S PERCEPTION: THE OBJECT OF FAITH (v. 17)

The object of Abraham's faith is very easy to discern. It was God alone, according to verse 17:

> As it is written: "I have made you a father of many nations." He is our father in the sight of God, in whom he believed — the God who gives life to the dead and calls things that are not as though they were.

The God "who gives life to the dead and calls things that are not as though they were" was clearly the object of the patriarch's faith. It is fundamental that we understand that the object of one's faith is most important. One's faith, outstanding as it may be, will never benefit its owner if it has the wrong object.

Some have had strong faith in thin ice but did not live to tell about it. They actually died by faith. Or to use another example, I may leave church next Sunday with the utmost faith that my car will get me home because it looks OK. However, if someone removes my hubcaps and lug bolts, then replaces the hubcaps, my faith will be to no avail — the wheels will fall off! On the other hand, if I have little faith in my car and drive it with trepidation, but no one has fooled with it, I'm perfectly safe despite my weak faith, because the object of my faith is strong.

When my son Carey was little, he used to hide on top of the refrigerator and jump on me when I passed. However, he had a misplaced faith in the object of his plunge (yours truly!)—and if he had tried it too many times, one of us would have been out of business!

By Scripture and by analogy we conclude that Abraham's faith was not exemplary due to its intrinsic strength, strong as it was, but because its object was God. We all have faith. The decisive issue is where we place the faith we have.

Abraham grasped two massive concepts about God. First, he understood that God "gives life to the dead." Although there had been no recorded resurrection at this point in history, and although God had not revealed any doctrine of resurrection, Abraham believed in God's resurrection power! This was borne out when he obediently raised the knife above Isaac. He knew that if Isaac died, God could resurrect him (cf. Genesis 22:5).

Second, he saw God as a God who "calls things that are not as though they were." God creates *ex nihilo*, from nothing. This is, of course, a towering concept. Perhaps, in retrospect, there is some suggestion here of God's restoration of Abraham and Sarah's procreation process. God for all purposes created Isaac *ex nihilo*.

Abraham's perception of God as the object of his faith was immense, and this gigantic concept dominated his entire experience of faith. It can makes all the difference in us too.

Robert Dick Wilson was one of the great professors at Princeton Theological Seminary. One of his students had been invited to preach in Miller Chapel twelve years after his graduation. Old Dr. Wilson came in and sat down near the front. At the close of the meeting, the old professor came up to his former student, cocked his head to one side in his characteristic way, extended his hand, and said, "If you come back again, I will not come to hear you preach. I only come once. I am glad that you are a big-godder. When my boys come back, I come to see if they are big-godders or little-godders, and then I know what their ministry will be." His former student asked him to explain, and he replied, "Well, some men have a little god, and they are always in trouble with him. He can't do any miracles. He can't take care of the inspiration and transmission of the Scripture to us. He doesn't intervene on behalf of his people. They have a little god and I call them little-godders. Then, there are those who have a great God. He speaks and it is done. He commands and it stands fast. He knows how to show himself strong on behalf of them that fear him. You have a great God; and he will bless your ministry." He paused a moment, smiled, said, "God bless you," and turned and walked out.[2]

If our view of God is as exalted as Abraham's, if we see God as so vast that he creates *ex nihilo* and gives life to the dead, if you and I really believe this, if we are "big-godders," it will make an equally immense difference in our faith and approach to life. Two questions are relevant here: 1) Is God the object of our faith? 2) How do we perceive the object of our faith?

We have seen Abraham's perception of the object of his faith. Now we come to his perception of the obstacles to his faith.

ABRAHAM'S PERCEPTION: THE OBSTACLES TO FAITH (vv. 18-20)

See if you can pick out the obstacles in these verses:

> Against all hope, Abraham in hope believed and so became the father of many nations, just as it had been said to him, "So shall your offspring be." Without weakening in his faith, he faced the fact that his body was as good as dead—since he was about a hundred years old—and that Sarah's womb was also dead. Yet he did not waver through unbelief regarding the promise of God. . . . (vv. 18-20a)

Abraham's faith faced two obstacles. The obvious barrier to his believing God would give him a child was the biological impossibility due to Sarah's and his age.

The less obvious obstacle was the staggering nature of the promise. That is, the promise was so wonderful, it was hard to believe — it was too good to be true! To think that his descendants would be as numerous as the stars above and the dust below, that all the earth would be blessed through him, that he would achieve a standing he did not deserve — this was difficult to believe. The first part of verse 20 touches on this when it says, "Yet he did not waver through unbelief regarding the promise of God." Though it was all so incredible, he did not vacillate. Birthdays came and went — eighty-seven, ninety-two, ninety-five, ninety-nine, and year after year another candle was placed on his *baklava* — and then God told him the promised son would be born the very next year! Through all of this Abraham did not waver regarding the fantastic promise.

The greatest obstacle, of course, was not the staggering promise, but the clear biological impossibility of Abraham and Sarah having offspring. He was impotent, and Sarah was barren. After all, Sarah was ninety and he was almost 100 when God gave him the covenant of circumcision and reaffirmed the promise of a son (cf. Genesis 17:1).

Interestingly, the older English translations based on the *Textus Receptus* render verse 19 as, "He considered *not* his own body now dead" (italics added). Apparently some scribe thought the verse made better sense by adding the word "not." However, the recent discovery of more ancient manuscripts confirm that Abraham took every relevant factor into consideration, including his great age. He contemplated the facts, which he fully understood, and believed God!

Some people are under the impression that when a person has "faith" he inwardly agrees to ignore the facts. They see faith and facts as mutually exclusive. Faith without reason is *fideism*; reason without faith is *rationalism*. In practice there must be no reduction of faith to reason. Likewise, there must be no reduction of reason to faith. Biblical faith is a composite of the two. Abraham did not take an unreasonable leap of faith.

How did Abraham come to such a massive exercise of faith? He weighed the human impossibility of becoming a father against the divine impossibility of God being able to break his word and decided that if God was God, nothing is impossible. As F. F. Bruce says, the patriarch believed "the bare word of God."[3] Genesis 17 reveals that God appeared before him and spoke directly to him, revealing himself as *El Shaddai*, the God of bounty and reproduction. And amidst involuntary laughter Abraham believed.

It must have been something when Abraham gave Sarah the news. I can imagine Sarah saying, "Where have you been?" Perhaps he said, "I have been outside having my devotions." And Sarah asked, "How was it?" Abraham may have replied, "It was great! I had a conversation with God. He told me something amazing." She replied, "What was it?" And he blurted out, as only a man will, "Well, you're going to have a baby!" I would like to have heard what Sarah said then.[4]

Abraham believed God! And we know exactly what he believed. He believed that God is the one "who gives life to the dead and calls things that are not as though they were" (v. 17).

Again, Abraham's majestic perception of his God was the ground on which he built his immense faith. To use Robert Dick Wilson's term, he was a "big-godder." Verse 18 says, "Against all hope, Abraham in hope believed." That is, against all human hope, Abraham in hope in God's promise believed, and so became the father of many nations."

> *In hope, against all human hope,*
> *Self-desperate, I believe; . . .*
> *Faith, mighty faith, the promise sees,*
> *And looks to that alone;*
> *Laughs at impossibilities,*
> *And cries: It shall be done!*
> (Charles Wesley)

Applying this to ourselves, if God is who he says he is (and he is!), none of his promises will fail because he forgets us or our situation is beyond his power. The problem is, many of us keep in the back of our minds unexorcised suspicions that what we say we believe about God's power is not really true. For all our lip service about trust in God, we rely chiefly upon what we can do ourselves. Some of us need to take deeper possession of the truths we have already believed about God. A good measure of how much spiritual truth we have appropriated is, how long is our worry list?

ABRAHAM'S PERCEPTION: THE OBJECTIVES OF FAITH (vv. 20B-22)

First, we saw Abraham's perception of the object of his faith, then his perception of faith's obstacles, and now we will consider Abraham's perception of the objectives of his faith. There were two.

The first objective of his faith was to glorify God, as the last line of verse 20 asserts: ". . . but was strengthened in his faith and gave glory to God." In this connection, we should emphasize that God is never glorified in a believer's life apart from faith — a full reliance on God. Abraham's life glorified God as few lives have because he demonstrated a faith that few mortals have shown. Some argue convincingly that verse 21 is one of the best definitions of faith in the Bible as it describes Abraham as "being fully persuaded that God had power to do what he had promised." May we glorify God in the same way, taking him at his word.

The second objective of Abraham's faith was righteousness. Verse 22 concludes the description of Abraham's faith by saying, "'it was credited to him as righteousness.'" Faith that makes one righteous before God perceives the immensity of God who creates from nothing and gives life to the dead (v. 17). Next, it is a faith that does not deny the existence of obstacles, but evaluates them in the light of God's Word and power (vv. 18-20). Ultimately, it brings the full assurance that what God has promised, he will perform (v. 21). That faith is reckoned for righteousness (v. 22). Faith is the only way any of us will ever be righteous before God.

Lest any of us try to relegate this to the moldy pages of ancient history, Paul says in verses 23, 24a: "The words 'it was credited to him' were written not for him alone, but also for us . . ." We can have righteousness too. Promises as staggering as those made to Abraham are ours. We are not only God's friends, but his sons and daughters! "Dearest Father" — "Abba, Father" is the language of our faith. And our present status will one day birth an entirely new state — "an eternal weight of glory far beyond all comparison" (2 Corinthians 4:17, NASB).

What are we to believe? What are we to put our faith in so as to be reckoned righteous? Paul is very explicit.

> The words "it was credited to him" were written not for him alone, but also for us, to whom God will credit righteousness — for us who believe in him who raised Jesus our Lord from the dead. He was delivered over to death for our sins and was raised to life for our justification. (vv. 23-25)

This is what we are to believe! We are to put our faith in God who raised up Christ who died for our sins and was resurrected for our justification.

That which Abraham believed and that which we are to believe are very similar. Anders Nygren put it this way: "When we believe in Jesus as 'put to death for our trespasses and raised for our justification,' we believe in the God 'who gives life to the dead.'"[5] In other words, to believe in Christ as described in verses 23-25 is to also believe in the stupendous God of Abraham.

How do we perceive the *object* of our faith — God? Hopefully as "the God who gives life to the dead and calls things that are not as though they were" — the God of the Resurrection.

How do we perceive the *obstacles* of our faith? Hopefully with realism and reason, weighing human possibilities against the divine impossibility of God breaking his word, and thus deciding that God is God and through him nothing is impossible.

How do we perceive the *objectives* of faith? Hopefully to glorify God through faith and find ourselves declared righteous. Abraham believed God, and it was reckoned to him as righteousness.

What is your perception of your state — righteous or unrighteous? Rest all on God and his Word.

Therefore, since we have been justified through faith, we have peace with God through our Lord Jesus Christ, through whom we have gained access by faith into this grace in which we now stand. And we rejoice in the hope of the glory of God. Not only so, but we also rejoice in our sufferings, because we know that suffering produces perseverance; perseverance, character; and character, hope. And hope does not disappoint us, because God has poured out his love into our hearts by the Holy Spirit, whom he has given us. You see, at just the right time, when we were still powerless, Christ died for the ungodly. Very rarely will anyone die for a righteous man, though for a good man someone might possibly dare to die. But God demonstrates his own love for us in this: While we were still sinners, Christ died for us. Since we have now been justified by his blood, how much more shall we be saved from God's wrath through him! For if, when we were God's enemies, we were reconciled to him through the death of his Son, how much more, having been reconciled, shall we be saved through his life! Not only is this so, but we also rejoice in God through our Lord Jesus Christ, through whom we have now received reconciliation. (5:1-11)

11

Justification – Exultation

ROMANS 5:1-11

Several years ago Lloyd Ogilvie wrote these heartening words, relevant to our present text:

> This past year has been the most difficult year of my life. My wife has been through five major surgeries, radiation treatment, and chemotherapy. I am thankful that I now know she is going to make it. During the same year, I suffered the loss of several key staff team-mates whose moves were very guided for them, but a source of pressure and uncertainty in my work. Problems which I could have tackled with gusto under normal circumstances seemed to loom in all directions. Discouragement lurked around every corner, trying to capture my feelings. Prayer was no longer a contemplative luxury, but the only way to survive. My own intercessions were multiplied by the prayers of others. Friendships were deepened as I was forced to allow people to assure me with words I had preached for years. No day went by without a conversation, letter, or phone call giving me love and hope. The greatest discovery that I have made in the midst of all the difficulties is that I can have joy when I don't feel like it — artesian joy.[1]

I personally have found this affirmation not only heartening but challenging. It is encouraging to hear of a fellow Christian who has undergone severe trials speak triumphantly of the joy which his faith gave him during those dark times. Unfortunately, such is not the experience of many believers. Their experience of faith has followed a course similar to many of the marriages we see. They begin with a boundless joy and promise which they never again attain. The buoyant optimism of the beginning fades to a dim memory.

That is not the way it is meant to be. Rather, our marriage to Christ is meant to begin on a high level and then go to even greater heights. The enviable joy that Ogilvie writes about can be the believer's through "thick and thin." I do not say this because of some sentimental idealism, but because that is the precise teaching of the Word in many, many passages, including Romans 5:1-11. This exultant section in Romans is the inevitable step for once hopelessly lost sinners who received through faith the righteousness of God and now stand justified before him. The true believer was once under wrath, but then was saved by faith, and now, as chapter 5 so powerfully maintains, he exults with great joy.

This passage is remarkable for several reasons. With its exalted language, it is hymn-like. There is also its air of confidence. Paul does not argue his case as he did in the preceding chapters. He simply states the facts in a marvelous chain of confident assertions. Our passage is also personal, as Paul switches to the first person plural — this is his experience along with all true believers. Lastly, the passage is remarkable because the joy of these verses is contagious. Every Christian can deepen his or her optimism and capacity for joy by understanding the benefits of justification as they are given by Paul in Romans 5:1-11.

THE GROUND OF EXULTING: PEACE AND GRACE (vv. 1-4)

Why does justification bring exultation? To begin with, through justification we receive the benefits of *"peace"* (v. 1) and *"grace"* (v. 2). Paul begins with a statement which many of us have committed to memory because of its importance: "Therefore, since we have been justified through faith, we have peace with God through our Lord Jesus Christ" (v. 1). Before we were Christians, we had not even the faintest chance for real peace because we were far from God. God had given us over to the destructive effects of our own sins and the sins of others (1:24, 26, 28). This resulted in profound alienation not only from God but from our fellow human beings, and also a constant tendency toward more depravity. To top it off, we stood under the ultimate wrath and judgment of God. No amount of personal bootstrap improvement could help us.

However, as Colossians 1:20 tells us, when we believed, God gave us peace with himself through the blood of the cross. The objective fact of that peace makes possible the inner subjective experience of peace with God. Whereas previously it was utterly impossible to experience true inner peace because God was not at peace with us, it is now ours because the Prince of Peace reigns in our hearts. That is why at the birth of Christ the angels chorused, "Glory to God in the highest, and on earth peace to men on whom his favor rests" (Luke 2:14).

I will never forget my first experience with peace. I was twelve and a half years old, and for about four months I had been sitting under the preaching of the gospel, hearing it clearly for the first time in my life. I came to a deep conviction of sin, and I met Jesus Christ. I can tell you without the slightest hyperbole or exaggeration that when I met him, the sky literally seemed to be bluer and the grass greener, and a great weight was lifted off my shoulders. For the first time in my life I knew the peace of God, and it was unlike any other peace I had ever known.

So as Paul begins this great chapter on exulting and boasting in God, he begins by stating the ground of the peace that God's children experience. At the very root of our joy is the peace of God.

Equally at the root of joy is the *grace* of God. Reading verses 1 and 2 together makes this very clear. "Therefore, since we have been justified through faith, we have peace with God through our Lord Jesus Christ, through whom we have gained access by faith into this grace in which we now stand." Grace is God's riches to us. Grace is the unsought, unde-served, and unconditional love of God. Grace is God pursuing us until he has found us and persevering with us ever afterwards. For Paul, grace and peace always go together. Even Paul's greeting in the opening verses of Romans show this: "Grace and peace to you . . ." (1:7). To stand in grace is to stand also in peace.

The effect of grace and peace together is to produce an exultant approach to life. First, as verse 2b says, "And we rejoice in the hope of the glory of God." Christians look forward to the day when they will fully behold the outward shining of God's inward being. The glory of God was seen in Jesus' life, as John tells us: "We have seen his glory, the glory of the one and only Son, who came from the Father" (John 1:14). There was also a time when his radiance broke through on the Mount of Transfigura-tion, where "His face shone like the sun" (Matthew 17:2). This is what all of us long for. Someday we will not only behold his glory, but will be glorified in him. Everything that now keeps us from being what God wants us to be will be gone forever!

Catch the force of Paul's words — "we rejoice in the hope of the glory of God." The word "rejoice" (*kaukaomai*) means to boast in the sense of jubilation — exultant rejoicing — to shout about it! We used to fall short of the glory of God (3:23), but now we boast in it! This sets us apart from the rest of the world. The Eastern religions offer no hope with their endless nightmare of reincarnations. Existentialists see the future as absurd. Evolutionists have no comfort. We Christians "rejoice in the hope of the glory of God" (v. 2).

It seems quite natural to exult in something which is positive. But the rejoicing that comes next (vv. 3, 4) is supernatural by anyone's standards: "Not only so, but we also rejoice in our sufferings, because we know that suffering produces perseverance; perseverance, character; and character, hope." As believers, we see our sufferings as potential for positive growth. Vance Havner in his book *It Is Toward Evening* tells the story about a small town that made its living entirely from growing cotton. It was not a great living, but it was a living. But calamity struck when the boll weevil invaded the community and threatened to ruin everyone. As it turns out, the farmers were forced to switch to peanuts and other crops that eventually brought them greater return than they would have made with cotton. Ultimately that which had seemed a disaster became the basis for undreamed prosperity. To register their appreciation, they erected a monument — to the boll weevil. To this very day in that little Southern town that monument stands.[2] We all have boll-weevil experiences: financial reversals, professional failure, relational disappointments, psychological or physical hurts. But these trials can bump us out of our old ways and force us to find new ways to live. Many tragedies can turn to triumphs through the Lord.

Verses 3 and 4 tell us that tribulation often becomes God's means to bring us to maturity. Look at the process. "Suffering produces perseverance" (v. 3b). The Greek word literally means "to abide under or stay under pressure." We naturally want to escape pressure, but tribulation forces us to stay under it — and ultimately this produces perseverance or stability. Next, "perseverance [produces] character." The word here derives from a group of words that have to do with the refining of metals, dross being burned away. Paul is speaking of sterling character — character without impurities. Hodge calls this "tried integrity."[3] This refined, pure character tends to confirm and strengthen our hope in the glory of God.

Are we experiencing this incredible exultation — this triumphant jubilation? Paul beautifully modeled it, as we see in 2 Corinthians 12:9 when he used exactly the same word saying, "Therefore I will boast all the more gladly about my weaknesses, so that Christ's power may rest on me." We exult in suffering because it is the path to spiritual maturity and glory. The great saints of God all agree. Ask Abraham and he will direct your attention to the sacrifice on Mount Moriah. Ask Jacob and he will point you to his stone pillow. Ask Joseph and he will tell you about the dungeon. Ask

Moses and he will remind you of his trials with Pharaoh. David will tell you his songs came in the night. Peter will speak of his denial, John of Patmos, and Jesus of the cross. Blessings are poured out in bitter cups.

THE GUARANTEE OF EXULTATION: UNBOUNDED LOVE (vv. 5-8)

It is a beautiful thing to experience God's peace and grace to the extent that we exult in tribulations as well as in the hope of glory. But how do we know this joy will not someday dissolve into delusion or that it is not a pipe dream now? The answer is, these great benefits are grounded in God's unbounded love. Verse 5 tells us: "And hope does not disappoint us, because God has poured out his love into our hearts by the Holy Spirit, whom he has given us."

The word used here for love is *agape*. Bishop Nygren tells us:

> When we realize that he never uses *agape* to express man's love to God, we shall not think that it is of man's love that Paul speaks in this verse. *Agape*, the love which God showed us in Christ, is for Paul so tremendous a fact that he regularly refrains from using the same word to express our love to God.[4]

God's love has been "poured out . . . into our hearts." The idea in the Greek is that God's love has been and continues to be poured out within our hearts. This is a picture of unstinting lavishness. The old commentator Bengel uses the Latin word "*abundantissime*."[5] Our hearts have been filled to overflowing with divine affection. The agent of this is the Holy Spirit, who personally represents God's love in our hearts.

What an amazing exposition of God's love Paul gives us. It is beyond the range of human experience. Realizing this, the apostle attempts to help us by commenting further on what Christ did:

> You see, at just the right time, when we were still powerless, Christ died for the ungodly. Very rarely will anyone die for a righteous man, though for a good man someone might possibly dare to die. But God demonstrates his own love for us in this: While we were still sinners, Christ died for us. (vv. 6-8)

The fine devotional publication *Daily Bread* has related the following story:

During the Revolutionary War there was a faithful preacher of the gospel by the name of Peter Miller. He lived near a fellow who hated him intensely for his Christian life and testimony. In fact, this man violently opposed him and ridiculed his followers. One day the unbeliever was found guilty of treason and sentenced to death. Hearing about this, Peter Miller set out on foot to intercede for the man's life before George Washington. The General listened to the minister's earnest plea, but told him he didn't feel he should pardon his friend. "My friend! He is not my friend," answered Miller. "In fact, he's my worst living enemy." "What!" said Washington. "You have walked 60 miles to save the life of your enemy? That, in my judgment, puts the matter in a different light. I will grant your request." With pardon in hand, Miller hastened to the place where his neighbor was to be executed, and arrived just as the prisoner was walking to the scaffold. When the traitor saw Miller, he exclaimed, "Old Peter Miller has come to have his revenge by watching me hang!" But he was astonished as he watched the minister step out of the crowd and produce the pardon which spared his life.

Peter Miller performed a noble act, and he -will be eternally commended. But this is just a shadow of what Christ did, because Christ not only obtained his enemies' pardons, but died for them to accomplish that.

Paul describes us here with four words: "powerless" (v. 6), "ungodly" (v. 6), "sinners" (v. 8), and "enemies" (v. 10). In so doing he tells us that God's love was totally unmotivated by anything in us. Because this love is unmerited and is not dependent upon us, it will never change. Think of it! We are lavished with a love that lies in God alone. God's love is the permanent possession of the child of God. The apostle hammers home this stupendous truth later in Romans as well:

Who shall separate us from the love of Christ? Shall trouble or hardship or persecution or famine or nakedness or danger or sword? . . . For I am convinced that neither death nor life, neither angels nor demons, neither the present nor the future, nor any powers, neither height nor depth, nor anything else in all creation, will be able to separate us from the love of God that is in Christ Jesus our Lord. (8:35, 38, 39)

Therefore we exult confidently in the hope of the glory of God — even in our tribulations! This is the reason for our unbounded optimism. This is why Lloyd Ogilvie could write God-honoring, optimistic words amidst his tribulation. This is why you and I can do the same.

THE HOPE OF FUTURE EXULTING: CONTINUAL BENEFITS (vv. 9-11)

We have already seen sufficient ground to never waver in our exultation. But God gives us even more. In verses 9 and 10 Paul uses an argument which the rabbis called *kal wahomer*, which means "light and heavy"[6] — an argument from the lighter to the heavier. We call it today in legal terms an *a fortiori* argument. We say, "If it was true in one place, it will be true in another." Paul's arguments in verses 9 and 10 are virtually identical and hinge on the term "much more."

> Since we have now been justified by his blood, how much more shall we be saved from God's wrath through him! For if, when we were God's enemies, we were reconciled to him through the death of his Son, how much more, having been reconciled, shall we be saved through his life!

The gist of this is: seeing what Christ did in dying to save us, how much more will he save us by his life! Jesus said, "Because I live, you also will live!" (John 14:19). The optimism this demands is boundless!

Paul concludes this section with these words in verse 11: "Not only is this so, but we also rejoice in God through our Lord Jesus Christ, through whom we have now received reconciliation."

Paul has stated that boasting is wrong (3:27). However, he means that boasting is wrong unless we are boasting in God. Verse 2 says we exult in the hope of God's glory. Verse 3 likewise shows that we exult in our tribulations, the road to glory. But above all, we exult in God himself (v. 11). Our rejoicing is not some theological chest-beating, but rather humble confidence of triumph through Jesus Christ.

We conclude with John Stott's summary of the significance of this section:

> We should be the most positive people in the world. We cannot mooch round the place with a dropping, hang-dog expression. We cannot drag our way through life, moaning and groaning. We cannot always be looking on the dark side of everything, as negative prophets of doom. No, "we exult in God." Then every part of our life becomes suffused with glory. Christian worship becomes a joyful celebration of God and Christian living a joyful service of God. So come, let us exult in God together![7]

Therefore, just as sin entered the world through one man, and death through sin, and in this way death came to all men, because all sinned — for before the law was given, sin was in the world. But sin is not taken into account when there is no law. Nevertheless, death reigned from the time of Adam to the time of Moses, even over those who did not sin by breaking a command, as did Adam, who was a pattern of the one to come. But the gift is not like the trespass. For if the many died by the trespass of the one man, how much more did God's grace and the gift that came by the grace of the one man, Jesus Christ, overflow to the many! Again, the gift of God is not like the result of the one man's sin: The judgment followed one sin and brought condemnation, but the gift followed many trespasses and brought justification. For if, by the trespass of the one man, death reigned through that one man, how much more will those who receive God's abundant provision of grace and of the gift of righteousness reign in life through the one man, Jesus Christ. Consequently, just as the result of one trespass was condemnation for all men, so also the result of one act of righteousness was justification that brings life for all men. For just as through the disobedience of the one man the many were made sinners, so also through the obedience of the one man the many will be made righteous. The law was added so that the trespass might increase. But where sin increased, grace increased all the more, so that, just as sin reigned in death, so also grace might reign through righteousness to bring eternal life through Jesus Christ our Lord. (5:12-21)

12

Grace Abounding

ROMANS 5:12-21

It is universally agreed that the passage before us is one of the greatest theological sections in the entire Bible. In its ten verses Paul summarizes the theology of the preceding chapters about the lostness of man and his rescue through God's provision.

It is also commonly agreed that Romans 5:12-21 is among the most difficult passages in Romans, if not in the entire New Testament. In this respect Anders Nygren says, "Paul's thoughts leap forth here like a torrential mountain stream. They rush on with such force that they do not always come to carefully formed expression."[1] As a result, when we read this section it is difficult to stay with the flow of thought.

Part of our task is to put this into simple terms — a commendable goal if we keep Einstein's advice before us that "we should make things as simple as possible, but not simpler than they are."

Though this is not a perfect outline, the flow of the passage follows this general plan:

I. The Ruin of Mankind (vv. 12-14)
II. The Rescue of Mankind (vv. 15-19)
III. The Reign of Mankind (vv. 20, 21)

There is a very positive progression here. The passage begins in the abyss with man's ruin and ascends through his rescue to the pinnacle of his reign. This is what the result can be in our lives if we interact with the magnificent flow of this passage. As believers we are intended to reign.

113

But the truth is, many of us are not reigning. We are like the Philistine king described in Judges 1:4-7 whom the Israelites captured and cut off his thumbs and big toes and who afterward remarked with amazing philosophical detachment, "Seventy kings with their thumbs and big toes cut off have picked up scraps under my table. Now God has paid me back for what I did to them" (v. 7). The Philistine was a king, but could no longer function as such. His hands could no longer hold scepter or sword. He could no longer stride across his realm. He was reduced to awkwardly picking scraps from under tables and tottering about. Some of us too no longer live like the kings and queens we are (see 1 Peter 2:9). Instead of dining, we are under the table hoping for morsels. A passage such as this can restore what we have lost so we can again reign as we ought.

THE RUIN OF MANKIND (vv. 12-14)

Verse 12 describes mankind's ruin in just twenty-seven English words: "Therefore, just as sin entered the world through one man, and death through sin, and in this way death came to all men, because all sinned . . ." The ruin that Paul describes is, of course, the fall of Adam as recorded in Genesis 2, 3. In 2:17 God gave the prohibition, "but you must not eat from the tree of the knowledge of good and evil, for when you eat of it you will surely die." But they sinned (Genesis 3:6, 7). The result, Paul tells us, is that sin and death spread to all men because, as the final words of our verse say, "all sinned." The verb "sinned" is in the aorist tense, which signifies a completed action in the past. The idea is, all of us sinned in that simple completed act — no exceptions! This is the foundational statement of our human condition of ruin and a basic truth of Christian theology.

We should stop here and take note that this idea is not easy for us to understand or accept because of our modern tendency toward "me — me — me." Our individualism makes many reject, with little thought, the idea that we could possibly share in Adam's sin.

But the Biblical mind did not have this problem. In Hebrew "Adam" means *mankind*. People in Bible times understood that the human race has a corporate solidarity in Adam. Thus all mankind was present and actually sinned in Adam. Adam was not a mere representative for mankind showing what we would do if we had the same temptation. *We were Adam.* "Adam is mankind," as F. F. Bruce says,[2] and as Adam we sinned. This is Biblical thinking, and it is therefore the only right thinking about man's condition. Any interpretation that departs from this thought or waters it down is mistaken. This is Pauline doctrine, the doctrine of Augustine, the Reformed position and that of orthodoxy. It is the only correct view.

So we all have an Adam-solidarity. We all are in the same boat. John Donne, a great poetic mind and a Biblical mind, spoke of our solidarity this way:

No man is an island, entire of itself; every man is a piece of the continent, a part of the main. If a clod be washed away by the sea, Europe is the less, as well as if a manor of thy friend's or of thine own were: any man's death diminishes me, because I am involved in mankind, and therefore never send to know for whom the bells tolls; it tolls for thee.[3]

Our sinful solidarity is profound — even to the very core of our natures. Bruce Catton, the great Civil War historian, gave an address when I was a freshman in college entitled, "What 1861 Has to Say to 1961" — the message being that human nature is ever the same and that the problem was identical in both eras. Paul has already stated this in Romans 3:9-11: "Jews and Gentiles alike are all under sin. As it is written: 'There is no one righteous, not even one; there is no one who understands, no one who seeks God.'"

Our ruin is universal. Logically, having explained the work of the first Adam in verse 12, Paul should have gone on to contrast the work of the Second Adam against that of the first. However, he leaves the sentence incomplete and goes on to demonstrate that this solidarity of sin and death through Adam has remained constant throughout man's history.

. . . for before the law was given, sin was in the world. But sin is not taken into account when there is no law. Nevertheless, death reigned from the time of Adam to the time of Moses, even over those who did not sin by breaking a command, as did Adam, who was a pattern of the one to come. (vv. 13, 14)

Realizing that Paul is arguing that sin and its deadly effect has remained constant throughout history, it seems confusing for Paul to say in verse 13, "But sin is not taken into account when there is no law." However, he does not mean that it is not counted, for it is because of sin that men died during the Law's absence. Paul means that *in comparison* with what happens when the Law is present, when God's Law is absent sin does not seem to be reckoned. The Law makes sin apparent and sharply defined.

Chuck Swindoll tells a story about his boyhood which makes the point. Like many boys he had a paper route, and like many he didn't particularly enjoy it. When delivering papers he would ride his bicycle across the lawns of homes that had the misfortune of being on a corner. At one particular place he had actually worn a narrow trail across the lawn. It wasn't right, but no one seemed to notice. But one day as he rode up he saw a sign which read, "KEEP OFF THE GRASS. NO BIKES." And — you guessed it — he rode right past it anyway on his well-worn trail — right up to the feet of the waiting author. As Swindoll put it, "The man shared with me a few things from his heart." Whereas before, Swindoll's transgression was not fully seen (and in a sense not reckoned), now it was sharply defined and accounted. This is what the Law does.

Paul's overall point is that all the human race remained under death and sin, whether under the Law or not, because death reigned. Genesis 5, which tells the story of those who died before the Law, says repeatedly, "and then he died," "and then he died," "and then he died."

So Paul's argument stands: the entire human race, because of its solidarity with Adam, stands under the ruin of sin and death. We all actually sinned in Adam! If we object, we should remember that if God had put each of us in Adam's place individually, we would have done the same! But more important, our solidarity with Adam not only condemns us through one man but makes possible our salvation through one Man — and this brings us to the matter of our rescue.

THE RESCUE OF MANKIND (vv. 15-19)

Our rescue came through a second and far greater Adam. The last phrase of verse 14 tells us that Adam was a "pattern" or "type" (Greek *tupos*) of him who was to come. This is not because they were similar, but because they were dissimilar. The only similarity between them was that what they did affected countless numbers of the human race. Adam could also be called an anti-type of Christ because what is true of Adam is only true of Christ in the opposite sense. There is greater distance between Christ and Adam than between a grasshopper and the highest archangel, for Christ is infinite. We must never commit the sacrilege of seeing the first and second Adams as perfectly parallel — one of the unforgivable sins of the cults, especially the Mormons.

Verses 15-17 tell us that the work of the Second Adam is far greater than of the first.

But the gift is not like the trespass. For if the many died by the trespass of the one man, how much more did God's grace and the gift that came by the grace of the one man, Jesus Christ, overflow to the many! (v. 15)

The sin of Adam brought death — a decaying degenerative force. But grace brought a far more dynamic power — life. It not only did away with death, but restored what had been destroyed. Moreover, "the trespass of Adam brought death once, the sacrifice and death of Jesus brings life a thousand times."[4]

Verse 16 tells us that Christ's work is far more powerful:

Again, the gift of God is not like the result of the one man's sin: The judgment followed one sin and brought condemnation, but the gift followed many trespasses and brought justification.

Adam's one transgression brought death. Jesus' death brought forgiveness for thousands of transgressions. Clearly, Jesus' work is far superior.

Verse 17 likewise emphasizes that Christ's work is far more efficacious:

For, if, by the trespass of the one man, death reigned through that one man, how much more will those who receive God's abundant provision of grace and of the gift of righteousness reign in life through the one man, Jesus Christ.

Christ gives to man far more than he lost in Adam — more indeed than Adam ever had! The blessing that comes from Christ is infinitely greater.

In verses 18, 19, Paul summarizes the greatness of our rescue:

Consequently, just as the result of one trespass was condemnation for all men, so also the result of one act of righteousness was justification that brings life for all men. For just as through the disobedience of the one man the many were made sinners, so also through the obedience of the one man the many will be made righteous.

Adam in disobedience grasped for equality with God. But Christ, in obedience, as Paul emphatically states,

did not consider equality with God something to be grasped, but made himself nothing, taking the very nature of a servant, being

117

made in human likeness. And being found in appearance as a man, he humbled himself and became obedient to death — even death on a cross! Therefore God exalted him to the highest place and gave him the name that is above every name, that at the name of Jesus every knee should bow, in heaven and on earth and under the earth, and every tongue confess that Jesus Christ is Lord, to the glory of God the Father. (Philippians 2:6-11)

So on the one hand we see the greatness of our ruin through our Adam-solidarity. But if we are in Christ, our Christ-solidarity far exceeds our ruin and results in our rescue. This ultimately means that we reign in life.

THE REIGN OF MANKIND (vv. 20, 21)

Now we come to the apex of Paul's expression: "The law was added so that the trespass might increase. But where sin increased, grace increased all the more" (v. 20). The Law was never given to make us do right. Paul will make this clear later in chapter 7, as he also does in Galatians 3:19-24. Where there is Law, we sin more, both in terms of quantity and of depth. But in doing this the Law also moves us closer to grace because the farther we descend, the nearer we are to brokenness and thus to Christ. This is why Paul says victoriously, "But where sin increased, grace increased all the more" (v. 20b).

The word translated "increased all the more" is scarcely translatable in few words. "Super-increased" is a possibility, or "super-abounded." It pictures unending, overflowing grace — a grace that knows no bounds. Grace is always more abundant than sin. Spurgeon has a sermon on this text entitled, "Grace Abounding over Abounding Sin."

This was the experience of Mel Trotter, who was such a great influence for Christ in Chicago and in fact the entire nation during the first half of this century. As an alcoholic he had fallen so low that on the evening he finally stumbled into the Pacific Garden Mission and found Christ, he was under the influence of alcohol he had purchased with the shoes taken from his little girl's feet as she lay in her coffin. So wondrous was the effect of God's abounding grace in his life that eight years later he was ordained to the Presbyterian ministry, became an outstanding evangelist, and founded more than sixty-seven rescue missions from coast to coast.[5] "But where sin increased, grace increased all the more." There is always more grace!

In the words of an old hymn:

Have you on the Lord believed?
Still there's more to follow.
Of his grace have you received?
Still there's more to follow.
Oh, the grace the Father shows,
Still there's more to follow
Freely He His grace bestows,
Still there's more to follow.
More and more and more and more,
Always more to follow;
Oh, His matchless, boundless love,
Still there's more to follow![6]

No matter how great your sin — in quantity or depth, God's grace superabounds to you! No one is beyond the grace of Christ.

Finally, what is the purpose of this grace? Verse 21 says, "so that, just as sin reigned in death, so also grace might reign through righteousness to bring eternal life through Jesus Christ our Lord." This includes our reigning in life, because as verse 17 says, "how much more will those who receive God's abundant provision of grace and of the gift of righteousness reign in life through the one man, Jesus Christ."

Practically, how does this happen for those of us who are believers but are not reigning?

We need, first, to review *the greatness of our ruin*. This is where we must always begin. This is why Christ so completely undressed mankind in the Beatitudes. Before we can reign we must be brought low. "Blessed are the poor in spirit," said Jesus (Matthew 5:3). Our solidarity with Adam and the rest of humanity in sin must be reiterated. All our existence is colored by sin. And our ruin in Adam is so great, there is no human remedy.

Having reviewed our ruin, we need next to review *the greatness of our rescue*. We must set before our consciousness the incomparable work of the matchless Second Adam. It is so supreme that it not only remedies Adam's own transgression, but all the sins ever committed by all the people who ever lived.

The profound contemplation of our ruin and our rescue can restore us so we will *reign* properly. At the risk of making this too simple, I believe this can all be summed up in one word — *LOVE*. Our healing and subsequent reign in life come as we contemplate and receive God's love.

Knowing God loves us, allowing his affection to permeate every corner of our lives, we will reign in life to his glory.

What shall we say, then? Shall we go on sinning so that grace may increase? By no means! We died to sin; how can we live in it any longer? Or don't you know that all of us who were baptized into Christ Jesus were baptized into his death? We were therefore buried with him through baptism into death in order that, just as Christ was raised from the dead through the glory of the Father, we too may live a new life. If we have been united with him in his death, we will certainly also be united with him in his resurrection. For we know that our old self was crucified with him so that the body of sin might be rendered powerless, that we should no longer be slaves to sin — because anyone who has died has been freed from sin. Now if we died with Christ, we believe that we will also live with him. For we know that since Christ was raised from the dead, he cannot die again; death no longer has mastery over him. The death he died, he died to sin once for all; but the life he lives, he lives to God. In the same way, count yourselves dead to sin but alive to God in Christ Jesus. Therefore do not let sin reign in your mortal body so that you obey its evil desires. Do not offer the parts of your body to sin, as instruments of wickedness, but rather offer yourselves to God, as those who have been brought from death to life; and offer the parts of your body to him as instruments of righteousness. For sin shall not be your master, because you are not under law, but under grace. (6:1-14)

13

Freedom from Sin

ROMANS 6:1-14

One of the dangers of preaching salvation by grace alone is that it can be interpreted as license to do whatever one wishes. The Apostle Paul was well aware of this tendency, as we saw in 3:8 where he mentioned that some were slanderously reporting that he and his followers were saying, "Let us do evil that good may result." Because of this type of misrepresentation, Paul was always on guard when he made a strong statement about grace. So when he said in 5:20b, "But where sin increased, grace increased all the more," he knew the worst would be made of it by some. He knew that a pernicious logic would be applied: "Well, if sin brings more grace, let's sin! Whoopie!" He also knew such thinking was not only logical to some minds, it was also natural because sin is enjoyable "for a short time" (Hebrews 11:25). He knew, too, that sinning could even be twisted into a religious duty, because it provides an opportunity for God to give his grace and love and thus glorify himself. Even people who have claimed to be Christians have thought this!

The church in Corinth had this problem, for when Paul insisted that an incestuous couple be excommunicated, there were some who saw nothing wrong with the incest, thinking it was an excellent display of Christian liberty (cf. 1 Corinthians 5).

A famous historical instance of such thought comes from the Russian monk Rasputin, who dominated the Romanov family in their final years. Rasputin taught that salvation came through repeated experiences of sin and repentance. He argued that because those who sin more require more forgiveness, those who sin with abandon will as they repent

121

experience greater joy; therefore, it is the believer's duty to sin. At times this type of thinking has been intellectualized, as in the last century in James Hogg's *Private Memoirs and Confessions of a Justified Sinner*.[1] Today this thinking is very common among those who wish to justify their sexual lifestyles. I have actually had such rationalizations seriously presented to me as if they were based on the Bible.

So when Paul said, "But where sin increased, grace increased all the more," he could sense the inevitable question coming and went ahead and voiced it himself: "What shall we say, then? Shall we go on sinning so that grace may increase?" (v. 1). His answer was: "By no means!" (v. 2a) ("May it never be," NASB; "Of course not!," TLB; "God forbid," KJV; "No, no!," NEB; "What a ghastly thought!" *Phillips*). Paul has no use for even the slightest intimation that grace encourages sin. In fact, he finishes verse 2 with a question to the contrary: "We died to sin; how can we live in it any longer?" The remainder of the chapter goes on to substantiate his position.

Verses 3-14 answer the question, How do those of us who are under grace live without being characterized by sin? How are we to live lives of victory? Paul answers logically. First, by *understanding* the nature of our identification with Christ (vv. 2-10). Second, by *accepting* our identification with Christ as true (v. 11). Third, by *yielding* to the Christ with whom we are so wonderfully identified (vv. 12, 13).

THE NATURE OF OUR IDENTIFICATION WITH CHRIST (vv. 2-10)

For Paul, what a believer understands is terribly important. Paul was convinced that Christian living depends on Christian learning, that duty follows doctrine. Therefore, it is natural that he attempts to increase our knowledge. The key word in verses 3 through 10 is "know," which occurs three times: "Or don't you know . . ." (v. 3), "For we know . . ." (v. 6), and "For we know . . ." (v. 9). Above all, Paul wants us to know or understand the nature of our union with Christ.

To help us, he employs the powerful metaphor of baptism. For Paul, a believer's being baptized symbolizes wondrous realities. Ron Ritchie, a pastor on the West Coast, experienced a beautiful illustration of this when he was conducting a baptism service in the Pacific Ocean.

> A woman came up to him and asked him to baptize her 9-year-old daughter. Ron was reluctant to do so without finding out whether the girl really understood what was happening, so he began to question

her and to teach her about the reality behind the water baptism. He was gesturing as he talked to her, and noticed the shadow of his hand as it fell on the sand. So he said to the little girl, "Do you see the shadow of my hand on the sand? Now that is just the shadow; the hand is the real thing. And when you came to Jesus, when you believed in Jesus, that was the real baptism. You were joined to him, and what happened to him happened to you. Jesus was alive; then he died, was buried, and then he arose from the dead. And that is what happened to you when you believed in him." He pointed to the shadow on the sand and said, "When you go down in the water and are raised up again, that is a picture of what has already happened." The girl immediately caught on and said, "Yes, that is what I want to do because Jesus has come into my life."[2]

Baptism is the shadow of what happened to us when we met Christ. Keeping that in mind, let us examine verses 3-5:

> Or don't you know that all of us who were baptized into Christ Jesus were baptized into his death? We were therefore buried with him through baptism into death in order that, just as Christ was raised from the dead through the glory of the Father, we too may live a new life. If we have been united with him in his death, we will certainly also be united with him in his resurrection.

The overall emphasis of these verses is upon our profound identity with Christ. Baptism bears with it the idea of *identification*, especially when it is linked to a person's name. For instance, 1 Corinthians 10:2 tells us that the Israelites were "baptized into Moses" — referring not to water baptism, but to the fact that they became united with him as never before as they recognized his leadership and their dependence on him. So it is with Christ. When we were baptized into him (Matthew 28:19), we achieved a profound identification.

Our text further emphasizes this identity in verse 5 which uses a botanical term in saying we have become "united with him." The word "united" (Greek: *symphytoi*, "grown together") pictures a branch bound to another — they are grafted together. That describes our union with Christ. The Scripture boldly affirms this in a number of places. Galatians 3:27 says, "for all of you who were baptized into Christ have been clothed with Christ." So close is our identification with Christ that we are, so to speak, robed with him. First Corinthians 12:13 adds: "For we were all baptized by one Spirit into one body" — the Body of Christ. There could not be a more profound identity or union. To state our union concisely:

> Our spiritual history began at the cross. We were there in the sense
> that in God's sight we were joined to Him who actually suffered on
> it. The time element should not disturb us, because if we sinned in
> Adam, it is equally possible to have died to sin with Christ.[3]

This is our position. We do not have to be conscious of it any more than of our conscious participation in Adam's sin. It is a fact: we are identified with Christ.

The specific emphasis of verses 3-5 is that we are so profoundly identified with Christ's death and resurrection that we actually did die with him and truly were raised with him, so that we now share in his resurrection life. Again the Scriptures attest to this. Galatians 2:20 tells us: "I have been crucified with Christ and I no longer live, but Christ lives in me." Galatians 6:14 says: ". . . the world has been crucified to me, and I to the world." Just as we died with him, we were also resurrected with him. "Since, then, you have been raised with Christ, set your hearts on things above, where Christ is seated at the right hand of God" (Colossians 3:1). Whereas before we had only a solidarity with Adam's sin, now that has been broken and we have a solidarity with Christ, the Second Adam, in his death and resurrection. We need to know and count on this if we are to experience victory over sin.

What that means practically in life is this: as Christ did not serve sin, neither must we. Verses 6 and 7 go on:

> For we know that our old self was crucified with him so that the
> body of sin might be rendered powerless, that we should no longer
> be slaves to sin — because anyone who has died has been freed from
> sin.

The "old self" is the kind of person we were before our conversion. That self was crucified with Christ. "The body of sin" — the body as it was, a vehicle of sin — has been rendered inoperative. Paul concludes this explanation of our union and deliverance in verses 8-10:

> Now if we died with Christ, we believe that we will also live with
> him. For we know that since Christ was raised from the dead, he can-
> not die again; death no longer has mastery over him. The death he
> died, he died to sin once for all; but the life he lives, he lives to God.

Paul emphasizes that when Christ died he died "once for all." This is a technical term used repeatedly in the book of Hebrews to emphasize the finality of Christ's work. Paul made this emphasis because the believer must have full confidence that the Captain of his salvation will never again come under the power of sin and death.

When we began this study we emphasized that in dealing with the problem of those who turn grace into license Paul would insist that the place to begin is our knowledge. We must know two things: First, we must know something of our immense identity (solidarity) with Christ. Though we cannot fully understand it, we actually did die with him and were resurrected with him in the historical events. Second, this shared death and resurrection means that the dominance of sin has been broken and we are freed from sin.

The argument that we should continue in sin because we are under grace is absolutely fallacious! The reverse is true. It is impossible to continue living unchanged when you become a Christian. In fact, I will put it even stronger: those who argue that grace allows a buffer for sin — that their sin will ultimately glorify God anyway — are revealing they are not under grace! They are not Christians, no matter how much they argue otherwise. When we have experienced solidarity with Christ, our lifestyle is affected, just as it was by our solidarity with Adam. If one's life has not changed and if there is no impulse for further change toward Christ, he or she is very probably not a Christian.

We have considered the truth of Paul's argument in verses 3-10 about our union with Christ. How do we make this work? Now we come to the practical application of everything we have said, and it has to do with the second key word of the text, the word "count" or "consider" (NASB) in verse 11.

THE REALITY OF OUR IDENTIFICATION
WITH CHRIST (v. 11)

"In the same way, count yourselves dead to sin but alive to God in Christ Jesus" (v. 11). The word translated "count yourselves" or "reckon" (KJV) or "consider" (NASB) is one of the most important words in Romans. Paul uses it nineteen times in the letter, and if one does not know what it means he or she will not understand Romans. It is a commercial term which means "to impute to one's account." The idea is, we are to reflect on our position in Christ. Then we are to set two things to our account: 1) We are "dead to sin." And 2) we are "alive to God in Christ Jesus."

Have you ever taken the time to consider the fact that you participated in the events of the cross, that you died and and that you were resurrected with Christ? If not, why not do it right now. This is prevention theology. So much of our time is spent in corrective theology — what to do when we sin, as for example in 1 John 1:9 ("If we confess our sins, he is faithful and just and will forgive us our sins and purify us from all unrighteousness"). This is good and necessary. But reflecting upon our identification with Christ is even better because it curbs our sinning. This reckoning to our account is something we are to constantly do, as the present tense of the verb indicates: "Keep on counting yourselves dead to sin but alive to God in Christ Jesus."

So far Paul has told us what we must know about our union with Christ. Then he explained about the necessity of reckoning. Now he tells us we must act. Theory must produce action.

THE RESPONSE TO OUR IDENTIFICATION WITH CHRIST (vv. 12, 13)

Verse 12 commands: "Therefore do not let sin reign in your mortal body so that you obey its evil desires." Exactly what does this mean? Paul is very precise and clear, and his answer falls into two corresponding halves. The first is *negative*: "Do not offer the parts of your body to sin, as instruments of wickedness" (v. 13a). That is, do not keep on making the parts of your body (your tongue, hands, feet) available as tools of unrighteousness. Be on constant guard against doing this. And while you are doing this, take *positive* actions: "but rather offer yourselves to God, as those who have been brought from death to life; and offer the parts of your body to him as instruments of righteousness" (v. 13b). The tense here demands a decisive once-and-for-all act. All of us must come to a time when we present everything to God for righteousness. This does not rule out subsequent commitments as well, but this initial time of surrender must come to all of us.

> *God, here I am — alive from the dead! I have died with Christ and have been resurrected with Christ. Praise your name. Now here is my body (my arms, my voice, my eyes). Take them all, that they might be instruments of righteousness and not of sin.*

Have you done this? Perhaps you have done the *no* — refusing to yield your body to the service of sin. That is good, but it is not enough. There must be the *yes* — "Take and use my entire life, Lord."

The logic of our passage is compelling in its three key words:

"know . . . count . . . offer." Do we know something of our amazing solidarity with Christ — that we actually participated in his death and resurrection? We do not completely understand it, but do we at least understand that the Scriptures claim this union for us? Then, have we consciously set to our account that we are dead to sin and alive to God in Christ Jesus? Finally, have we yielded our entire lives to him?

If so, then we know the answer to those who argue that grace encourages sin. As verse 14 tells us: "For sin shall not be your master, because you are not under law, but under grace." Grace has delivered us from the old system.

When as a young teenager Stuart Briscoe was drafted into the Royal Marines during the Korean War, he came under the control of a particularly imposing regimental sergeant major who strode around the barracks leaving a train of tough men quaking in their boots. Briscoe did not realize how dominant this man had become in his life until the day he was released from the Marines. Clutching his papers in one hand, he was luxuriating in his newfound freedom to the extent of putting the other hand in his pocket, slouching a little, and whistling — sins so heinous that if they had been observed by the sergeant major, they would have landed him in big trouble! Then Briscoe saw him striding toward him. On an impulse he sprang into the posture of a Marine until he realized that he had died to him. He was not dead, and neither was the sergeant major. But as far as the sergeant major's domination of his life was concerned, it was all a matter of history. So Briscoe did some reckoning, decided not to yield to the man's tyranny, and demonstrated that fact by refusing to swing his arms high and march as if on parade and keep his back at ramrod stiffness. Instead he presented his feet, hands, and back to his newfound freedom as a *former* Marine — and the sergeant major could not do a thing about it![4]

Let us continue considering ourselves dead to sin but alive to God in Christ Jesus.

What then? Shall we sin because we are not under law but under grace? By no means! Don't you know that when you offer yourselves to someone to obey him as slaves, you are slaves to the one whom you obey — whether you are slaves to sin, which leads to death, or to obedience, which leads to righteousness? But thanks be to God that, though you used to be slaves to sin, you wholeheartedly obeyed the form of teaching to which you were entrusted. You have been set free from sin and have become slaves to righteousness. I put this in human terms because you are weak in your natural selves. Just as you used to offer the parts of your body in slavery to impurity and to ever-increasing wickedness, so now offer them in slavery to righteousness leading to holiness. When you were slaves to sin, you were free from the control of righteousness. What benefit did you reap at that time from the things you are now ashamed of? Those things result in death! But now that you have been set free from sin and have become slaves to God, the benefit you reap leads to holiness, and the result is eternal life. For the wages of sin is death, but the gift of God is eternal life in Christ Jesus our Lord. (6:15-23)

14

Freedom in Slavery

ROMANS 6:15-23

As we have seen, Paul was very careful to make sure that his famous grace statement at the end of chapter 5 ("But where sin increased, grace increased all the more," v. 20b) would not be misunderstood as promoting sin. He covered his statement by posing the rhetorical question that opens chapter 6: "What shall we say, then? Shall we go on sinning so that grace may increase?" (v. 1). To which he answered, "By no means! We died to sin; how can we live in it any longer?" (v. 2). This was a great answer, and Paul went on to expand it, emphasizing that the key to living a life free from sin's dominance is to reckon ourselves dead to sin but alive to God in Christ Jesus, and then to stop presenting ourselves as instruments of unrighteousness, but rather as instruments of righteousness to God. Paul seemingly ended his argument in verse 14 with the summary statement, "For sin shall not be your master, because you are not under law, but under grace." It was an excellent closing statement. The argument of verses 1-14 is powerful and conclusive.

However, Paul, who had made this argument other times as well, realized that some person somewhere would pervert this closing statement. Someone would undoubtedly reason, "Well, if we really are under grace and free from the penalty of sin, what difference will a little sin make?" I have heard such a comment many times, and perhaps you have too. Recently I heard a fallen minister use the same argument: "I know it is wrong, but I am a child of God — he will forgive me. I am under grace." Such thinking is not only wrong but precarious! Interpreting the freedom we have in Christ in an unqualified sense empowers sin to pull

129

believers back under its authority. And if this kind of perverse reasoning becomes a permanent part of our thinking, it may reveal that we are not under grace and never have been. F. F. Bruce says, "To make being 'under grace' an excuse for sinning is a sign that one is not really 'under grace' at all."[1]

Such thinking is deadly. Paul meets it head-on in verse 15 with another rhetorical question similar to that in verse 1: "What then? Shall we sin because we are not under law but under grace? By no means!" To make his reasoning stick, he appropriates the powerful, attention-getting metaphor of slavery in the following verses.

THE EXPLANATION OF THE
SLAVERY PRINCIPLE (vv. 16-19)

With this mention of slavery, Paul got their attention indeed! It is estimated that the population of Rome in the first century was about one-third slaves. So vast was the slave population that a suggestion that slaves be made to wear a distinctive style of clothing was abandoned because it would reveal their numerical strength. Moreover, many free men had once been slaves. Thus, it is very likely that more than one-half of the Roman church either were or had been enslaved.[2] There was not a member of the church at Rome who was not keenly aware of the implications of what Paul was saying in verse 16.

Obedience was the universal hallmark of slavery, and it is the same for the various enslavements we experience today. It is very possible to sit next to a slave and not realize it. It is also possible that the person sitting next to you is sitting next to a slave! Some people are enslaved to their work. They have one abiding allegiance in life and that is the job, where they live out slavish obedience. Some are enslaved to things — possessions. All their waking thoughts are given to taking care of what they have or dreaming about how they can acquire more. Others are enslaved to habits which dominate their existence. The examples are limitless. The ill-tempered are slaves to their tempers, the sensual to their bodies. We obey the things which enslave us. Here Paul applies this principle spiritually. Look at the verse carefully.

> Don't you know that when you offer yourselves to someone to obey
> him as slaves, you are slaves to the one whom you obey — whether
> you are slaves to sin, which leads to death, or to obedience, which
> leads to righteousness? (v. 16)

All humanity serves under one of two slaveries — either "sin, which leads to death" or "obedience, which leads to righteousness." There is no middle ground. Everyone who has ever lived has been subject to the first slavery. This was made perfectly clear by Jesus in an exchange with his contemporaries. They said,

> "We are Abraham's descendants and have never been slaves of anyone. How can you say that we shall be set free?" Jesus replied, "I tell you the truth, everyone who sins is a slave to sin." (John 8:33, 34)

Jesus called his self-righteous countrymen slaves of sin, and the indictment applies to every mortal who ever lived. Characteristically, the most enslaved argue that they are the most free. Suggest to the herpes-carrying Casanova that he is a slave and you will receive a jovial denial; push him about it and the conversation will become unpredictably unpleasant. John Calvin said over 400 years ago, "The greater mass of vices anyone is buried under, the more fiercely and bombastically does he extol his freedom." The end of such slavery, according to our text, is death — "sin, which leads to death."

The second slavery is to Christ. Paul calls it "obedience, which leads to righteousness" — ultimate justification which issues in eternal life.[3] Instead of bondage, this slavery brings freedom. Elisabeth Elliot tells of visiting in Scotland and observing a Scottish collie in his glory — tending sheep. He was doing what he was bred for and trained to do. He was beautiful to watch as he circled right and left, ". . . barking, crouching, racing along, herding a stray sheep here, nipping at a stubborn one there, his eyes always glued to the sheep, his ears listening for a tiny metal whistle from his master. . . ." As she watched, she reflected,

> I saw two creatures who were in the fullest sense "in their glory": A man who had given his life to sheep, who loved them and loved his dog; and a dog whose trust in man was absolute, whose obedience was instant and unconditional, and whose very meat and drink was to do the will of his master.

The dog did not understand the pattern — only obedience — and he was in glory. That is what obedience, slavery to God, and righteousness bring to us! We know, of course, that God shares his glory with no one. Yet, through obedience there is a human glory which comes through being what he made us to be. Obedience to God liberates us to be all we can be.

As our Master, he completely knows us. He wrote the manual. To use Elisabeth Elliot's words,

> He is our Creator, the One whose spoken Word called into being the unimaginable thing called space and the equally unimaginable thing called time. He set the stars in trajectories and put the sliding shutter on the lizard's eye.[4]

That is why when we obey him we become all we are meant to be.

So we have before us the two slaveries. There is no middle ground. We either choose to obey the world and thus death, or we choose obedience to Christ and eternal righteousness. The key to a full life is profound slavery and obedience.

Now we turn from obedience (the principle of slavery) to the example of the Romans' obedience in verses 17, 18:

> But thanks be to God that, though you used to be slaves to sin, you wholeheartedly obeyed the form of teaching to which you were entrusted. You have been set free from sin and have become slaves to righteousness.

Notice the phrase "form of teaching" because it is the key to understanding what is meant here. The word "form" refers to a specific pattern of apostolic teaching. F. F. Bruce says that it ". . . is probably the summary of Christian ethics, based on the teaching of Christ, which was regularly given to converts in the primitive church to show them the way of life they ought to follow."[5] Such commentators as Cranfield, Dodd, Harrison, and Murray agree. In other words, the Romans' slavery to Christ was not just a vague commitment to follow him. It was a commitment to live by specific standards of behavior derived from the teaching of Christ. Some think they did this publicly at baptism.[6] At any rate, they realized that their Christianity demanded a profound slavery.

Paul says beautifully of them, "You wholeheartedly obeyed the form of teaching to which you were entrusted" (v. 17b). The heart is the wellspring of man's spiritual life, and that is where the Roman Christians' obedience was rooted. It was not just a formal obedience — it came from the center of their being. This is the example of slavery Paul holds up for us all: a heartfelt obedience to Christ and his Word. It is an obedience which brings liberation. "You have been set free from sin and have become slaves to righteousness" (v. 18). Their obedience was to Christ. Consequently, they could no longer be slaves of sin.

THE CALL TO OBEDIENT SLAVERY (v. 19)

With the slavery principle explained and the example of it set forth, Paul extends an outright call to slavery:

> I put this in human terms because you are weak in your natural selves. Just as you used to offer the parts of your body in slavery to impurity and to ever-increasing wickedness, so now offer them in slavery to righteousness leading to holiness. (v. 19)

This is a powerful call to commitment. It is a call to slavery — a call to total obligation, total commitment, total accountability.[7]

Obedience is not a popular word today. It is something of a cultural obscenity. Bonhoeffer's oft-quoted words are more relevant today than they have ever been:

> . . . cheap grace, the grace which amounts to the justification of sin without the justification of the repentant sinner who departs from sin and from whom it departs. Cheap grace is not the kind of forgiveness of sin which frees us from the toils of sin. Cheap grace is the grace we bestow on ourselves.
>
> Cheap grace is the preaching of forgiveness without requiring repentance, baptism without church discipline, communion without confession, absolution without personal confession. Cheap grace is grace without discipleship, grace without the cross, grace without Jesus Christ, living and incarnate. . . .
>
> Such grace is costly because it calls us to follow, and it is grace because it calls us to follow Jesus Christ . It is costly because it costs a man his life, and it is grace because it gives a man the only true life.[8]

Paul calls us to obedience — profound slavery! He has presented us with two slaveries, one which leads to death, and one which leads to righteousness and eternal life. Ultimately, we are either of one slavery or the other. However, practically speaking there is a third slavery, a most unhappy state. It is the lot of one who has chosen to become a slave of Christ, has obeyed from the heart, but then pulled away. This one never knows the glory of obedience and becoming all he can be. My family's dog, Chad, is a beloved animal. But it has been years since he knew anything like the glorious freedom of the Scottish collie mentioned earlier. Why so? Well, he used to play with our children in the front yard without a leash. However, one day though he was called, he took off on a dead run. When he returned, he was duly repentant, was disciplined, and was reinstated. But he did it again and again and again! Now poor Chad never goes outside without a leash around his neck. Some of us are like that. God loves us. We are his forever. But it has been years since we have really been free. We know little of the liberty of obedience.

The truth is: in slavery to God there is freedom; in obedience to God there is liberation. What is God's slavery like? I enjoy what Chrysostom said: "It is better than any freedom." Paul unashamedly calls us to such slavery:

> I put this in human terms because you are weak in your natural selves. Just as you used to offer the parts of your body in slavery to impurity and to ever-increasing wickedness, so now offer them in slavery to righteousness leading to holiness. (v. 19)

THE GLORIOUS BENEFITS OF OBEDIENT SLAVERY (vv. 21-23)

In concluding this argument, Paul speaks about the benefits:

> What benefit did you reap at that time from the things you are now ashamed of? Those things result in death! But now that you have been set free from sin and have become slaves to God, the benefit you reap leads to holiness, and the result is eternal life. (vv. 21, 22)

Our past slavery brought only shame and death. But our enslavement to God brings not only freedom from sin but sanctification and eternal life — the practical experience of growing to be more like the Master and the experience of knowing we have eternal life now.

Verse 23 gives us the triumphant summation: "For the wages of sin is death, but the gift of God is eternal life in Christ Jesus our Lord." The old slavemaster (sin) pays wages — death. Death works now in the lives of those under his pay, and one day he will make the final payment. The new slavemaster does not pay wages. What he gives cannot be earned. All is of grace. Eternal life is not in the future, but exists in us and for us today. There is an inheritance waiting for us (1 Peter 1:4, 5), but even now there is a bud which will fully blossom when we see him.

Paul began with the rhetorical question and answer, "What then? Shall we sin because we are not under law but under grace? By no means!" (v. 15). Why? Because we are slaves of Christ, we have been called to a profound obedience and have become the recipients of the glorious benefits that are ours as his slaves.

The abiding truth is this: obedience is the key to our liberation. Irenaeus said, "The glory of God is a man fully alive!" Our spiritual life comes, of course, through our union with Christ. But the fullness of that life comes through obedience. G. K. Chesterton said, "Obedience is but the other side of the Creative will." Obedience looses the creative power of God in our lives. God will do great and wondrous things in and through the life of an obedient soul. Samuel said:

> "Does the Lord delight in burnt offerings and sacrifices as much as
> in obeying the voice of the Lord? To obey is better than sacrifice,
> and to heed is better than the fat of rams." (1 Samuel 15:22)

If God is speaking to you about any area of your life, obey him now.

Do you not know, brothers — for I am speaking to men who know the law — that the law has authority over a man only as long as he lives? For example, by law a married woman is bound to her husband as long as he is alive, but if her husband dies, she is released from the law of marriage. So then, if she marries another man while her husband is still alive, she is called an adulteress. But if her husband dies, she is released from that law and is not an adulteress, even though she marries another man. So, my brothers, you also died to the law through the body of Christ, that you might belong to another, to him who was raised from the dead, in order that we might bear fruit to God. For when we were controlled by the sinful nature, the sinful passions aroused by the law were at work in our bodies, so that we bore fruit for death. But now, by dying to what once bound us, we have been released from the laws so that we serve in the new way of the Spirit, and not in the old way of the written code. What shall we say, then? Is the law sin? Certainly not! Indeed I would not have known what sin was except through the law. For I would not have known what it was to covet if the law had not said, "Do not covet." But sin, seizing the opportunity afforded by the commandment, produced in me every kind of covetous desire. For apart from law, sin is dead. Once I was alive apart from law; but when the commandment came, sin sprang to life and I died. I found that the very commandment that was intended to bring life actually brought death. For sin, seizing the opportunity afforded by the commandment, deceived me, and through the commandment put me to death. So then, the law is holy, and the commandment is holy, righteous and good. Did that which is good, then, become death to me? By no means! But in order that sin might be recognized as sin, it produced death in me through what was good, so that through the commandment sin might become utterly sinful. We know that the law is spiritual; but I am unspiritual, sold as a slave to sin. I do not understand what I do. For what I want to do I do not do, but what I hate I do. And if I do what I do not want to do, I agree that the law is good. As it is, it is no longer I myself who do it, but it is sin living in me. I know that nothing good lives in me, that is, in my sinful nature. For I have the desire to do what is good, but I cannot carry it out. For what I do is not the good I want to do; no, the evil I do not want to do — this I keep on doing. Now if I do what I do not want to do, it is no longer I who do it, but it is sin living in me that does it. So I find this law at work: When I want to do good, evil is right there with me. For in my inner being I delight in God's law; but I see another law at work in the members of my body, waging war against the law of my mind and making me a prisoner of the law of sin at work within my members. What a wretched man I am! Who will rescue me from this body of death? Thanks be to God — through Jesus Christ our Lord! So then, I myself in my mind am a slave to God's law, but in the sinful nature a slave to the law of sin. (7:1-25)

15

Freedom in Christ

ROMANS 7:1-25

Romans 7 has helped thousands shed the graveclothes of death — and especially the bindings which come from the Law. Borrowing T. E. Lawrence's term "pillars of wisdom," I would like to suggest that Romans 7 gives us four pillars of wisdom regarding our relationship to the Law which, if understood, will aid our liberation from sin. Every Christian can experience greater freedom if he or she will make these pillars part of his or her life.

THE FIRST PILLAR:
OUR RELATION TO THE LAW (vv. 1-6)

Paul chooses the analogy of marriage to illustrate how we relate to the Law.

> Do you not know, brothers — for I am speaking to men who know the law — that the law has authority over a man only as long as he lives? For example, by law a married woman is bound to her husband as long as he is alive, but if her husband dies, she is released from the law of marriage. So then, if she marries another man while her husband is still alive, she is called an adulteress. But if her husband dies, she is released from that law and is not an adulteress, even though she marries another man. (vv. 1-3)

Whether by Roman or Jewish law, a woman was bound to her husband for life. The only way she could be freed was through the death of her husband. When this happened, she was perfectly free to marry again.

Applying the analogy to the believer and his relationship to the Law, the woman is the believer and the Law is the husband. However, because the Law cannot die, Paul has the woman (the believer) die in verse 4:

> So, my brothers, you also died to the law through the body of Christ, that you might belong to another, to him who was raised from the dead, in order that we might bear fruit to God.

Although Paul's application of the marriage analogy is not altogether perfect, the meaning is clear:

> As death breaks the bond between husband and wife, so death — the believer's death with Christ — breaks the bond which formerly yoked him to the law, and now he is free to enter into union with Christ.[1]

So the first pillar of wisdom regarding our relationship with the Law is that our marriage to it has been dissolved by our identification with the death of Christ. As a result we are married to him and the Law has no claims on us.

Paul describes our new freedom in verses 5, 6:

> For when we were controlled by the sinful nature, the sinful passions aroused by the law were at work in our bodies, so that we bore fruit for death. But now, by dying to what once bound us, we have been released from the law so that we serve in the new way of the Spirit, and not in the old way of the written code.

The result of the dissolution of our marriage to the Law is "that we serve in the new way of the Spirit." Instead of despair, there is joy! Instead of bondage, there is freedom! Instead of death, there is life! We no longer belong to the Law, but to Christ. This is the primary pillar of our wisdom.

The second pillar of wisdom is our understanding of how the Law and sin interact in our experience. Here Paul becomes very personal. The marriage analogy was a hypothetical illustration, but now the apostle turns autobiographical.

THE SECOND PILLAR: THE RELATION OF LAW TO SIN (vv. 7-13)

Paul begins this autobiographical section by answering an anticipated objection in verse 7:

> What shall we say, then? Is the law sin? Certainly not! Indeed I would not have known what sin was except through the law. For I would not have known what it was to covet if the law had not said, "Do not covet."

The Living Bible expresses verse 7 this way:

> Well then, am I suggesting that these laws of God are evil? Of course not! No, the law is not sinful, but it was the law that showed me my sin. I would never have known the sin in my heart — the evil desires that are hidden there — if the law had not said, "You must not have evil desires in your heart."

Paul's first point here is that *the Law reveals sin*. Scholars suggest that Paul's personal experience of this may have taken place at about the time of his Bar Mitzvah when he became, as the term translates, "a son of the Law." Whether before or after that time, he began to seriously reflect on the Ten Commandments, and he found that he did pretty well until he came to the Tenth which says, "You shall not covet . . ." (Exodus 20:17). As his sharp young mind grappled with the concept, he began to see that his inner life was filled with coveting. Moreover, he saw that the rest of the Ten Commandments are broken through sins which originate in coveting.

As a result young Saul began to see himself as he really was. The Scriptures witness that this is indeed what the Law does. "Through the law we become conscious of sin" (3:20). James 1:22-25 tells us that the Law is a mirror which reveals the inner man. What a gift the Law is!

But the Law not only reveals sin, it *activates* sin, as verses 8, 9 teach:

> But sin, seizing the opportunity afforded by the commandment, produced in me every kind of covetous desire. For apart from law, sin is dead. Once I was alive apart from law; but when the commandment came, sin sprang to life and I died.

An expanded paraphrase of this statement may be helpful: "But sin, setting up a base of operations through the commandment not to covet, produced in me coveting of every kind; for apart from the Law sin is dead or dormant. And I was alive, blissfully indifferent, to the searching demands of the Law; but when the commandment not to covet came, sin sprang to life, and I felt the sentence of death."

Poor young Saul. Once he realized what covetousness was, all he could do was covet! Other Scriptures also attest to sin's active power. Romans 5:20 contends, "The law was added so that the trespass might increase." And in 1 Corinthians 15:56 we read, "The power of sin is the law."

Saint Augustine, in his *Confessions*, describes how this principle worked in his life:

> There was a pear tree near our vineyard, laden with fruit. One stormy night we rascally youths set out to rob it and carry our spoils away. We took off a huge load of pears . . . not to feast upon ourselves, but to throw them to the pigs, though we ate just enough to have the pleasure of forbidden fruit. They were nice pears, but it was not the pears that my wretched soul coveted, for I had plenty better at home. I picked them simply in order to become a thief. The only feast I got was a feast of iniquity, and that I enjoyed to the full. What was it that I loved in that theft? Was it the pleasure of acting against the law, in order that I, a prisoner under rules, might have a maimed counterfeit of freedom by doing what was forbidden, with a dim similitude of omnipotence? The desire to steal was awakened simply by the prohibition of stealing.[2]

Things have not changed much in 1500 years, have they? The Law says, "Don't covet." but my nature says, "It sounds exciting." I recall being in Boston several years ago and walking south on the Common toward the gardens — beautifully manicured lawns and flowers, with a pond and swan boats. There were signs everywhere which read KEEP OFF THE GRASS. However, literally hundreds of people were lying on the grass and hanging their clothes on the signs! It is pleasurable to lie on forbidden grass.

Have you considered what would happen if on Main Street of your town one of the stores painted this sign on their window: YOU ARE FORBIDDEN TO THROW STONES THROUGH THIS WINDOW. The window would not last twenty-four hours. Even human law's prohibitions are to us like shaking is to a can of cola.

Not only does the Law reveal and activate sin, but *it kills*, as verses 10, 11 tell us:

> . . . the very commandment that was intended to bring life actually brought death. For sin, seizing the opportunity afforded by the commandment, deceived me, and through the commandment put me to death.

The commands perfectly kept would bring life (cf. Leviticus 18:5), but broken they bring death. ". . . for the letter kills, but the Spirit gives life" (2 Corinthians 3:6).

Lastly, the Law brings recognition of *the magnitude of sin.*

> So then, the law is holy, and the commandment is holy, righteous and good. Did that which is good, then, become death to me? By no means! But in order that sin might be recognized as sin, it produced death in me through what was good, so that through the commandment sin might become utterly sinful. (vv. 12, 13)

Before we came under the teaching of the gospel, some of us were blissfully unaware of the depth of our sin. Then we began to see something of God's righteous requirements, and our sinfulness became painfully apparent. Now we have become Christians, and life is a continuing revelation of the radical nature of our sin. Every year as I grow in the Lord I become more aware that though I have been born again and my sin is covered by Christ's blood, I am in myself thoroughly, disgustingly sinful! The more I understand God's Law, the more I see my sin as "utterly sinful" (v. 13). Is this morbid introspection? I do not think so. It is rather a key to liberation, as we shall see.

The first pillar of wisdom is that we are dead to the Law and the Law has no right over us. The second pillar of wisdom shows the utter pervasiveness of sin. Knowledge of the Law is indispensable to our salvation and growth. The third pillar of wisdom brings an understanding of what it is like for the believer to struggle against the Law on his own.

THE THIRD PILLAR:
THE CONFLICT OF THE LAW AND SELF (vv. 14-24)

This section of Romans 7 has known centuries of controversy: who is their subject? There are basically three views. The first is that this passage describes a *non-Christian* Pharisee under the Law (this was the view of the Greek Fathers). The second view is that it describes a *normal Christian* (the view of Augustine, Luther, and Calvin). The third position is that it describes a *carnal Christian*.[3] I believe the second view is correct, mainly because Paul continues to write in the first-person singular but in the present tense. It seems most natural to understand this section as Paul talking about what he was then experiencing.

We should note right at the start that chapters 7 and 8 are simultaneous. Chapter 8 (the chapter of victory) is not subsequent to chapter 7 in Paul's experience, for he experienced both alternately and continued to do so in the years that followed.

In this self-portrait Paul describes himself not as a so-called carnal Christian, but as one who loves the Law of God and longs to please God, but is trying to do so in his own strength. A so-called carnal Christian does not have such a goal. Here Paul speaks with a candor to be praised. He does not put on any prissy piety.

This is Paul's autobiography, but it is also the experience of every Christian. Anyone who has seriously followed Christ has known something of this. This is reality!

Paul states the problem of the struggling Christian in verses 14-16:

> We know that the law is spiritual; but I am unspiritual, sold as a
> slave to sin. I do not understand what I do. For what I want to do I
> do not do, but what I hate I do. And if I do what I do not want to do,
> I agree that the law is good.

Someone said after reading this that Paul must have been a golfer, because all golfers know that what you want to do you do not do, and what you do not want to do, that is the very thing you do.[4] The problem here, though, is more important than one's golf score. How many thousands have said words like these to their pastors or counselors in recent months. It is the cry of the believer who is trying, but is relying on himself. Paul finds himself dominated by sin.

> As it is, it is no longer I myself who do it, but it is sin living in me.
> I know that nothing good lives in me, that is, in my sinful nature.
> For I have the desire to do what is good, but I cannot carry it out.
> For what I do is not the good I want to do; no, the evil I do not want
> to do — this I keep doing. Now if I do what I do not want to do, it
> is no longer I who do it, but it is sin living in me that does it. (vv.
> 17-20)

Twice Paul says, "it is no longer I myself who do it." He is not actually saying he does not do it, but that it is not what his deep inner self, renewed in Christ, wants to do. He is dominated by sin. Thomas a Kempis wrote of the same frustration:

> I desire to enjoy Thee inwardly, but I cannot take Thee. I desire to cleave to heavenly things, but fleshly things and unmortified passions depress me. I will in my mind to be above all things, but in spite of myself I am constrained to be beneath, so I, unhappy man, fight with myself and am made grievous to myself while the spirit seeketh what is beneath. O what I suffer within while as I think on heavenly things in my mind; the company of fleshly things cometh against me when I pray.[5]

Thomas a Kempis writes for us all. How often we have tried with all our might to follow Christ, but have been pulled down by our flesh and failed. Paul understands what is happening at such times and records:

> So I find this law at work: When I want to do good, evil is right there with me. For in my inner being I delight in God's law; but I see another law at work in the members of my body, waging war against the law of my mind and making me a prisoner of the law of sin at work within my members. (vv. 21-23)

The principle Paul recognizes is that he is a man with two natures. One delights in the Law of God. The other wages war against God's Law. The Christian is subject to two forces simultaneously and thus lives in a state of tension.

> For the sinful nature desires what is contrary to the Spirit, and the Spirit what is contrary to the sinful nature. They are in conflict with each other, so that you do not do what you want. (Galatians 5:17)

The seventh chapter of Romans is a passionate piece of writing. Paul wants us to feel the emotion he experiences in trying to live up to God's standards in his own strength. And here we have the third pillar of wisdom defined: A believer who tries to please God in his or her own strength will always come to disheartening, aching frustration — *always*! Moreover, this will happen to "good Christians" — even super-Christians. Paul was perhaps the greatest Christian ever, and this was his experience. He had more theology and passion in his little finger than most of us have in our entire life. Despite this, he sometimes tried to live up to God's standards on his own. It would be naive to say that after Paul came to an understanding of how sin defeats us through the Law, he never came under bondage again. I personally believe that with time he came less and less under bondage, but he never came to perfection.

THE FOURTH PILLAR:
THE BELIEVER'S POWER (vv. 24, 25)

"What a wretched man I am! Who will rescue me from this body of death?" (v. 24). The adjective "wretched" means "a miserable distressed condition."[6] Paul has come to the end of himself, and this is the ground of the fourth pillar of wisdom. How so? Because such a cry takes us to the very place that the Lord Jesus began the Sermon on the Mount: "Blessed are the poor in spirit, for theirs is the kingdom of heaven" (Matthew 5:3). "Blessed are the bankrupt . . . Blessed are the wretched." Actually Paul is now in fine shape because when the believer realizes his helplessness he will receive God's help. As long as we think we can do it ourselves, we are in Romans 7. Now I must admit, this is not only Paul here, it is Kent Hughes — time and time again. When will I ever learn? Paul is every man or woman who truly seeks to follow Christ.

How does Paul handle coming to the end of himself? Beautifully! "Who will rescue me from this body of death?" (v. 24b). Notice that he does not say, "What must I do?" but "Who will rescue me?" Then he answers, "Thanks be to God — through Jesus Christ our Lord!" (v. 25). Here he anticipates something else he knew so very well — the victory of the power of the indwelling Spirit (see chapter 8). "Now that I have come to the end, I know where to look — to Christ and his indwelling Spirit. Praise God!"

Paul's words can help us rid ourselves of the graveclothes of the Law. He has suggested four pillars of wisdom.

First Pillar: Our marriage to the Law has been broken by our death and resurrection in Christ. The Law has no more power over us.

Second Pillar: The Law is good, for it reveals to us the righteous demands of God. It reveals the utter pervasiveness of sin. To the believer this is grace.

Third Pillar: When a believer tries to live a life that is pleasing to God in his own strength, he will fail every time.

Fourth Pillar: That very failure makes him ready for God's grace. Ray Stedman writes:

There are teachers who teach that this passage in Romans 7 is something a Christian goes through but once. Then he gets out of it and moves into Romans 8, never to return to Romans 7 again. Nothing could be further from the truth! Even as mighty a man as Paul went through it again and again. This is a description of what every believer will go through many times in his experience because sin has the power to deceive us and to cause us to trust in ourselves, even when we are not aware we are doing so. The law is what will expose that evil force and drive us to this place of wretchedness that we might then, in devotion of spirit, cry out, Lord Jesus, it is your problem; you take it.[7]

May we learn these lessons well, for they are the key to an increasing experience of the heady atmosphere of Romans 8.

Therefore, there is now no condemnation for those who are in Christ Jesus, because through Christ Jesus the law of the Spirit of life set me free from the law of sin and death. For what the law was powerless to do in that it was weakened by the sinful nature, God did by sending his own Son in the likeness of sinful man to be a sin offering. And so he condemned sin in sinful man, in order that the righteous requirements of the law might be fully met in us, who do not live according to the sinful nature but according to the Spirit. Those who live according to the sinful nature have their minds set on what that nature desires; but those who live in accordance with the Spirit have their minds set on what the Spirit desires. The mind of sinful man is death, but the mind controlled by the Spirit is life and peace, because the sinful mind is hostile to God. It does not submit to God's law, nor can it do so. Those controlled by the sinful nature cannot please God. You, however, are controlled not by the sinful nature but by the Spirit, if the Spirit of God lives in you. And if anyone does not have the Spirit of Christ, he does not belong to Christ. But if Christ is in you, your body is dead because of sin, yet your spirit is alive because of righteousness. And if the Spirit of him who raised Jesus from the dead is living in you, he who raised Christ from the dead will also give life to your mortal bodies through his Spirit, who lives in you. Therefore, brothers, we have an obligation — but it is not to the sinful nature, to live according to it. For if you live according to the sinful nature, you will die; but if by the Spirit you put to death the misdeeds of the body, you will live, because those who are led by the Spirit of God are sons of God. For you did not receive a spirit that makes you a slave again to fear, but you received the Spirit of sonship. And by him we cry, "*Abba*, Father." The Spirit himself testifies with our spirit that we are God's children. Now if we are children, then we are heirs — heirs of God and co-heirs with Christ, if indeed we share in his sufferings in order that we may also share in his glory. (8:1-17)

16

Liberation by the Spirit

ROMANS 8:1-17

Scotland's greatest preacher, Dr. Alexander Whyte, was once speaking on Romans 7, and said this:

> As often as my attentive bookseller sends me on approval another new commentary on Romans, I immediately turn to the seventh chapter. And if the commentator sets up a man of straw in the seventh chapter, I immediately shut the book. I at once send the book back and say, "No, thank you. That is not the man for my hard-earned money."[1]

I think perhaps Dr. Whyte was a bit severe because it is possible for a writer to take a different position on Romans 7 than the one Dr. Whyte and I have taken and still write an excellent commentary on Romans. Some of the best Bible teachers see the matter differently. Nevertheless, I have some sympathy for what Alexander Whyte was saying because I think it is misleading, and thus not spiritually healthy, to imagine that Romans 7:14-25 is anything other than the Apostle Paul describing his own struggle as a Christian trying to please God in his own strength (to measure up to God's standards as revealed in the Law). But of course Paul is also talking about the experience of everyone who has come to Christ. To argue that Romans 7 cannot be the experience of a great Christian is to espouse an unrealistic and unhealthy approach to the Christian life.

Now, there is nothing wrong with God's Law. It is good and perfect. The problem lies with us. Paul's passionate conclusion is the cry of every Christian who has ever tried to please God on his own:

So I find this law at work: When I want to do good, evil is right there with me. For in my inner being I delight in God's law; but I see another law at work in the members of my body, waging war against the law of my mind and making me a prisoner of the law of sin at work within my members. What a wretched man I am! Who will rescue me from this body of death? (7:21-24)

This has been and is my cry. It has been yours too. We want to do good, but we end up doing the very thing we did not want to do. Our inner being wants to please God, but the power to do so is out of our grasp. We are in bondage.

But there is another experience which also belongs to Everyman, and it is described fully in Romans 8. If we have been Christians for any length of time, we have known something of the life of Romans 8, but all of us would like to spend more time in its liberating heights.

Paul memorably introduces this great treatise by saying: "Therefore, there is now no condemnation for those who are in Christ Jesus" (v.1a). This is an arresting statement. But it is even more gripping when we understand that the term "condemnation" carries the idea of penal servitude. F. F. Bruce paraphrases it this way:

> There is no reason why those who are in Christ Jesus should go on doing penal servitude as though they had never been pardoned and liberated from the prison house of sin.[2]

In this way Paul introduces the grand theme of Romans 8: the work of the Holy Spirit in effecting our liberation.

The theme of chapter 8 is the Holy Spirit. Until this point, there have only been two mentions of the Spirit in Romans. The first was a passing reference to "the Spirit of holiness" (1:4), and the other described the Holy Spirit as pouring out the love of God within our hearts (5:5). Now chapter 8 mentions the Holy Spirit twenty times! Second Corinthians 3:17 says, "Where the Spirit of the Lord is, there is freedom." Romans 8 is the chapter of *liberation through God's Spirit*. My hope is that our study of it will enable us to live more and more in "the glorious freedom of the children of God" (v. 21) so that chapter 7 will become less and less our experience.

The structure of the argument of verses 2-17 is as follows:

I. The Holy Spirit's Liberating Work (vv. 2-4)
II.The Holy Spirit's Liberating Gifts (vv. 5-17)

A. A new mind-set (vv. 5-8)
B. A new sense of life (vv. 9-11)
C. A new obligation (vv. 12, 13)
D. A new identity (vv. 14-17)

THE HOLY SPIRIT'S LIBERATING WORK (vv. 2-4)

Verse 2 introduces the work of the Holy Spirit in bringing liberation: "because through Christ Jesus the law of the Spirit of life set me free from the law of sin and death." Here "law" carries the idea of principle: "You were under the old principle of sin and death, but that has been transcended by the new principle of life in Christ — and so you are free." The old principle showed us our sin, stirred up our sin so that we sinned even more, and then brought us to condemnation. But the new principle liberates us. Death has been replaced with life.

Here Paul gives the Holy Spirit one of his more magnificent titles: "the Spirit of life." It reminds us of the first mention of the Spirit in the Bible (Genesis 1:2), when the Spirit brought forth creation *ex nihilo*. That same creative power is characteristic of this new principle. The Spirit of God "gives life to the dead and calls things that are not as though they were" (4:17b).

This "Spirit of life" administers the work of God the Father, thus securing our liberation. God's work is described in verses 3, 4:

> For what the law was powerless to do in that it was weakened by the sinful nature, God did by sending his own Son in the likeness of sinful man to be a sin offering. And so he condemned sin in sinful man, in order that the righteous requirements of the law might be fully met in us, who do not live according to the sinful nature but according to the Spirit.

The Law held up its perfect standard, but was unable to empower us to live up to that standard because of the weakness of our flesh. There was nothing wrong with the Law. The problem lay with the weakness of our flesh.

> For what the law was powerless to do in that it was weakened by the sinful nature, God did by sending his own Son in the likeness of sinful man to be a sin offering. And so he condemned sin in sinful man. . . . (v. 3)

Since our flesh was inadequate, God sent Christ in "the likeness of sinful man." Paul was very careful about his words here. He did not say Christ came "in sinful flesh" because that would imply sin was in him. Nor did he say, "likeness of flesh" because that might imply Christ only seemed to be in the flesh. He said, "the likeness of sinful man" because Christ took on man's flesh (human nature) without becoming a sinner. Cranfield writes, ". . . the Son of God assumed the selfsame fallen human nature that is ours, but . . . in His case that fallen human nature was never the whole of Him."[3] Christ became "a sin offering" as he took our sin without sinning. Thus his flesh (his human nature) remained strong and unfallen. As a result "he condemned sin in sinful man." That is, he conquered sin.

What this means *for us* is given in verse 4. He condemned sin in his flesh "in order that the righteous requirements of the law might be fully met in us, who do not live according to the sinful nature but according to the Spirit." The Holy Spirit creates a new humanity which is characterized by walking "according to the Spirit." This new humanity, through its union with Christ, whose flesh never sinned, is infused with the power to live in a way that is pleasing to God. Everything the Law required is now realized in the lives of those who are controlled by the Holy Spirit.

> *To run and work the law commands,*
> *Yet gives me neither feet or hands;*
> *But better news the gospel brings:*
> *It bids me fly, and gives me wings.*[4]

The principle of the Spirit of life in Christ Jesus has set us free from the principle of sin and death. Thus when we yield to the power of the Holy Spirit, we are liberated. We no longer have to sin. Through the Holy Spirit the virtue and perfection and power of Christ's life is communicated to us. We actually do the Law of God from the heart. We love him with all our hearts, and we love our neighbors as ourselves. This is as great a miracle as when the Spirit hovered over the face of the deep and with power materialized a new creation at the spoken word of the Father. The Holy Spirit liberates us through Christ!

THE HOLY SPIRIT'S LIBERATING GIFTS (vv. 5-17)

Now we will consider what the Holy Spirit gives us in our liberation. Four things are mentioned in verses 5-17. First, he gives us *a new mind-set.*

Verses 5-8 describe two mind-sets — one without Christ and the other with Christ. The bulk of the description is of the non-Christian mind-set.

> Those who live according to the sinful nature have their minds set on what that nature desires; but those who live in accordance with the Spirit have their minds set on what the Spirit desires. The mind of sinful man is death, but the mind controlled by the Spirit is life and peace, because the sinful mind is hostile to God. It does not submit to God's law, nor can it do so. Those controlled by the sinful nature cannot please God.

The mind-set of those without Christ has distinct characteristics: death, hostility toward God, and an *inability to subject itself* to God. These govern its orientation to all of life. How sad! First Corinthians 2:14 says, "The man without the Spirit does not accept the things that come from the Spirit of God, for they are foolishness to him, and he cannot understand them." On the other hand, "the mind controlled by the Spirit is life and peace" (v. 6).

What Paul is saying here is immensely important because our mind-set makes all the difference when it comes to daily living. We all, whatever our spiritual state, live in a storm-tossed world. The rain falls on the just and the unjust. The set of our minds will determine not only eternity but the quality of our life now.

> One ship drives east and another drives west
> With the selfsame winds that blow.
> 'Tis the set of the sails
> And not the gales
> Which tells us the way to go.
>
> Like the winds of the sea are the ways of fate,
> As we voyage along through life—
> 'Tis the set of a soul
> That decides its goal
> And not the calm or the strife.[5]

The Holy Spirit gives the believer a new set of mind which brings life and peace. This is liberation!

Second, the Holy Spirit gives *a new sense of life*. Verse 9 tells us our life is permeated by the personality of Christ.

You, however, are controlled not by the sinful nature but by the Spirit, if the Spirit of God lives in you. And if anyone does not have the Spirit of Christ, he does not belong to Christ.

As believers we have "the Spirit of Christ" — that is, the indwelling Holy Spirit. The clear implication of Paul's use of the phrase "the Spirit of Christ" is that through the Spirit we experience something of Jesus' disposition — his kindness, his gentle care, his love in our lives. As we allow the Holy Spirit to fill us, we are filled with the ethos of Jesus, and life becomes more and more to us what it was and is to him. Paul continues in verses 10, 11:

But if Christ is in you, your body is dead because of sin, yet your spirit is alive because of righteousness. And if the Spirit of him who raised Jesus from the dead is living in you, he who raised Christ from the dead will also give life to your mortal bodies through his Spirit, who lives in you.

This could be paraphrased:

If Christ dwells within you, then, while your body is still subject to that temporal death which is the consequence of sin, the Spirit who has taken up His abode in you, the living and quickening Spirit, imparts to you that eternal life which is the consequence of justification.[6]

Through the Spirit we have a sense of new life now and the assurance of eternal life in the Resurrection. The Holy Spirit confirms and intensifies our assurance of immortality. The "now" of living becomes Technicolor!

When evangelist D. L. Moody described his conversion experience, he said: "I was in a new world. The next morning the sun shone brighter and the birds sang sweeter . . . the old elms waved their branches for joy, and all nature was at peace."[7] I found the same thing to be true. When I was twelve years old, I came to know Christ. I remember saying the next day, "The sky is bluer and the grass is greener." Jesus Christ enriches the "now" of life!

But the "then" of living is assured by the Holy Spirit as well. Carlos Baker's standard biography of Ernest Hemingway records this sad description of him the year before he died:

The only resemblance to the man we had imagined was in the fullness of the face. And even the face was pale and red-veined, not
ruddy or weather-beaten. We were particularly struck by the thin-
ness of his arms and legs. . . . He walked with the tentativeness of a
man well over sixty-one. The dominant sense we had was of
fragility.

They were equally surprised by his apparent inability to talk. He "spoke
in spurts of a few words, hardly ever in sentences. . . ."[8]

When Hemingway died, everything was lost!

This is not so for the believer. Second Corinthians 4:16 says:
"Therefore we do not lose heart. Though outwardly we are wasting away,
yet inwardly we are being renewed day by day." This positive sense of
immortality is one of the liberating gifts of the Holy Spirit.

The third element the Holy Spirit gives us is *a new obligation.*

Therefore, brothers, we have an obligation — but it is not to the sinful nature, to live according to it. For if you live according to the sinful nature, you will die; but if by the Spirit you put to death the
misdeeds of the body, you will live. (vv. 12, 13)

Paul realizes that though we all have the privilege of victorious
Christian living through the Holy Spirit, we will not automatically follow God's will. Therefore he exhorts us to live "by the Spirit." Day by
day we are constantly solicited to follow the flesh, and that is why Paul
encourages us to constantly be putting to death the deeds of the body. The
freedom of the Spirit brings obligation — the obligation of liberation.

Lastly, the Holy Spirit gives us *a new identity.*

. . . those who are led by the Spirit of God are sons of God. For you
did not receive a spirit that makes you a slave again to fear, but you
received the Spirit of sonship. And by him we cry, "*Abba,* Father."
The Spirit himself testifies with our spirit that we are God's children.
(vv. 14-16)

The identity the Spirit gives us is that of being sons and daughters of God.
Verse 16 tells us, "The Spirit himself testifies with our spirit that we are
God's children." In Hebrew culture the testimony of two witnesses was
required to establish a truth, and we have two witnesses: that of our inner-
most being, and that of the Holy Spirit. Paul calls our identity "the Spirit
of sonship." F. F. Bruce says:

The term "adoption" may smack somewhat of artificiality in our ears; but in the first century A.D. an adopted son was a son deliberately chosen by his adoptive father to perpetuate his name and inherit his estate; he was no whit inferior in status to a son born in the ordinary course of nature and might well enjoy the father's affection more fully and reproduce the father's character more worthily.[9]

We sense that we really are God's sons! So intense is the reality of our adoption that we cry, "*Abba*, Father." The Aramaic word "Abba," which means "Dear Father" in the sense that we might say "Dad" or "Daddy," was never used by the Jews to address God, nor do they use it today. Jesus alone used it, and this was no doubt considered scandalous by his enemies. He used it in Gethsemane when he cried, "*Abba*, Father . . . everything is possible for you. Take this cup from me. Yet not what I will, but what you will" (Mark 14:36). We believe it was the word he used in the Aramaic original of what we call "the Lord's prayer." And here in Romans the Holy Spirit compels us to cry, "*Abba*, Father!" Galatians 4:6 says, "Because you are sons, God sent the Spirit of his Son into our hearts, the Spirit who calls out, '*Abba*, Father.'" It is not a reasoned cry, but a reflexive one, the cry of children.

Can anything be more beautiful in this world of cold steel and computers? Jesus, through the Spirit, has given us his own special name for God, and it has become our natural cry to a loving Father. Could we offer anything more enticing than this to a lonely world? Many have never known a meaningful relationship with an earthly Father. Or some have, but now he is gone. God offers his soul-satisfying paternity to all who come to him. "Abba, Father."

Paul began by saying that we are no longer under penal servitude to sin. We are free because the Holy Spirit has applied the work of Christ to us. The Law could not save us because of the weakness of our flesh, but Christ came to our rescue as he came in "the likeness of sinful man to be a sin offering" (v. 3).

Then he addressed the dynamic role of the Holy Spirit in our liberation: a *new* mind-set, a *new* sense of life, a *new* identity, and a *new* obligation.

The key to personal enjoyment of all this is twofold: first, experiencing the renewal of the Holy Spirit; second, living according to the Spirit.

May all this be ours today and always!

I consider that our present sufferings are not worth comparing with the glory that will be revealed in us. The creation waits in eager expectation for the sons of God to be revealed. For the creation was subjected to frustration, not by its own choice, but by the will of the one who subjected it, in hope that the creation itself will be liberated from its bondage to decay and brought into the glorious freedom of the children of God. We know that the whole creation has been groaning as in the pains of childbirth right up to the present time. Not only so, but we ourselves, who have the firstfruits of the Spirit, groan inwardly as we wait eagerly for our adoption as sons, the redemption of our bodies. For in this hope we were saved. But hope that is seen is no hope at all. Who hopes for what he already has? But if we hope for what we do not yet have, we wait for it patiently. In the same way, the Spirit helps us in our weakness. We do not know what we ought to pray, but the Spirit himself intercedes for us with groans that words cannot express. And he who searches our hearts knows the mind of the Spirit, because the Spirit intercedes for the saints in accordance with God's will. (8:18-27)

17

Three Groans and
One Glory

ROMANS 8:18-27

The opening verses of Romans 8 introduce the profound liberation which comes from the Holy Spirit. Verses 2-4 reveal *how* the Holy Spirit liberates us through Christ. Verses 5-17 tell us *what* the Holy Spirit gives us as he liberates us. As we followed the argument of these verses we saw an exhilarating intensification of hope culminating in the cry, "*Abba*, Father."

Now in verses 17 and 18 Paul contrasts this rising hope with the inescapable reality of the pain of human existence and declares that our pain is not worthy to be compared with the coming glory. He says in verse 18, "I consider that our present sufferings are not worth comparing with the glory that will be revealed in us."

This is an astounding statement. It is even more astounding that Paul should apply it to himself. When his ship was not sinking or he was not being stoned or robbed, he was being whipped to within an inch of his life (cf. 2 Corinthians 11:23-27). He wasn't speaking poetically when he told the Galatians, "Finally, let no one cause me trouble, for I bear on my body the marks of Jesus" (Galatians 6:17). Yet he says that the present sufferings are not worthy to be compared with the coming glory. Amazing!

Some believers down through the ages have had it worse than Paul. Some have known years of imprisonment in vermin-filled prisons and medieval tortures — finally expiring as they were drawn and quartered. Yet the future glory is greater! That is the plain meaning of Paul's words.

He begins verse 18 by saying, "I consider," meaning "I have thought it over carefully — I have weighed the evidence and thus reckon it to be so." He says essentially the same thing in 2 Corinthians 4:17 — "For our light and momentary troubles are achieving for us an eternal glory that far outweighs them all." No matter what we have gone through, are presently going through, or will go through, the sum total is not worth comparing with the glory that awaits us. We can compare a thimble of water with the sea, but we cannot compare our sufferings with the coming glory.

What, then, must this glory be like? We know that the universe will be transformed (cf. Revelation 21:1). We also know that we will have bodies like Christ's glorified body (cf. Philippians 3:21). These are thrilling truths, especially when we reflect on how marvelous our own bodies are even now! When C. S. Lewis preached the sermon "The Weight of Glory" in the Church of St Mary the Virgin, Oxford on June 8, 1941, he gave as eloquent an explanation as has ever been given. In his homily he noted that the promises of Scripture may be reduced to five headings: 1) we shall be with Christ, 2) we shall be like him, 3) we shall have "glory," 4) we shall be feasted, and 5) we shall have some official position in the universe. In speculating on what our glorification may involve, Lewis noted that the Scriptures indicate that as part of our glory we will shine like the sun (Matthew 13:43). He concluded:

> Some day, God willing, we shall get in. When human souls have become as perfect in voluntary obedience as the inanimate creation is in its lifeless obedience, then they will put on its glory, or rather that greater glory of which Nature is only the first sketch. For you must not think that I am putting forward any heathen fancy of being absorbed into Nature. Nature is mortal; we shall outlive her. When all the suns and nebulae have passed away, each one of you will still be alive. Nature is only the image, the symbol; but it is the symbol Scripture invites me to use. We are summoned to pass in through Nature, beyond her, into that splendour which she fitfully reflects.[1]

This hope was as real to Paul as meat and drink. Lewis was right when he said:

> Indeed, if we consider the unblushing promises of reward and the staggering nature of the rewards promised in the Gospels, it would seem that Our Lord finds our desires not too strong, but too weak. We are half-hearted creatures fooling about with drink and sex and

ambition when infinite joy is offered us, like an ignorant child who wants to go on making mud pies in a slum because he cannot imagine what is meant by the offer of a holiday at the sea.[2]

Belief in what the Scriptures say will change our lives. Some of us need to have our eyes lifted from the dirt toward the heavens. There is simply no comparison of our pleasure or pain with the glory yet to be revealed.

As we continue on with our study of verses 18-27, Paul presents the hope as so substantive that creation groans for it, believers groan for it, and even the Holy Spirit aids believers with his own groans. Christian hope that eventuates in groans is a marvelous asset to living.

CREATION'S GROAN AND HOPE (vv. 19-22)

The first groan that Paul introduces is that of creation (vv. 19-21).

The creation waits in eager expectation for the sons of God to be revealed. For the creation was subjected to frustration, not by its own choice, but by the will of the one who subjected it, in hope that the creation itself will be liberated from its bondage to decay and brought into the glorious freedom of the children of God.

In a marvelous blend of poetic and prophetic impulse, Paul pictures animate and inanimate creation as an audience eagerly waiting for the sons of God to come into their true glory. In verse 19 the phrase, "waits in eager expectation" comes from a group of words that carry the idea of craning the neck or stretching forward. Here the form of the word is intensive.[3] Phillips translates this, "The whole creation is on tiptoe to see the wonderful sight of the sons of God coming into their own." Creation longs for the day of liberation.

Next Paul gives the reason for the creation's longing: "For the creation was subjected to frustration, not by its own choice, but by the will of the one who subjected it" (v. 20). Paul is referring, of course, to the curse that came upon creation when mankind sinned. In Genesis 1:29 God described creation to Adam and Eve like this:

"I give you every seed-bearing plant on the face of the whole earth and every tree that has fruit with seed in it. They will be yours for food."

The earth was immensely productive. It was kind to itself and kind to its masters. It was a *paradise*. But after the Fall came the curse:

> To Adam he said "Because you listened to your wife and ate from the tree about which I commanded you, 'You must not eat of it,' Cursed is the ground because of you; through painful toil you will eat of it all the days of your life. It will produce thorns and thistles for you, and you will eat the plants of the field. By the sweat of your brow you will eat your food until you return to the ground, since from it you were taken; for dust you are and to dust you will return."
> (Genesis 3:17-19)

Creation became a sufferer and was imbued with futility, decay, and death. So now at times the forces of nature seem to work against themselves, as well as against man. M. Reuss says,

> Everywhere our eyes meet images of death and decay; the scourge of barrenness, the fury of the elements, the destructive instincts of beasts, the very laws which govern vegetation, everything gives nature a somber hue.[4]

The animal world was invaded by fear and violence. The loveliest scenes in nature, while remaining beautiful, are also witness to bloody horrors. Floods, hurricanes, droughts, tornadoes, blights, avalanches, and earthquakes stalk the earth.

Mankind's abuse exacerbates the disharmony. I have lived where the air is too polluted to comfortably breathe and a walk on the beach coats one's feet with tar. It is probably true that if mankind goes its way unhindered, the last man will stand at the edge of a petroleum-clogged sea while behind him rise the twisted skeletons of his great cities. Paul says in verse 22, "We know that the whole creation has been groaning as in the pains of childbirth right up to the present time." The earth groans like a woman in labor. It wants desperately to be delivered.

Sometimes there appears to be no hope. But there is! Verses 20, 21 indicate that God subjected nature "in hope that the creation itself will be liberated from its bondage to decay and brought into the glorious freedom of the children of God." Many of us have pictures of our wives after they have delivered a child, and typically the baby is in their arms and mother is radiant. None of us have a picture of our wives in labor. We do not reach into our wallets saying, "Let me show you a picture of Margaret groaning in labor. Isn't the agony terrific?" Creation will one day be delivered — and the difference between then and now is the difference between agony and ecstasy! Someone our groaning creation will come into "the glorious freedom of the children of God." Think what will happen when nature is free to produce as it was designed to produce, free from pestilence and danger. We are going to see that day!

We see the *principle* of the groan for glory all about us. Now Paul moves to *personal application*. Creation groans, and Christians groan too.

THE CHURCH'S GROAN AND HOPE (vv. 23-25)

> Not only so, but we ourselves, who have the firstfruits of the Spirit, groan inwardly as we wait eagerly for our adoption as sons, the redemption of our bodies. (v. 23)

The thing we groan for is our adoption as sons, which will be completed by the redemption of the body. We are already God's sons and daughters, but we will not be complete for eternity until we get our new bodies. Second Corinthians 5:2 is a parallel passage: "Meanwhile we groan, longing to be clothed with our heavenly dwelling." We cry, "Who will rescue me from this body of death?" (7:24).

We also groan because of the misery of living in our fallen bodies in this fallen world. Ray Stedman writes:

> Our lives consist of groans. We groan because of the ravages that sin makes in our lives, and in the lives of those we love. Also we groan because we see possibilities that are not being captured and employed. And then we groan because we see gifted people who are wasting their lives, and we would love to see something else happening. It is recorded that, as he drew near the tomb of Lazarus, Jesus groaned in his spirit because he was so burdened by the ravages that sin had made in a believing family. He groaned, even though he knew he would soon raise Lazarus from the dead. So we groan in our spirits—we groan in disappointment, in bereavement, in sorrow. We groan physically in our pain and our limitation. Life consists of a great deal of groaning.[5]

We also groan for a positive reason — we have "the firstfruits of the Spirit" (v. 23). We have the first installment (or down payment) of the inconceivably fabulous heritage God has prepared for us. When Abraham's servant was sent to find a bride for Isaac and met Rebekah, he gave silver and gold garments and presents to Laban as indications of what was to come. That is what God has done for us by his Holy Spirit. That indescribable peace we knew when we first experienced the forgiveness of our sins, the power of God that calms our heart despite circumstances, the joy that floods our souls — these are mere foretastes of what is yet to come!

We are described as waiting "eagerly" (v. 23). This same strong word is used of creation's waiting (v. 19). We are on tiptoe waiting for our deliverance. Paul underlines this hope in verses 24, 25:

> For in this hope we were saved. But hope that is seen is no hope at
> all. Who hopes for what he already has? But if we hope for what we
> do not yet have, we wait for it patiently.

Here we again find the same strong word — "wait for it patiently." We are on tiptoe, and we wait with perseverance. Life right now is very good for me. But in the future there will be joys supreme. I look forward to that time of deliverance from this body of sin, glory ineffable, seeing the face of Christ, experiencing without restriction the perpetual adventure of getting to know him. And so do you! We groan . . . we have an inconsolable longing which our greatest joys dimly foreshadow. Someday we will know the fullness of our salvation.

THE HOLY SPIRIT'S GROAN AND HOPE (vv. 26, 27)

Creation groans, we groan, and even the Holy Spirit groans. Verses 26, 27 tell us:

> In the same way, the Spirit helps us in our weakness. We do not
> know what we ought to pray, but the Spirit himself intercedes for us
> with groans that words cannot express. And he who searches our
> hearts knows the mind of the Spirit, because the Spirit intercedes for
> the saints in accordance with God's will.

If we are honest with ourselves, we must all admit there are times when we cannot pray. There have been times when my children were so desperately ill and the urgency so great that I could scarcely converse with God. At best I may have said a few words, "but the Spirit himself intercedes for us with groans that words cannot express."

There have been times when something has been said to us that is so devastating and we are so hurt we cannot pray, "but the Spirit himself intercedes for us with groans that words cannot express."

One day some of us will lie in hospitals with catheters and IVs, and we will not have the will to pray or even put two thoughts together, "but the Spirit himself intercedes for us with groans that words cannot express." The Holy Spirit expresses those things we feel but cannot articulate.

The Holy Spirit says those things we want to say but cannot mouth. How beautiful! May we appreciate our wealth.

The word indicating the Holy Spirit "helps" our weakness gives us further insight into how he intercedes for us. A. T. Robertson says:

> The Holy Spirit lays hold of our weaknesses along with (*syn*) us and carries His part of the burden facing us (*anti*) as if two men were carrying a log, one at each end.[6]

The Holy Spirit does not give armchair advice. He rolls up his sleeves and helps us bear our weakness. That is real help.

How marvelous this all is! We have two intercessors: one in Heaven — our Lord Jesus who intercedes for our sins (v. 34), and one in our hearts — the Holy Spirit himself. How greatly we are loved!

A glory awaits us that exceeds the wildest imaginations of our most gifted science fiction writers. You and I are going to be creatures so glorious that if we saw such ones today we would be tempted to fall down and worship them.

Because of the greatness of the coming glory and because of our weakness, we groan. But we are not alone, for we are surrounded by the sympathetic groanings of creation and even of the Holy Spirit. And one day our groanings will be replaced by glory!

> *When all my labors and trials are o'er,*
>   *And I am safe on htat beutiful shore*
> *Just to be near the dear Lord I adore*
>   *Will through the ages be glory for me.*
> *O that will be glory for me,*
>   *Glory for me, glory for me.*

Charles H. Gabriel, 1900

And we know that in all things God works for the good of those who love him, who have been called according to his purpose. For those God foreknew he also predestined to be conformed to the likeness of his Son, that he might be the first-born among many brothers. And those he predestined, he also called; those he called, he also justified; those he justified, he also glorified. What, then, shall we say in response to this? If God is for us, who can be against us? He who did not spare his own Son, but gave him up for us all — how will he not also, along with him, graciously give us all things? Who will bring any charge against those whom God has chosen? It is God who justifies. Who is he that condemns? Christ Jesus, who died — more than that, who was raised to life — is at the right hand of God and is also interceding for us. Who shall separate us from the love of Christ? Shall trouble or hardship or persecution or famine or nakedness or danger or sword? As it is written: "For your sake we face death all day long; we are considered as sheep to be slaughtered." No, in all these things we are more than conquerors through him who loved us. For I am convinced that neither death nor life, neither angels nor demons, neither the present nor the future, nor any powers, neither height nor depth, nor anything else in all creation, will be able to separate us from the love of God that is in Christ Jesus our Lord. (8:28-39)

18

Super Conquerors

ROMANS 8:28-39

Two great men stood side by side in the early Reformation movement. One was, of course, Martin Luther, the activist. The other was Philipp Melanchthon, the scholar. Luther once said of their relationship:

> I am rough, boisterous, stormy, and altogether warlike, fighting against innumerable monsters and devils. I am born for the removing of stumps and stones, cutting away thistles and thorns, and clearing the wild forests; but master Philippus comes along softly and gently, sowing and watering with joy, according to the gifts which God has abundantly bestowed upon him.[1]

What Luther said of Melanchthon was eminently true. Melanchthon's friend Camerarius wrote of him that as a boy he was gentle, winsome, unassuming, and scholarly, with an abiding look of innocence. Melanchthon liked people, and people liked him. He was a favorite person in his tiny village on the Rhine. At the same time, he was absolutely brilliant! In the year 1516, when Melanchthon was only nineteen years old, Erasmus wrote of him, "What purity and elegance of style! What rare learning! What comprehensive reading! What tenderness and refinement in his extraordinary genius!"[2]

Because of his remarkable brilliance, Melanchthon's family name of Schwartzert was changed to its Greek equivalent "Melanchthon." His mastery of the Greek and Roman classics helped spark a new enthusiasm for those languages. In fact, the great church historian Philip Schaff gives

Melanchthon more credit than anyone, even Erasmus, for reviving the study of Greek literature.[3] And the study of Greek opened the way for the triumph of the Reformation. (Melanchthon often said that the ancient languages were the swaddling clothes of the Christ Child.)

Melanchthon was also a gifted preacher. At the age of twenty-one he became a professor at the University of Wittenberg, where Luther taught. Melanchthon's specialty was preaching in Latin to the students who did not know German, and his Sunday sermons drew crowds of 1,500 to 2,000.

Luther and Melanchthon made a great pair. Luther knew that Melanchthon was all gold, and he never attempted to disguise his appreciation. Nor could Luther ever forget the day when his friend showed him that the word which had always been translated "penance" really meant "repentance," a change of heart. Melanchthon likewise loved Luther. Luther was his hero. He wrote simply, "If there is anyone whom I dearly love, and whom I embrace with my whole heart, it is Martin Luther."[4] They were a perfect match. J. W. Richard wrote about Melanchthon:

> In matters of intellect he had a quick perception, an acute penetration, a retentive memory, an ardent thirst for knowledge, and the ability to express his thoughts with accuracy and precision.[5]

They stood together to the end. When Luther died, Melanchthon gave the funeral oration over his grave. And when Melanchthon died a few years later, his body was lowered into the same grave, where they now sleep side by side in the Castle Church of Wittenberg.

Where did Melanchthon get his strength? What made this gentle, retiring man stand with Luther against the world? The heart of the text we will now consider, verse 31, gives the answer: "If God is for us, who can be against us?" In his lectures and correspondence that verse is quoted more than any other Scripture. It still hangs on his study wall in Wittenberg where visitors can see it.

As the record has it, when Melanchthon sensed he was dying he asked to be placed on the traveling bed in his study because that is where he was happiest. When the pastor read Romans 8:31, Melanchthon exclaimed, "Read those words again!" The pastor read, "If God is for us, who can be against us?" Melanchthon murmured in a kind of ecstasy, "That's it! That's it!" This text had always been the greatest comfort to him. In the darkest hours of his life when destruction threatened, he comforted himself again by reciting, "If God is for us, who can be against us?"[6]

These words are the crowning expression of confidence in a text which exudes Christian confidence as much as any section of Scripture. As we examine the final section of Romans 8, we will see why it meant so much to Melanchthon and to thousands of believers over the years. If we are interested in a life crowned with confidence, this could be our foundational text.

CROWNED WITH CONFIDENCE IN GOD'S SOVEREIGNTY (vv. 28-30)

This section begins with an immensely confident statement so familiar to all of us: "And we know that in all things God works for the good of those who love him, who have been called according to his purpose" (v. 28). The text is so familiar that sometimes we do not even take time to say it, we just quote the reference. "Having trouble today, my friend? Well, remember Romans 8:28. Chin up!" It is good advice, although I am not sure it should be used so glibly. For one thing, the text is for Christians only, "those who love him" — that is, those who have experienced the love of God and have responded to it. Romans 8:28 has become so popular that those with no faith in Christ obtain from it a false security. Believers, however, can wrap their souls in it!

Romans 8:28 does not mean, as is commonly thought, that "everything will turn out okay in this life." It means, rather, that everything will work out for our ultimate good. These words have our eternal rather than our temporal good in mind. Bishop Anders Nygren writes:

> Just as the present aeon is to be followed by eternity, it has already been preceded by an eternity. Only when we see our present existence set in God's activity, which goes from eternity to eternity, do we get it in right perspective. Then man comes to see that *everything* that comes to the Christian in this life — and consequently the sufferings of the present too — must work together for good to him.[7]

The specific good will be seen when we are glorified as we are conformed to the image of Christ. The Christian should not view present distresses and reversals as ultimately destructive. In some manner they are preparing us for the future revelation of God's glory. At that time we will clearly see what we have always known: ". . . that in all things [pleasures, pains, experiences of tremendous suffering, disappointments] God works for the good of those who love him, who have been called according to his purpose." Thus we have the foundation for a massive confidence such as that of Philipp Melanchthon. It really is true! God does cause everything that happens to us (even the evils inflicted by others, even the presently inexplicable disappointments) to work out for every believer's eternal good.

This immense confidence rests on the certainty of our redemption, which began before time with God's foreknowledge and will end beyond time with our glorification. This certainty is described in verses 29, 30 in what commentators have called "the golden chain." Notice that the emphasis is on God doing everything:

> For those God foreknew he also predestined to be conformed to the likeness of his Son, that he might be the firstborn among many brothers. And those he predestined, he also called; those he called, he also justified; those he justified, he also glorified.

Our confidence is that all who begin will finish — 100 percent. The same number he called will be justified. The same number he justified will be glorified. Whatever else may be said about this, one thing is clear: the entire initiative in our salvation lay with God. Before time began he "foreknew" us and "predestined" us to be "conformed to the likeness of his Son." Then within history he "called" us. This was and is the mysterious work of the Holy Spirit as he appeals to our hearts to respond in faith to the free offer of pardon and new life in the gospel of Christ (2 Thessalonians 2:13, 14). The effectual call came to us individually in many ways, but the outcome was the same — justification.

Further, someday when history is over and time is no more, the golden chain will conclude: "those he justified, he also glorified." James Denny, one-time principal of Free Church College, Edinburgh, called this, "the most daring anticipation of faith that . . . the New Testament contains. . . ."[8] Denny said this because "glorified" is in the past tense. Believers are spoken of as already glorified — their glorification is that certain! Here on earth we comprise an incredible array of individuals. But when we get to Heaven, we will all be like Jesus. We will retain our individuality, but we will also have Christ's character — the same gentleness, the same self-control, the same perfect love. John Donne put it this way:

> I shall be so like God, as that the devil himself shall not know me from God, so farre as to finde any more place to fasten a temptation upon me, then upon God; not to conceive any more hope of my falling from that kingdome, then of God's being drivern out of it.

This ought to fuel our confidence! Everything that happens in life is used by God to prepare us in some way for the future revelation of glory. The immense certainty of this rests on the fact that everything is of God. Each of the five links in the golden chain of our redemption are his work. *We are going to be like Jesus.* The family resemblance both in body and spirit is unmistakable.

CROWNED WITH CONFIDENCE IN
OUR PERSEVERANCE (vv. 31-39)

The challenge in verse 31 is noted for its elevated eloquence and poetic fervor: "What, then, shall we say in response to this? If God is for us, who can be against us?" The story is told that during a crisis in the Civil War a timid civilian sought out President Lincoln and said, "Oh, Mr. President, I am most anxious that the Lord should be on our side!" Lincoln replied, "That gives me no anxiety at all. The thing I worry about is being on the Lord's side!" Lincoln was correct in his application for that moment. But in the context of salvation there is no doubt — "God is for us." Melanchthon found this to be true. When Martin Luther stood tall at Worms, it was, to use Carlyle's words, "the greatest moment in the modern history of man." But there was another man with him, a shy man of peace. He was there because he believed "If God is for us, who can be against us?" Luther and Melanchthon *contra mundum.* The logic of our text, seriously applied, pushes us to the heights of confidence. It means more than God being graciously disposed toward us. It means he is for us in all that he does. We may be defeated at this moment, but evil will never prevail. We are always being led to victory in Christ. "God is for us." We can write our names in the verse: "God is for Kent Hughes, God is for_____."

Paul goes on to substantiate this boast of confidence in the remainder of the chapter, giving three arguments. First, he says God will withhold nothing in taking care of us. "He who did not spare his own Son, but gave him up for us all — how will he not also, along with him, graciously give us all things?" (v. 32). Again we are compelled to take our thinking to its logical conclusion. Since God gave his only Son for us, he will withhold nothing beneficial from us.

For sake of illustration, suppose on a whim you visit a Rolls Royce dealership, enter a drawing, and win a brand-new Rolls Silver Cloud. When you go to pick it up, they say, "It's all yours — tax free. Take it home!" But they refuse to give you the key. Ridiculous! If the car is yours, whatever you need to drive it is yours. Likewise, since we have received the incredible gift of God's Son and salvation in him, it is ridiculous to suppose God will not give us everything else we need. Second Peter 1:2, 3a tells us:

Grace and peace be yours in abundance through the knowledge of God and of Jesus our Lord. His divine power has given us everything we need for life and godliness. . . .

Because of the immensity of the gift of God's Son, we may be confident he will freely give us all things.

> *What will He not bestow?*
> *Who freely gave this mighty gift unbought,*
> *Unmerited, unheeded and unsought,*
> *What will He not bestow?*
> *He spared not His Son!*
> *'Tis this that silences each rising fear,*
> *'Tis this that bids the hard thought disappear.*
> *He spared not His Son!*
>
> (Horatius Bonar)

Next we read that God will allow nothing to condemn us:

Who will bring any charge against those whom God has chosen? It is God who justifies. Who is he that condemns? Christ Jesus, who died — more than that, who was raised to life — is at the right hand of God and is also interceding for us. (vv. 33, 34)

If accusations are brought against us, we need not fear, for the charges are silenced by the upraised, pierced hands of our Intercessor. If we are to be condemned, it will have to be over Christ's dead and now resurrected body, which actually is the basis of our salvation! How is that for confidence?

Finally, God will allow nothing to separate us from his love:

Who shall separate us from the love of Christ? Shall trouble or hardship or persecution or famine or nakedness or danger or sword? As it is written: "For your sake we face death all day long; we are considered as sheep to be slaughtered." No, in all these things we are more than conquerors through him who loved us. (vv. 35-37)

In verse 35 Paul is speaking autobiographically having experienced all that he writes about here, and he affirms that none of this — in fact, absolutely nothing — can separate us from Christ's love. In verse 36 he quotes Psalm 44:22 to show that the tribulations believers face are nothing new, but have always been characteristic of God's people. And in verse 37 he concludes, "In all these things we are more than conquerors through him who loved us." Literally he says, "We are super conquerors!" Not just victors, but super victors! "More than conquerors" — that is what we are now and how we will regard ourselves through all eternity.

When Chrysostom was brought before the Roman Emperor, the Emperor threatened him with banishment if he remained a Christian. Chrysostom replied,

"Thou canst not banish me for this world is my father's house." "But I will slay thee," said the Emperor. "Nay, thou canst not," said the noble champion of the faith, "for my life is hid with Christ in God." "I will take away thy treasures." "Nay, but thou canst not for my treasure is in heaven and my heart is there." "But I will drive thee away from man and thou shalt have no friend left." "Nay, thou canst not, for I have a friend in heaven from whom thou canst not separate me. I defy thee; for there is nothing that thou canst do to hurt me."[10]

At this point Paul lets it all out. If he were sitting at the keyboard of a great organ, all the stops would be completely out — *fortissimo*. In his emotion he even switches to the first person:

For I am convinced that neither death nor life, neither angels nor demons, neither the present not the future, nor any powers, neither height nor depth, nor anything else in all creation, will be able to separate us from the love of God that is in Christ Jesus our Lord. (vv. 38, 39)

Death will not pull me away from God's love. Neither will life and its allurements, nor cosmic spiritual powers — benevolent or malevolent, nor anything in time, nor power, nor the height of Heaven or the depth of Hell, nor anything else — disappointment, neurosis, disease, a broken romance, financial crisis, insanity — nothing "will be able to separate us from the love of God that is in Christ Jesus our Lord."

Philipp Melanchthon died in 1560 with verse 31 on his lips. Exactly 100 years later John Bunyan sat at his desk in deep depression wondering if he could go on, worrying about the future, when the same text came to his rescue.

"I remember," he says, "that I was sitting in a neighbor's home, and was very sad, that word came suddenly to me. 'What shall we say to these things? If God be for us, who can be against us?' That was a help to me."[11]

May it be a help to all of us.

I speak the truth in Christ — I am not lying, my conscience confirms it in the Holy Spirit — I have great sorrow and unceasing anguish in my heart. For I could wish that I myself were cursed and cut off from Christ for the sake of my brothers, those of my own race, the people of Israel. Theirs is the adoption as sons; theirs the divine glory, the covenants, the receiving of the law, the temple worship and the promises. Theirs are the patriarchs, and from them is traced the human ancestry of Christ, who is God over all, forever praised! Amen. It is not as though God's word had failed. For not all who are descended from Israel are Israel. Nor because they are his descendants are they all Abraham's children. On the contrary, "It is through Isaac that your offspring will be reckoned." In other words, it is not the natural children who are God's children, but it is the children of the promise who are regarded as Abraham's offspring. For this was how the promise was stated: "At the appointed time I will return, and Sarah will have a son." Not only that, but Rebecca's children had one and the same father, our father Isaac. Yet, before the twins were born or had done anything good or bad — in order that God's purpose in election might stand: not by works but by him who calls — she was told, "The older will serve the younger." Just as it is written: "Jacob I loved, but Esau I hated." What then shall we say? Is God unjust? Not at all! For he says to Moses, "I will have mercy on whom I have mercy, and I will have compassion on whom I have compassion." It does not, therefore, depend on man's desire or effort, but on God's mercy. For the Scripture says to Pharaoh: "I raised you up for this very purpose, that I might display my power in you and that my name might be proclaimed in all the earth." Therefore God has mercy on whom he wants to have mercy, and he hardens whom he wants to harden. One of you will say to me: "Then why does God still blame us? For who resists his will?" But who are you, O man, to talk back to God? "Shall what is formed say to him who formed it, 'Why did you make me like this?'" Does not the potter have the right to make out of the same lump of clay some pottery for noble purposes and some for common use? What if God, choosing to show his wrath and make his power known, bore with great patience the objects of his wrath — prepared for destruction? What if he did this to make the riches of his glory known to the objects of his mercy, whom he prepared in advance for glory — even us, whom he also called, not only from the Jews but also from the Gentiles? As he says in Hosea: "I will call them 'my people' who are not my people; and I will call her 'my loved one' who is not my loved one," and, "It will happen that in the very place where it was said to them, 'You are not my people,' they will be called 'sons of the living God.'" Isaiah cries out concerning Israel: "Though the number of the Israelites be like the sand by the sea, only the remnant will be saved. For the Lord will carry out his sentence on earth with speed and finality." It is just as Isaiah said previously: "Unless the Lord Almighty had left us descendants, we would have become like Sodom, and we would have been like Gomorrah." What then shall we say? That the Gentiles, who did not pursue righteousness, have obtained it, a righteousness that is by faith; but Israel, who pursued a law of righteousness, has not attained it. Why not? Because they pursued it not by faith but as if it were by works. They stumbled over the "stumbling stone." As it is written: "See, I lay in Zion a stone that causes men to stumble and a rock that makes them fall, and the one who trusts in him will never be put to shame." (9:1-33)

19

Sovereign Election

ROMANS 9:1-33

I remember sitting in a local restaurant on a warm morning when through the window I saw the trees suddenly bend to the rushing wind. The sky darkened as black clouds bore down from the north. By the time I left, the temperature had dropped twenty degrees.

The switch from Romans 8 to 9 is like that. Romans 8 is all sunshine, ending in ecstatic declaration:

> For I am convinced that neither death nor life, neither angels nor demons, neither the present nor the future, nor any powers, neither height nor depth, nor anything else in all creation, will be able to separate us from the love of God that is in Christ Jesus our Lord. (vv. 38, 39)

Then comes the gloom of chapter 9:

> I speak the truth in Christ — I am not lying, my conscience confirms it in the Holy Spirit — I have great sorrow and unceasing anguish in my heart. For I could wish that I myself were cursed and cut off from Christ for the sake of my brothers, those of my own race, the people of Israel. Theirs is the adoption as sons; theirs the divine glory, the covenants, the receiving of the law, the temple worship and the promises. Theirs are the patriarchs, and from them is traced the human ancestry of Christ, who is God over all, forever praised! Amen. (vv. 1-5)

Paul hurt so much at the thought of Israel's rejection of Christ that he was willing to forego Heaven and suffer damnation if that would bring their salvation. Though Paul knew such a bargain was impossible, his emotions were intensely real. Why? He loved his fellow countrymen and longed for their salvation. He was proud of his Jewish heritage. His hurt was intensified by his awareness of the vast privileges from which they had not benefitted — especially the fact that the Messiah "who is God over all, forever praised!" (v. 5) came from them.

Those of us who have loved ones who are lost know something of this. We may enjoy them, laugh with them, even play with them, but there is always pain underneath. Luther put it this way: "Love is not only pure joy, and delight, but also great and deep heaviness of heart and sorrow."[1] Paul's immense heart bore an ache for all Israel.

This needs to be underscored because in the following verses he says some of the hardest things in all of Scripture. Paul knew from his constant interaction with his fellow Jews that his insistence that they were lost evoked this objection: "Paul, indeed we have had all the privileges that you mention, and they are so great that if we are lost God has failed. He does not keep his word!" In anticipation of such a response Paul now defends the character of God. Technically, this is called a "theodicy" — a vindication of the justness of God. Paul traces the history of God's dealings with Israel and shows God to be righteous and just.

A word of caution before we proceed: This is one of the least popular passages in the Scriptures because Paul bases his defense of God's character on the doctrine of *election*, which teaches that before the world was created God chose who would receive salvation. This does not jibe with our natural way of thinking. In fact, this section runs so counter to man's normal thought that I know of one pastor who simply skipped it as he preached through Romans. We must avoid such a mistake for the sake of our own souls and of the church.

What is taught here is beyond our complete understanding. Isaiah records God as saying,

> "For my thoughts are not your thoughts, neither are your ways my ways," declares the Lord. "As the heavens are higher than the earth, so are my ways higher than your ways and my thoughts than your thoughts." (55:8, 9)

God is beyond us! If anyone completely understands his ways, the Trinity will have to make room for another member.

Despite our frailty, it is of the greatest importance that though we may not fully grasp the doctrine of election, we understand as much as we can what the Scriptures teach and believe it, for it bears heavily on the doctrine of God. In our day of horizontal focus, when so much is being attributed to man, the concept of God has become decadent and vacuous for many. The need for Scriptural teaching on this matter has never been greater.

We should also note that the doctrine of election is nothing new. It was the view of Tyndale and Wycliffe, of the hymn-writers Isaac Watts and John Newton, of the evangelist George Whitefield, of the revivalist-theologian Jonathan Edwards, of the founder of modern missions William Carey, of the Reformers Melanchthon, Luther, Calvin, Zwingli, Hus, Knox, and of a host of Puritans and great preachers such as C. H. Spurgeon and Alexander Whyte. It is a basic element of Christian theology.

THEODICY A: THE FAITHFULNESS OF GOD (vv. 6-13)

Now, as we turn to our text, Paul answers those who say that if the Jews are not saved, God has failed.

> It is not as though God's word had failed. For not all who are descended from Israel are Israel. Not because they are his descendants are they all Abraham's children. On the contrary, "It is through Isaac that your offspring will be reckoned." (vv. 6, 7)

In other words, natural descent (the Jewish bloodline) was not sufficient. In verses 8, 9 Paul uses the famous example of Isaac and Ishmael to illustrate the principle of divine choice. Though Ishmael was descended from Abraham, God chose Isaac. In fact, God arranged for Isaac's birth by working a miracle in the darkness of Sarah's womb. Paul realizes that his detractors would argue that God chose Isaac because he was the son of Abraham's full wife Sarah, whereas Ishmael was born of Hagar, so he submits another case — that of Jacob and Esau, who were the sons of one mother.

> Not only that, but Rebecca's children had one and the same father, our father Isaac. Yet, before the twins were born or had done anything good or bad — in order that God's purpose in election might stand: not by works but by him who calls — she was told, "The older will serve the younger." Just as it is written: "Jacob I loved, but Esau I hated." (vv. 10-13)

Jacob became the heir because of God's sovereign "choice" (v. 11, NASB; literally "election," as in NIV). This was not because of moral virtues or good works, because the twins were not even born when the choice was made. Not only that, but God's choice went beyond the individuals to nations. We know this because the context of the quotation from Malachi 1:2, 3 ("I have loved Jacob, but Esau I hated") refers to the descendants of Jacob (the Jews) and of Esau (the Edomites) who spent long periods in bondage to the Jews. The selection of Jacob individually and the Israelites corporately was solely God's sovereign choice. God did not hate Esau and the Edomites, but in comparison with his choice of Jacob and the Israelites he loved them less.

This relative use of hate is also found in Luke 14:26 when Jesus says, "If anyone comes to me and does not hate his father and mother, his wife and children, his brothers and sisters — yes, even his own life — he cannot be my disciple." Jesus obviously does not mean his followers are to hate their relatives, but that they are to love him so much that love for family appears as hatred in comparison.

God loves sinners. John 3:16 says, "For God so loved the world that he gave his one and only Son, that whoever believes in him shall not perish but have eternal life." "The Lord . . . is patient with you, not wanting anyone to perish, but everyone to come to repentance" (2 Peter 3:9). But at the same time, "Whoever believes in the Son has eternal life, but whoever rejects the Son will not see life, for God's wrath remains on him" (John 3:36).

The point Paul is making is, God has not failed because Israel has failed, because true Israel (true believers) have always come to God through his sovereign choice. God could have chosen Esau and rejected Jacob if he wanted. If you know anything about those two scoundrels, the marvel is not in God's rejection of Esau, but in his choice of Jacob. God has not failed!

THEODICY B: THE JUSTICE OF GOD (vv. 14-18)

Again Paul anticipates his antagonists' outcry and says it for them in verse 14: "What then shall we say? Is God unjust? Not at all!" Or as Phillips renders it, "Do we conclude that God is monstrously unfair? Never!" At first it appears that Paul does not really answer the question but simply says it is impossible for God to do anything unjust. But the answer is sufficient. Luther comments, "Why, then should man complain that God acts unjustly, when this is impossible? Or, could it be possible that God is not God?"[2]

If we say God cannot be fair and be a God who elects, we show a faulty concept of God. If we think of God as an enlarged man, with human emotions and motives, how misled we are. God is infinite — we are finite. He knows all — our knowledge is incomplete and ephemeral. A. W. Tozer wrote:

> The Church has surrendered her once lofty concept of God and has substituted for it one so low, so ignoble, as to be utterly unworthy of thinking, worshiping men. This she has done not deliberately, but little by little and without her knowledge; and her very unawareness only makes her situation all the more tragic.[3]

The fact is, God is perfect. Perfect in knowledge, wisdom, power, presence, faithfulness, goodness, justice, mercy, grace, love, and holiness. Therefore, he is perfect in his choices.

God does not answer to anyone, is not responsible to anyone. He is totally, absolutely sovereign. Paul vindicates the assault on God's character with the examples of Moses and Pharaoh.

> For he says to Moses, "I will have mercy on whom I have mercy, and I will have compassion on whom I have compassion." It does not, therefore, depend on man's desire or effort, but on God's mercy. (vv. 15,16, quoting Exodus 33:19)

This took place on Mt. Sinai after Moses had made intercession for his people's sin in making the golden calf and then asked God to show him his glory. "I will have mercy on whom I have mercy, and I will have compassion on whom I have compassion" means that God's mercy and compassion cannot be subject to any cause outside his free grace.[4] God had mercy on the Israelites (not destroying them for their idolatry), not because they deserved it, but simply because he chose to be merciful.

In verses 17, 18 the thought moves from Moses to Pharaoh — from the leader to the oppressor:

> For the Scripture says to Pharaoh: "I raised you up for this very purpose, that I might display my power in you and that my name might be proclaimed in all the earth." Therefore God has mercy on whom he wants to have mercy, and he hardens whom he wants to harden.

Pharaoh deserved death, but God did not strike him down. Rather, he allowed him to continue to live and reign so that God could demonstrate his power in the repeated defeats of Pharaoh. Pharaoh became an international illustration of God's supremacy.

Paul mentions that God hardened Pharaoh's heart, but does not take time to indicate the other side of the coin — that Pharaoh hardened his own heart. (The Exodus account reveals both.) In truth, God gave Pharaoh opportunity to repent, but Pharaoh resisted God and therefore hardened himself to divine rule. Sunlight melts ice but hardens clay. God was not unrighteous with Pharaoh. He gave him repeated opportunities to believe. The point is, God is sovereign and acts according to his own will and purposes. He is perfectly just, for he is God.

THEODICY C: GOD'S JUSTICE CONTINUED (vv. 19-29)

Paul anticipates another angry question in verse 19: "One of you will say to me: 'Then why does God still blame us? For who resists his will?'" The reasoning goes like this: "Paul, you say that Pharaoh was manipulated to work out God's plan — that Pharaoh's evil actually brought glory to God. How can Pharaoh be held accountable for his actions since he was used by God? Your God is unfair!" What is the answer to this?

To begin with, "But who are you, O man, to talk back to God?" (v. 20). Tiny man — whose life is just a breath, whose history proves over and over that despite all his learning and technological triumphs he repeatedly makes colossal errors and falls into unspeakable barbarisms — this puny man stands before the God who knows the end from the beginning, who has never learned anything because he knows everything, who is the perfection of wisdom and love — and talks back to him. How absurd!

In verses 20, 21 Paul continues this point by drawing the ancient analogy of a potter and his clay (taken from Jeremiah 18:1-10 and Isaiah 45:9): "Shall what is formed say to he who formed it, 'Why did you make me like this?' Does not the potter have the right to make out of the same lump of clay some pottery for noble purposes and some for common use?" Does clay ever talk back to the potter? Of course not! Moreover, the clay of mankind is sinful through and through. There is no neutrality in man — he is an enemy of God. So the question is not, "Why are some made to dishonor?" because dishonor is the natural state of the clay. The question is rather, "Why are some selected for honor?"

In this respect, Dr. Barnhouse wrote:

> Calvin was very guilty at this point. He attempted to deduce from this passage what has come to be called "double predestination."

The Bible nowhere announces the predestination of the lost. It would seem that Calvin and others have drawn an inference in purely human logic. They would hold that the choice of Jacob implies the reprobation of Esau. Both of these brothers were born in sin; they both had the nature of Adam. They both grew up in sin. They both were children of wrath, disobedient by nature. If there had been any merit in these two sons, God would have been unjust in not rewarding that merit. The choice of one deserving man over another deserving man would have been favoritism. When we see that the two were equally undeserving, the whole picture becomes different. Everything that is said in the entire Bible about the nature of fallen man may be said — must be said — about both Jacob and Esau. God determined, for causes that are to be found in Himself and have not been revealed to us, to show favor to Jacob.[5]

As believers, we must rest in this: God is not answerable to man for what he does. However, he can be relied upon to act consistently with his character, which has been disclosed supremely in Christ. With such a God, why should any of us question his ways?

In addition, God has purposes which we are incapable of seeing. Paul suggests this by posing a hypothetical example:

> What if God, choosing to show his wrath and make his power known, bore with great patience the objects of his wrath — prepared for destruction? What if he did this to make the riches of his glory known to the objects of his mercy, whom he prepared in advance for glory — even us, whom he also called, not only from the Jews but also from the Gentiles? (vv. 22-24)

Sometimes we wonder why God withholds judgment of the ungodly. It may be that he does it to better display his glory to his beloved. We must bow before God, realizing he has noble purposes we cannot see.

Lastly, Paul calls us to realize that Israel's failure and his choices of Gentiles was prophesied in the Scriptures, namely Hosea and Isaiah.

> As he says in Hosea: "I will call them 'my people' who are not my people; and I will call her 'my loved one' who is not my loved one," and, "It will happen that in the very place where it was said to them,'You are not my people,' they will be called 'sons of the living God.'" Isaiah cries out concerning Israel: "Though the number of the Israelites be like the sand by the sea, only the remnant will be

saved. For the Lord will carry out his sentence on earth with speed and finality." It is just as Isaiah said previously: "Unless the Lord Almighty had left us descendants, we would have become like Sodom, and we would have been like Gomorrah." (vv. 25-29, quoting Hosea 2:23; 1:10; Isaiah 10:22, 23; 1:9)

"My friends," Paul is saying, "the failure of the Jews and the inclusion of the Gentiles has been in God's plan from the beginning. God is just. His word has not failed." Paul succeeds in defending God.

ALL BY FAITH (vv. 30-33)

Paul asks, "What then shall we say?" That is, what are we to conclude? The answer is: It is all is of faith.

> What then shall we say? That the Gentiles, who did not pursue righteousness, have obtained it, a righteousness that is by faith; but Israel, who pursued a law of righteousness, has not attained it. Why not? Because they pursued it not by faith but as if it were by works. They stumbled over the "stumbling stone." As it is written: "See, I lay in Zion a stone that causes men to stumble and a rock that makes them fall, and the one who trusts in him will never be put to shame." (vv. 30-33, quoting Isaiah 8:14; 28:16)

Paul here paints a mental picture of a roadway with a great stone (representing Christ) placed right in the middle and all humanity streaming toward it. Those who are pursuing righteousness by works refuse to see it and stumble over it headlong to destruction, but others come and rest on it in faith and thus find salvation.

Paul has been emphasizing divine choice, but now presents us with human responsibility. There are two wrong responses to all this. One is, "I'll do it myself. Somehow I'll make it, by hook or by crook." The end of this attitude is to fall headlong to destruction. The other response is to say, "God will do everything, I'll do nothing." This too will end in destruction. But there is a third, correct response, and that is: "I stand on the Rock that is higher than I." The Scriptures never say, "Try to determine whether you are elect." They say rather:

> "*Believe* in the Lord Jesus, and you will be saved." (Acts 16:31)
> Yet to all who *received* him, to those who *believed* in his name, he gave the right to become children of God. (John 1:12)

Have you really trusted Christ? Have you believed in him? Are you resting in him?

I trust we are each resting on the Rock today.

Brothers, my heart's desire and prayer to God for the Israelites is that they may be saved. For I can testify about them that they are zealous for God, but their zeal is not based on knowledge. Since they did not know the righteousness that comes from God and sought to establish their own, they did not submit to God's righteousness. Christ is the end of the law so that there may be righteousness for everyone who believes. Moses describes in this way the righteousness that is by the law: "The man who does these things will live by them." But the righteousness that is by faith says: "Do not say in your heart, 'Who will ascend into heaven?'" (that is, to bring Christ down) "or 'Who will descend into the deep?'" (that is, to bring Christ up from the dead). But what does it say? "The word is near you; it is in your mouth and in your heart," that is, in the word of faith we are proclaiming: That if you confess with your mouth, "Jesus is Lord," and believe in your heart that God raised him from the dead, you will be saved. For it is with your heart that you believe and are justified, and it is with your mouth that you confess and are saved. As the Scripture says, "Everyone who trusts in him will never be put to shame." For there is no difference between Jew and Gentile — the same Lord is Lord of all and richly blesses all who call on him, for, "Everyone who calls on the name of the Lord will be saved." How, then, can they call on the one they have not believed in? And how can they believe in the one of whom they have not heard? And how can they hear without someone preaching to them? And how can they preach unless they are sent? As it is written, "How beautiful are the feet of those who bring good news!" But not all the Israelites accepted the good news. For Isaiah says, "Lord, who has believed our message?" Consequently, faith comes from hearing the message, and the message is heard through the word of Christ. But I ask, Did they not hear? Of course they did: "Their voice has gone out into all the earth, their words to the ends of the world." Again I ask, did Israel not understand? First, Moses says, "I will make you envious by those who are not a nation; I will make you angry by a nation that has no understanding." And Isaiah boldly says, "I was found by those who did not seek me; I revealed myself to those who did not ask for me." But concerning Israel he says, "All day long I have held out my hands to a disobedient and obstinate people." (10:1-21)

20

God's Sovereignty – Man's Responsibility

ROMANS 10:1-15

A recurring argument which confronted Paul in his ongoing dialogue with his lost Jewish brethren was: If Israel with all its immense spiritual privilege is rejected, then God's word has failed. Paul's answer was that throughout their history God had repeatedly demonstrated that he operates by sovereign choice. Thus Isaac had been chosen over Ishmael and Jacob over Esau. Moses and Pharaoh provided further examples. God is the potter, humanity is the clay, and God can do as he pleases. Let God be true and every man a liar. And so from Heaven we have the majestic, inscrutable doctrine of God's sovereign election. This is a marvelous doctrine to be believed, though we cannot fully understand it.

Now we come to chapter 10, which presents us with the other side of the coin: *human responsibility.* The fact is, the Word of God teaches both God's elective sovereignty and man's responsibility, though it does not show us how to reconcile this paradox. In this respect it is parallel to the doctrine of the Trinity. How can three be one and one three? Those who insist they can resolve this mystery do so at the expense of one truth or the other. Very often the Deity of Jesus Christ or of the Holy Spirit is sacrificed to uphold the idea of one God, or the truth of the unity of God is compromised. The mystery of the Trinity is to be believed rather than entirely understood.

Romans 9 teaches divine election — chapter 10 teaches human responsibility. I emphasize this because it is possible to get just enough of the vertical theology of chapter 9 to make us horizontally irresponsible. Some believers have abdicated their duty because of a misappropriation of the doctrine of election, and some unbelievers have remained frozen in their unbelief because they have been told that they can do nothing about it. We humans like being absolved of responsibility. Will Rogers once remarked that there are two eras in American history — the passing of the buffalo and the passing of the buck. The Metropolitan Insurance Company once published some excuses for auto accidents received from its clients. These included:

> One said, "The guy was all over the road. I had to swerve a number
> of times before I hit him." Another reported, "The other car collided
> with mine without warning me of its intention."

It is very natural to place the responsibility on others.

Here in chapter 10 God places the responsibility for Israel's lostness on Israel. God rejected Israel because Israel rejected the gospel. If you are without Christ, it is not because you are non-elect, but because you are rejecting Christ. You cannot place the blame on anyone else. At least five times in this chapter (vv. 8, 11, 12, 16, and 21) the responsibility of the Jews is implicitly emphasized, concluding with the poignant plea of verse 21: "But concerning Israel he [God] says, 'All day long I have held out my hands to a disobedient and obstinate people.'"

As we examine chapter 10 we want to see what the Jews (God's privileged people) need to know if they are to have salvation. However, this truth is also for us because we too are an immensely privileged people. The call of salvation is all around us.

As Paul launches into the subject, he again lets his readers know where his heart is: "Brothers, my heart's desire and prayer to God for the Israelites is that they may be saved" (v. 1). Paul's continued prayer for Israel is evidence that he did not regard their rejection as final. Moreover, what he now says about their spiritual condition is said from a heart of love and intercession. He prays for nothing short of their redemption. To such a caring heart we are compelled to listen.

MAN'S RESPONSIBILITY: ZEALOUS WORKS BUT LOST (vv. 2-5)

Paul recognized that the Jews had a genuine zeal: "For I can testify about them that they are zealous for God" (v. 2). Ever since returning from the Babylonian captivity, the Jews had been cured of idolatry. They never again fell to national apostasy. When Antiochus Epiphanes conquered Jerusalem and forced pork down the priests' throats and placed an altar to Venus in the Temple in an attempt to Hellenize their religion, the nation did not succumb. In fact, they ultimately prevailed in the Maccabean revolt. They had a heroic zeal for the God of Israel!

Even today Orthodox Judaism puts many Christians to shame with its zeal. Those who have read the writings of Chaim Potok and Isaac Bashevis Singer have been captivated with this zeal. But zeal alone will not suffice, as Paul shows. The sad fact is, there are thousands of zealous people who are abysmally lost. There are few people more dedicated than the Bahai missionary. The zeal in our home-grown American cults is proverbial. And what can we say of committed Marxists? Even an orthodox zeal for the God of the Bible will not guarantee Heaven. Paul's words ought to do away with such muddled sentimental rationalizations as "He is such a sincere young man" or "I just cannot believe such a good, honest, sincere person will be lost." Sincerity never replaces truth!

Paul explains the situation this way:

> For I can testify about them that they are zealous for God, but their zeal is not based on knowledge. Since they did not know the righteousness that comes from God and sought to establish their own, they did not submit to God's righteousness. Christ is the end of the law so that there may be righteousness for everyone who believes. (vv. 2-4)

The Law was given as a tutor to lead the Jewish nation to Christ. God never intended that the Jews would be saved through perfect obedience to the Law, but rather that by their failure to live up to it they would be driven to grace. In Galatians 3:24 Paul states this truth explicitly: "So the law was put in charge to lead us to Christ that we might be justified by faith." The futility and frustration of falling short of the Law's demands were meant to open them up to God's grace and imputed righteousness — the righteousness which he bestows apart from works on the basis of faith (3:21, 22; Philippians 3:9). However, instead of turning to God in repentance the Jews "sought to establish their own" righteousness (v. 3). They saw the Law as a way to lift themselves up to God.

There are many people like that today, both Jews and Gentiles. A letter by a rabbi to a young man who had turned to Christ gives this classic expression:

The basic question about religion is how to elevate man, and bring
him into closer relationship with God. (That is the rabbis' view of
the purpose of religion. It is to elevate man, not to change him.) We
believe that God revealed to us in the Torah (the Law of Moses) how
he wants us to live, so that we can be in harmony with his divine purpose. Our role and religious purpose is to obey God's laws — to love
him and to obey him. We exercise our free will by proper intention
and, through having done the good deeds, are elevated so that it
becomes progressively easier and more natural to continue to do
good and to resist evil.[1]

From this we see that one of the current Jewish positions on how to be
right before God is to simply keep working at it until it becomes easier
and easier. Then one is elevated finally to a place of righteousness before
him.

Paul brings this false thinking into perfect focus: "Christ is the end
of the law so that there may be righteousness for everyone who believes"
(v. 4). That is, Christ perfectly fulfilled the Law through his perfect obedience, something none of us could ever do. Therefore Christ offers a new
righteousness to those who will receive it. The fact that the Jews would
not accept what Christ had done on their behalf demonstrates that they
had never understood what the Law was.

It is so easy for a zealous person to be lost if one thinks religion
exists as a ladder to elevate oneself to righteousness and acceptance
before God. Now, I do not want to be misunderstood: a true believer
ought to be filled with zeal (a lack of zeal may even mean one is not a
believer). But religious zeal is not an infallible sign that one knows the
truth. The fact is, a man or woman can be zealous for the Scriptures, zealous for Sunday school, zealous for the programs of the Church, zealous
for body life, zealous for all of these things, and still be unregenerate.

Each person must ask himself or herself where he or she is in relation to Christ. Paul wanted the Romans to see that zealous people can be
lost people. This was (and is) a matter of life and death.

MAN'S RESPONSIBILITY:
SIMPLE FAITH BUT SAVED (vv. 6-13)

Religious people, like the Jews of Jesus' time, have a tendency to compli-
cate the matter of salvation. Paul warns of this in verses 6-13, using a loose
quotation from Moses' farewell address in Deuteronomy 30:12-14:

But the righteousness that is by faith says: "Do not say in your heart, 'Who will ascend into heaven?'" (that is, to bring Christ down) "or 'Who will descend into the deep?'" (that is, to bring Christ up from the dead). But what does it say? "The word is near you; it is in your mouth and in your heart," that is, the word of faith we are proclaiming: That if you confess with your mouth, "Jesus is Lord," and believe in your heart that God raised him from the dead, you will be saved. For it is with your heart that you believe and are justified, and it is with your mouth that you confess and are saved.

Simply stated, we do not have to go to Heaven or into the world of the dead to find Christ. He is near us. Nor does salvation belong to the elite who have taken mystical journeys to Heaven or Hell. For those who knew something of the Scriptures (as the Jews knew the Law) the saving word was on their lips and heart. That is, the gospel of Christ — the word of faith — was (and is) available, accessible, and simple.

My eyes drank in this text when I came to know Christ as a twelve-year-old — especially verses 9 and 10. I can still see them in my King James Bible. I can see the floor below it, a concrete floor wet with my tears. My eyes were wide open to the truth of these verses when I was saved. (I do not apologize for using the word "saved." It is the Biblical word in the text here, and it precisely describes what happened to me.)

Why do so many people miss the point? Because it does not jibe with the concept of religious self-elevation. It is just too simple.

The Good News is the ultimate both in simplicity and mystery. We will never completely understand it in this world. Yet it is so simple that a twelve-year-old can understand enough to truly come to Christ.

In simplest terms, what does Romans 10:9, 10 require? It requires a belief in two things: First, that "Jesus is Lord." C. E. B. Cranfield writes:

> The confession that Jesus is Lord meant the acknowledgment that Jesus shares the name and the nature, the holiness, the authority, power, majesty and eternity of the one and only true God . . . there is expressed in addition the sense of His ownership of those who acknowledge Him and of their consciousness of being His property. . . .[2]

And secondly, Romans 10:9, 10 requires that you believe that God raised Christ from the dead. Further, true faith always leads to confession. Jesus said, "For out of the overflow of the heart the mouth speaks" (Matthew 12:34). Do we believe like that?

Further, this message is for everyone. It is universal!

> As the Scripture says, "Everyone who trusts in him will never be put
> to shame." For there is no difference between Jew and Gentile —
> the same Lord is Lord of all and richly blesses all who call on him,
> for, "Everyone who calls on the name of the Lord will be saved."
> (vv. 11-13)

This universal offer is grounded in two Old Testament quotations: "the
one who trusts will never be dismayed" (Isaiah 28:16), and "everyone
who calls on the name of the Lord will be saved" (Joel 2:32). This is the
way God has always operated. We must say with all gentleness and
firmness, each man and woman is responsible for his or her destiny.

The responsibility which the gospel brings is not only to accept its
offer, but to afterwards take the Good News out to the world. Paul exhorts
us to do this with four rhetorical questions:

> How, then, can they call on the one they have not believed in? And
> how can they believe in the one of whom they have not heard? And
> how can they hear without someone preaching to them? And how
> can they preach unless they are sent? As it is written, "How beauti-
> ful are the feet of those who bring good news!" (vv. 14, 15)

Those closing words were first spoken (in Isaiah 52:7) about those
who brought Jerusalem the good news that the days of captivity in
Babylon were over. Our job is similar, and it is indeed beautiful!

I ask then, Did God reject his people? By no means! I am an Israelite myself, a descendant of Abraham, from the tribe of Benjamin. God did not reject his people, whom he foreknew. Don't you know what the Scripture says in the passage about Elijah — how he appealed to God against Israel: "Lord, they have killed your prophets and torn down your altars; I am the only one left, and they are trying to kill me"? And what was God's answer to him? "I have reserved for myself seven thousand who have not bowed the knee to Baal." So too, at the present time there is a remnant chosen by grace. And if by grace, then it is no longer by works; if it were, grace would no longer be grace. What then? What Israel sought so earnestly it did not obtain, but the elect did. The others were hardened, as it is written: "God gave them a spirit of stupor, eyes so that they could not see and ears so that they could not hear, to this very day." And David says, "May their table become a snare and a trap, a stumbling block and a retribution for them. May their eyes be darkened so they cannot see, and their backs be bent forever." Again I ask, Did they stumble so as to fall beyond recovery? Not at all! Rather, because of their transgression, salvation has come to the Gentiles to make Israel envious. But if their transgression means riches for the world, and their loss means riches for the Gentiles, how much greater riches will their fullness bring! I am talking to you Gentiles. Inasmuch as I am the apostle to the Gentiles, I make much of my ministry in the hope that I may somehow arouse my own people to envy and save some of them. For if their rejection is the reconciliation of the world, what will their acceptance be but life from the dead? If the part of the dough offered as firstfruits is holy, then the whole batch is holy; if the root is holy, so are the branches. If some of the branches have been broken off, and you, though a wild olive shoot, have been grafted in among the others and now share in the nourishing sap from the olive root, do not boast over those branches. If you do, consider this: You do not support the root, but the root supports you. You will say then, "Branches were broken off so that I could be grafted in." Granted. But they were broken off because of unbelief, and you stand by faith. Do not be arrogant, but be afraid. For if God did not spare the natural branches, he will not spare you either. Consider therefore the kindness and sternness of God: sternness to those who fell, but kindness to you, provided that you continue in his kindness. Otherwise, you also will be cut off. And if they do not persist in unbelief, they will be grafted in, for God is able to graft them in again. After all, if you were cut out of an olive tree that is wild by nature, and contrary to nature were grafted into a cultivated olive tree, how much more readily will these, the natural branches, be grafted into their own olive tree? I do not want you to be ignorant of this mystery, brothers, so that you may not be conceited: Israel has experienced a hardening in part until the full number of the Gentiles has come in. And so all Israel will be saved, as it is written: "The deliverer will come from Zion; he will turn godlessness away from Jacob. And this is my covenant with them when I take away their sins." As far as the gospel is concerned, they are enemies on your account; but as far as election is concerned, they are loved on account of the patriarchs, for God's gifts and his call are irrevocable. Just as you who were at one time disobedient to God have now received mercy as a result of their disobedience, so they too have now become disobedient in order that they too may now receive mercy as a result of God's mercy to you. For God has bound all men over to disobedience so that he may have mercy on them all. (11:1-32)

21

Israel's Future

ROMANS 11:1-32

There is no doubt that the Jews are a unique people. They can trace their lineage back thousands of years to one man, Abraham. It was into the Jewish tribe of Judah that the Son of God was born. God was a Jew — not, as the book title says, an Englishman. Also, the Jews have proven to be second to none in battle. The battle cry "After thee, O Benjamin" has often brought unflinching resolve, and Masada was an illustration of that commitment. In addition, the intellectual contributions of the Jews to Western thought are incalculable.

Despite all this, Jews are subject to divided sympathies throughout the world, whether in Hong Kong, Mexico City, or Chicago. Sometimes even whole societies have fallen into anti-Semitism, as we know all too well, though generally those having a living faith in Christ have been friends to the Jews.

C. S. Lewis himself seems to have had some prejudice toward the Jews which reversed as he grew in Christ. In 1921 he wrote to his brother:

> I am very glad you have become a convert to Milton . . . what parts are you reading? I wonder, will you ever get to the end of the Bible; the undesirable "primitives" around you will enable you to appreciate the Hebrews who were class A primitives after all. . . .[1]

Again, in 1921 he wrote,

Paradise Regained I only read once; it is a bit too much for me. In
it the Hebrew element finally gets the better of the classical and
romantic elements. How can people be attracted to things Hebrew?[2]

Lewis came to Christ in 1931, and in 1941 he wrote to Dom Bede
Griffiths:

My enjoyment of the Psalms has been greatly increased lately. The
point has been made before, but let me make it again: what an
admirable thing it is in the divine economy that the sacred literature
of the world should have been entrusted to a people whose poetry,
depending largely on parallelism, should remain poetry in any language you translate it into.[3]

In 1955 Lewis penned these words to an unidentified lady:

I think myself that the shocking reply to the Syrophoenician woman
(it came alright in the end) is to remind all us Gentile Christians —
who forget it easily enough and even flirt with anti-Semitism — that
the Hebrews are spiritually senior to us, that God *did* entrust the
descendants of Abraham with the first revelation of Himself. . . .[4]

So apparently C. S. Lewis grew in his appreciation for the Jews as
he grew in faith.

Unfortunately, this is not always so, even for believers. Martin
Luther was initially very sympathetic toward the Jews. In an early pam-
phlet, *Jesus Was Born a Jew*, he wrote:

Our fools, the popes, bishops, sophists and monks, these coarse
blockheads, dealt with the Jews in such a manner that any Christian
would have preferred to be a Jew. Indeed had I been a Jew and had
I seen such idiots and dunderheads expound Christianity, I should
rather have become a hog than a Christian. . . . I would advise and
beg everybody to deal kindly with the Jews and to instruct them in
the Scriptures; in such a case we could expect them to come over to
us.[5]

However, in later years, after no success in Jewish evangelization,
Luther reversed himself, writing a series of anti-Semitic pamphlets. In
one entitled *Concerning the Jews and Their Lies* he admonished
Christians to destroy Jewish homes and synagogues with fire and cover

them with dirt, to silence rabbis on pain of death, seizure of Jewish wealth, and the enslavement of young Jews at hard labor.

> To sum up, dear princes and nobles who have Jews in your domains, if this advice of mine does not suit you, then find a better one so that you and we may all be free of this insufferable devilish burden — the Jews.[6]

To be sure Luther was a man of his times. Similar actions in other areas were perpetrated by the other Reformers. But nevertheless, his conduct was sub-Christian. Many literate Jews have not forgotten this, and some even argue that Adolf Hitler simply brought to flower the seed planted by Martin Luther. Sadly, it is possible for Christians to be anti-Semites. As one Jew put it to a Christian:

> *How odd of God*
> *To choose the Jew,*
> *But not so odd*
> *As those who choose*
> *The Jewish God*
> *And hate the Jew.*

Anti-Semitism is indeed well within the capabilities of professing believers, as patently un-Christlike as it is! I do not doubt for a moment that the Church at large could fall to it under certain economic and political circumstances, the clear teaching of the Bible notwithstanding. It is amazing how we can squeeze God's Word through our cultural and social grid to suit the times.

What should be our attitude toward Israel in light of what God has to say about the Jews in Romans 11?

In this chapter Paul concerns himself with the question of whether God has given up on Israel. It was a natural question because much of the nation was spiritually lost in Old Testament times, and likewise the bulk of the nation rejected the Messiah when he came. Paul's answer here will be that God is in no way done with the Jews — there is a future for the Jewish nation. This answer, as we shall see, carries with it some advice on how we are to regard the Jews.

Paul states the question in verse 1: "I ask then, Did God reject his people?" This was a logical question after the description of Israel's failure to respond to Christ (chapter 10), and the apostle answers it with three sweeping thoughts. The first is found in verses 1-10, where he shows that God had not discarded his people, for there was a believing remnant.

ANSWER ONE: THE BELIEVING REMNANT (vv. 1-10)

Paul's own conversion was evidence of a believing remnant. He says in verse 1b: "By no means! I am an Israelite myself, a descendant of Abraham, from the tribe of Benjamin." Paul's case is encouraging. He had been the foremost calculating, implacable, bloodthirsty enemy of the Church. He was so odious to Christians that after Saul's conversion only Barnabas, a peacemaker *par excellence*, could effect his acceptance. God had sovereignly hunted him down, smote him on the Damascus Road, and brought him kicking and struggling into the Kingdom. Paul, a hardened, religious man with blood on his hands, came to Christ, so there is hope for anyone. By the authority of the Word of God we can say that no one is beyond the grace of God. People like Paul are living demonstrations that God is not through with the Jews. What a beautiful gospel to preach!

The remnant of believing Jews is larger than it may appear. Paul notes in verses 2-5 that Elijah discovered this very truth. Elijah had withstood the prophets of Baal, then outran Ahab's chariot to Jezreel — a distance of eighteen miles (he must have been some jogger!). By the end of the day he was absolutely worn-out, even in the flush of victory. Hearing that Jezebel wanted him dead, he fled for his life, finding a place in the wilderness where he cast himself down and said, "Lord, they have killed your prophets and torn down your altars; I am the only one left, and they are trying to kill me" (v. 3). "And what was God's answer to him? 'I have reserved for myself seven thousand who have not bowed the knee to Baal'" (v. 4). Poor old Elijah thought he was all alone, but there were 7,000 others! Paul perhaps felt a special kinship with Elijah, sometimes feeling as if he were the only one left.

Today Israel is in national apostasy, but there are more Jewish believers than many of us think. They are a reminder that God is not through with his covenant people.

Why have the rest remained in unbelief? Paul explains that they have been judicially hardened because they persist in the pattern of works, thinking they can make themselves righteous.

> And if by grace, then it is no longer by works; if it were, grace would
> no longer be grace. What then? What Israel sought so earnestly it

did not obtain, but the elect did. The others were hardened. . . . (vv. 6, 7)

That is, they were hardened as a judgment for their unbelief. Hardening happened to Pharaoh, but it was no surprise in him. But here it is God's own people who are hardened to him.

Paul drives the point home by using Old Testament quotations:

> . . . as it is written: "God gave them a spirit of stupor, eyes so that they could not see and ears so that they could not hear, to this very day." And David says: "May their table become a snare and a trap, a stumbling block and a retribution for them. May their eyes be darkened so they cannot see, and their backs be bent forever." (vv. 8-10; cf. Deuteronomy 29:4; Isaiah 29:10; Psalm 69:22, 23)

This is a terrible judgment, but one brought on by the Jews' own actions. Everett Harrison, after carefully assessing these Scriptures in their Old Testament contexts, says this:

> From an observation of the setting of the quotations, it is clear that God did not give his people deaf ears to mock them any more than he gave them blind eyes to taunt them. What was involved was a judicial punishment for failure to use God-given faculties to perceive His manifested power and to glorify Him.[7]

What Paul says here about hardening should be sobering to both Jew and Gentile, for the principle is universal: If anyone hears the truth and does not respond to it, the time can come in which he or she will be incapable of responding. As a pastor preaches week after week to a congregation, he senses that over the years there are some who are dead to the Word of God, and that is a terrifying thing. The Lord Jesus, speaking of this principle, said in Matthew 13:12, "Whoever has will be given more, and he will have an abundance. Whoever does not have, even what he has will be taken from him." Then he went on to explain in verses 13-15:

> "This is why I speak to them in parables: 'Though seeing, they do not see; though hearing, they do not hear or understand.' In them is fulfilled the prophecy of Isaiah: 'You will be ever hearing but never understanding; you will be ever seeing but never perceiving. For this people's heart has become calloused; they hardly hear with their ears, and they have closed their eyes. Otherwise they might see with

their eyes, hear with their ears, understand with their hearts and turn,
and I would heal them.'"

Some of the Pharisees could not understand what Jesus was saying because they had not appropriated the truth of God they had already received. This is a warning for all of us to never hear the Word of God without responding.

Whenever Bonhoeffer was listening to a student's sermon, he would set his pen aside and listen intently. He was guarding his heart against the possibility of hearing God's Word but not responding to it. We should always be ready to obey the Word of God when it is presented to us.

Returning to Paul's overall point, God is not through with Israel. The existence of a believing remnant today, just as in Elijah's day, is evidence that God still has a plan for his people — and that he has the power to bring it about.

ANSWER TWO:
THE TEMPORARY REJECTIONOF JEWS (vv. 11-24)

In verses 11-24 Paul enlarges his argument by showing that the rejection of the majority is not permanent. "Again I ask, Did they stumble so as to fall beyond recovery? Not at all!" (v. 11). Or as *The Living Bible* says, "Does this mean that God has rejected his Jewish people forever? Of course not!"

Why, then, has this happened? One of the reasons is to make them jealous of the blessing given to Gentile believers. Notice the last half of verse 11: "because of their transgression, salvation has come to the Gentiles to make Israel envious." Now consider verses 13, 14:

> I am talking to you Gentiles. Inasmuch as I am the apostle to the
> Gentiles, I make much of my ministry in the hope that I may some-
> how arouse my own people to envy and save some of them.

Individual believers and the corporate Body of Christ are meant to lead lives that radiate such reality that unbelieving Jews will be provoked to spiritual jealousy.

Sometimes this indeed happens. My dean during seminary days was a brilliant Jew, Dr. Charles Feinberg. He was so intelligent that he could continue lecturing to his class without missing a syllable while writing a note to his secretary! How did this brilliant Jew come to Christ? Just after

Dr. Feinberg graduated Phi Beta Kappa from the University of Pittsburgh he lived in an Orthodox Jewish household. That household had a "Sabbath Gentile," a Gentile woman who was hired to serve them on the Sabbath. Though Feinberg was not aware of it, this woman had taken the rites of purification simply so she could bear witness in that home.

Feinberg was attracted by the quality of this believer's life and began to ask questions. Although the woman could not give him all the answers, she took him to Dr. John Solomon, then resident head of the American Board of the Mission to the Jews, and Dr. Feinberg was led to Christ. He had been made thirsty — jealous so to speak, beautifully jealous — by this cleaning woman. The Church is to be a place where there is such love for Christ and such love for each other that Jews and Gentiles become thirsty for Christ. What a challenge!

Are the Jews we meet provoked to jealousy or just provoked? We Christians ought to be so alive, so full of Christ, and so full of love for one another that Jews and Gentiles say to themselves, "They have something I don't have, and I must have it."

Now Paul alludes to a coming blessing that will extend to all when Israel is restored:

> But if their transgression means riches for the world, and their loss means riches for the Gentiles, how much greater riches will their fullness bring! (v. 12)

A worldwide quickening and spread of spiritual life will come when Israel is restored. Israel will become a tonic to the nations. The difference will be so dramatic that it can only be described as the difference between life and death.

Paul pictures the temporariness of the Jews' rejection and the certainty of their restoration through two illustrations. The first is in verse 16: "If the part of the dough offered as firstfruits is holy, then the whole batch is holy; if the root is holy, so are the branches." While we may wonder at what is meant here, the Jews had no problem understanding it. Paul is referring to Old Testament offerings and sacrifices, and specifically the offering of the firstfruits. In that offering the priest took some of the dough from the larger lump and offered it to God. Paul reasoned that if the lump offered to God was acceptable, the rest would naturally be as well. The firstfruit was Abraham, the father of the Jewish nation, and he was accepted before God. Thus it is natural for his descendants to be also accepted. Paul is making the point, how natural the Jews' return and acceptance by God will be. Put another way, "if the root is holy, so are the branches." Israel's origins make her restoration the most *natural* thing!

In verses 17-22 Paul extends this argument with the illustration of grafting branches onto an olive tree. The normal practice was to upgrade a wild olive tree by grafting healthy fruit-producing branches to it. While grafting does not affect the rest of the tree, the new branches become very productive. But here Paul talks about grafting wild, *fruitless* branches onto a good tree, something he knew was "contrary to nature" (v. 24), but he wanted to make a point:

> After all, if you were cut out of an olive tree that is wild by nature, and contrary to nature were grafted into a cultivated olive tree, how much more readily will these, the natural branches, be grafted into their own olive tree? (v. 24)

It will be so natural for Israel to return to health because she originally came from a productive tree. If God could engraft wild branches like you and me, how much more a natural branch!

Lewis put it this way:

> In a sense, the converted Jew is the only normal human being in the world. Everyone else is, from one point of view, a special case dealt with under emergency conditions.[8]

What should this mean to Gentile believers? It means we should not be arrogant.

> . . . do not boast over those branches. If you do, consider this: You do not support the root, but the root supports you. You will say then, "Branches were broken off so that I could be grafted in." Granted. But they were broken off because of unbelief, and you stand by faith. Do not be arrogant, but be afraid. For if God did not spare the natural branches, he will not spare you either. (vv. 18-21)

It is so easy to fall into a reverse elitism. Maybe this is what Luther did. Just as the Jew regards himself as God's special person, so the Gentile can assume such an attitude, even despising the Jews! Nothing could be more un-Scriptural than discriminating against unbelieving Jews. We who are Gentiles are fortunate to have any part in the tree at all. This is a call to profound humility.

ANSWER THREE:
THE FUTURE SALVATION OF ISRAEL (vv. 25-32)

Finally, Paul assures us that there is a future salvation for Israel. In verse 25 Paul lays open the secret:

> I do not want you to be ignorant of this mystery, brothers, so that you may not be conceited: Israel has experienced a hardening in part until the full number of the Gentiles has come in.

Things are going to remain pretty much as they are with the Jews until the "full number of the Gentiles" is realized. This fullness could refer to a specific number in God's mind or it could refer to a sweeping revival among the Gentiles, or perhaps to the spread of the gospel to every tongue and nation — universal evangelization. Whatever this phrase means, it refers to a positive outflow of the gospel of grace among the Gentiles before Christ comes.

At that time Israel will be restored:

> And so all Israel will be saved, as it is written: "The deliverer will come from Zion; he will turn godlessness away from Jacob. And this is my covenant with them when I take away their sins." (vv. 26, 27)

There is no way "Israel" here can be spiritualized, considering the context of chapters 9 — 11. It clearly refers to ethnic Israel, the Jewish people. Alan Johnson writes:

> "All" Israel, then, must refer to the forgiveness of the whole people or nation, the whole ethnic group in contrast to the saved remnant of Jews in Paul's day and ours. It is the whole people, rather than a small part, that will be converted to the Messiah.[9]

This is spectacular! It will take place in the millennial reign of Christ. Jesus will reign from Jerusalem, and all his promises will be completely brought to reality.

How, then, are we to look upon the Jew? Paul suggests:

> As far as the gospel is concerned, they are enemies on your account; but as far as election is concerned, they are loved on account of the patriarchs, for God's gifts and his call are irrevocable. Just as you who were at one time disobedient to God have now received mercy

as a result of their disobedience, so they too have now become disobedient in order that they too may now receive mercy as a result of
God's mercy to you. For God has bound all men over to disobedience so that he may have mercy on them all. (vv. 28-32)

There will be a great pouring out of God's mercy in the future. No one
knows the exact time, but we do know there will be extensive proclamation of the gospel among the Gentiles before Israel's restoration — and
the stage is certainly set for that. The incredible expansion of the church
in South America and in countries like Korea demonstrate the possibility of explosive evangelism like we have never seen before. The growth
of missions and the flood of volunteers to such difficult places as North
Africa is likewise encouraging.

   Also, Israel's presence in Palestine is in keeping with the fact that the
Old Testament covenants equate the land and the blessing (Genesis 12:1-
3; 13:14-17; 17:7, 8; Deuteronomy 30:1-10; 2 Samuel 7:16). Jesus himself
tells us, "Jerusalem will be trampled on by the Gentiles until the times of
the Gentiles are fulfilled" (Luke 21:24). No matter how insurmountable the
difficulties, the land and the people will one day be reunited, and Israel will
fulfill its destiny in Palestine. The stage appears well set. In Israel the Bible
is increasingly becoming the center of cultural focus.

   Each young person must memorize in Hebrew the entire historical
   books (Genesis through Chronicles) plus the prophets (Isaiah
   through Zechariah) before he can graduate from high school! While
   largely of historical and moral emphasis, this preparation of Jewish
   minds and hearts might in the future play a significant role in the
   nation's conversion to the Messiah.[10]

   Finally, the question of our attitude toward Israel is certainly to be
one of love.

> How odd of God
>   To choose the Jew,
> But not so odd
>   As those who choose
> The Jewish God
>   And hate the Jew.

In the Church there is no room whatsoever for anti-Semitism.
However, it is also sad when Christians take Israel's side on every issue,

as if they were taking the side of God. Sympathy for Israel must never hide injustice to the Arabs. Christians must think critically and clearly on ethical issues. God does not need a compromised theology to help keep Israel in the land.

Similarly, the Christian who believes the present state of Israel is not God's doing but man's cannot dismiss the injustices of the Arabs to the Jews.

Lastly, we should evangelize Jews as aggressively as we do Gentiles. Susan Perlman, a missionary to the Jews, recently wrote: "A subtle form of anti-Semitism is to deny Jewish people a hearing of the gospel and not care about their eternal destiny."[11] May God help us avoid such a trap.

Oh, the depth of the riches of the wisdom and knowledge of God! How unsearchable his judgments, and his paths beyond tracing out! "Who has known the mind of the Lord? Or who has been his counselor?" "Who has ever given to God, that God should repay him?" For from him and through him and to him are all things. To him be the glory forever! Amen. (11:33-36)

22

From Theology to Doxology

ROMANS 11:33-36

$\mathbf{W}$e are now at the end of the doctrinal section of the book of Romans, the greatest theological treatise in the entire New Testament, containing truths which have often brought reformation and revival to the Church. In 1:18 — 3:20 we encountered an explanation and condemnation of the sinful human race. From that grim theme, 3:21 — 5:11 moved on to the grand hope of justification. Then chapters 6 — 8 presented principles of living the Christian life. And finally in chapters 9 — 11 we saw a defense of God's righteousness in his dealings with the Jews and Gentiles in history, eventuating in great blessing for both in the future.

So wonderful is God's plan that having voiced it, Paul now can scarcely contain himself. So he breaks into praise:

> Oh, the depth of the riches of the wisdom and knowledge of God!
> How unsearchable his judgments, and his paths beyond tracing out!
> "Who has known the mind of the Lord? Or who has been his counselor?" "Who has ever given to God, that God should repay him?"
> For from him and through him and to him are all things. To him be the glory forever! Amen. (vv. 33-36)

Paul's theology has turned to doxology. This is typical of Paul. In the book of Ephesians, after laying a magnificent theological foundation in chapters 1 — 3, he breaks into song:

Now to him who is able to do immeasurably more than all we ask
or imagine, according to his power that is at work within us, to him
be glory in the church and in Christ Jesus throughout all generations,
forever and ever! Amen. (3:20, 21)

Our study of God and his ways among us should turn our hearts to
music. The term *theology* produces in the mind of the man on the street
visions of damp libraries and musty tomes and somber monasteries.
Instead, *theology* should suggest light and dancing! And that is what our
present passage should do for us. Formally stated, Romans 11:33-36
identifies the proper response of our hearts to God's sovereign working.
Any person who truly appropriates something of Paul's response in these
verses will experience a marked increase in joy.

THE PROPER WONDER
OF THE BELIEVING HEART (vv. 33-35)

The expression of Paul's wonder begins with the two exclamations in
verse 33. First we read, "Oh, the depth of the riches of the *wisdom* and
knowledge of God!" "Knowledge" is the gathering of information; "wisdom" is knowing what to do with it. The old commentator Albert Bengel
put it this way: "*Wisdom* directs all things to the best end; *knowledge*
knows the end. . . ."[1] Paul marvels at how deep and rich God's wisdom
is, especially in reference to his dealings with Israel.

God had not failed Israel as a nation, even though Israel was then
(and is now) rejected by him, for God had always worked through the
principle of election (for example, Jacob and Esau). He is the potter, and
fallen humanity is the clay. Israel, however — i.e., the individuals who
make up Israel — is responsible to accept the simple gospel by which
God lovingly stretches out his hands to sinners. But they were hardened,
so the gospel went out to the Gentiles. However, one day the blessing is
going to return to Israel and there will be a great national repentance (cf.
vv. 25-27). Paul experienced a sense of wonder at a God who can so work
in history. "Oh, the depth of the riches of the wisdom and knowledge of
God!"

One exclamation was not enough for the apostle, so he used another
as well: "How unsearchable his judgments, and his paths beyond tracing
out!" (v. 33). How beyond us God is! The word "unfathomable" (NASB;
NIV "beyond tracing out") literally means "untraceable." Tracing God's
ways in his dealings with man is as futile as tracking his footprints on the

sea (cf. Psalm 77:19). God's methods of operation do not conform to man's preconceptions.

> "For my thoughts are not your thoughts, neither are your ways my ways," declares the Lord. "As the heavens are higher than the earth, so are my ways higher than your ways and my thoughts than your thoughts." (Isaiah 55:8, 9)

God is by nature incomprehensible to us. One of the reasons for this is, of course, that our experience limits us. We cannot think in categories beyond our range of experience or sensation.

Lewis uses the example of a shellfish which, trying to tell other shellfish what man is like, has to speak in terms of their common experience. So he tells them that man has no shell, is not attached to a rock, and does not reside in water. To help the first shellfish get the idea across, other learned shellfish expand on his statements, finally concluding that man is a ". . . sort of amorphous jelly (he has no shell), existing nowhere in particular (he is not attached to a rock) and never taking nourishment (there is no water to drift it toward him)." Conclusion? Man is a famished jelly existing in a dimensionless void.[2] In the same way our human limitations keep us from thinking rightly about our infinite God.

Likewise, our language is incapable of communicating about a God who is above nature. That is why the Scriptural writers constantly use "like" and similar terms when describing God, as safeguards against misrepresentation. For example, "And the one who sat there had the appearance of jasper" (Revelation 4:3). God is incomprehensible! Does that mean we can know nothing about him? No, for the Scriptures and nature teach us much about what he is like. But we will never know him fully or exhaustively.

In his exclamations Paul wonders at the greatness of his God, and his thoughts naturally flow into worship: "Who has known the mind of the Lord? Or who has been his counselor?" (v. 34a). The prophet Isaiah put it this way:

> Who has understood the Spirit of the Lord, or instructed him as his counselor? Whom did the Lord consult to enlighten him, and who taught him the right way? Who was it that taught him knowledge or showed him the path of understanding? (40:13, 14)

Who could ever suggest anything God had not thought of first? God knew all things before human history began and has never learned anything during the history of the world, because he has known all things forever. Thus, no man can call God to account, saying, "What are you doing?" To argue with God is to argue with the one who makes it possible to argue!

Paul continues in verse 35: "Who has ever given to God, that God should repay him?" God does not, and never will, owe anything to anyone. He is no man's debtor.

Paul bows in awe at the depth of God's knowledge and wisdom. Who can fathom his wondrous salvation of the lost human race . . . the miracle of justification . . . our sanctifying identification with him . . . the victory of the Christian life . . . the mystery of his dealings with Israel? Worshiping God for his knowledge and wisdom fills us with mystery and hope for the future.

THE PROPER AFFIRMATION
OF THE BELIEVING HEART (v. 36)

We now come to what is, I think, the most uplifting doxological statement in the entire New Testament. Certainly it is the proper affirmation of the believing heart. "For from him and through him and to him are all things. To him be the glory forever! Amen" (v. 36).

To facilitate our appreciation of this, I would like us to think of our tiny solar system for a moment:

Imagine a perfectly smooth glass pavement on which the finest speck can be seen. Then shrink our sun from 865,00 miles in diameter to only two feet . . . and place the ball on the pavement to represent the sun. Step off 83 paces (about two feet per pace) and to represent proportionately the first planet, Mercury, put down a tiny mustard seed. Take 60 steps more and for Venus, put an ordinary BB. Mark 78 more steps . . . put down a green pea representing Earth. Step off 108 paces from there, and for Mars put down a pinhead. Sprinkle around some fine dust for the asteroids, then take 788 steps more. For Jupiter, place an orange on the glass at that spot. After 934 *more* steps, put down a golf ball for Saturn. Now it gets really involved. Mark 2,086 steps, and for Uranus . . . a marble. Another 2,322 steps from there you arrive at Neptune. Let a cherry represent Neptune. This will take 2 1/2 miles, and we haven't even discussed Pluto! If we swing completely around, we have a smooth, glass surface five miles in diameter, yet just a tiny fraction of the heavens — excluding Pluto. On this surface, five miles across, we have only a seed, BB, pea, pinhead, some dust, an orange, golf ball, a marble and a cherry. Guess how far we'd have to go on the same scale before we could put down another two-foot ball to represent the nearest star. Come on, guess. Seven hundred paces? Two thousand steps more? Forty-four hundred feet? No, you're way off. We'd have to go 6,720 miles before we could arrive at that star. Miles, not feet. And that's just the first star among millions. In one galaxy among perhaps hundreds, maybe thousands. And all of it in perpetual motion, perfectly synchronized, the most accurate time-piece known to man.[3]

Incredible, and all from the hand of Almighty God. "For from him and through him and to him are all things." "From him . . . are all things." There was a time when there was nothing but God. Matter and created mind were yet unmade or unborn. There was no sun, yet Jehovah dwelt in light ineffable. There was no earth, yet his throne stood fast and firm. There was no Heaven, yet his glory was unbounded. God is completely self-sufficient. "I am who I am" (Exodus 3:14) — this was and is his unqualified statement of independent being. He was complete, and everything came from him. Since he created everything, the first idea had to come from him. No one could have suggested anything, because there was no one to suggest. The atomic structure of the atom, supernova, and pulsar — all came from him.

Not only that, but "through him . . . are all things." There was no raw material with which to work. He created the universe out of nothing, *ex nihilo*. John 1:3 tells us: "Through him all things were made; without him nothing was made that has been made." Everything came from the womb of his omnipotence. He simply spoke, and the heavens flashed into being, and the world began to turn on its axis.

Some time back I joined some friends for dinner. It was a beautiful evening. I marveled at God's creation as the orange ball of the sun descended. Fireflies flitted about over a couple of acres of grass. I thought to myself, "God's word spoke all this into existence." He spoke the sun into being, he spoke the firefly into being, he spoke the rainbow into being. "Through him . . . are all things."

An elementary but correct way to think of God is as the one who contains all, who gives all that is given, but who Himself can receive nothing that He has not first given.[4]

One second without God's power and everything would disappear!

> For by him all things were created: things in heaven and on earth,
> visible and invisible, whether thrones or powers or rulers or author-
> ities; all things were created by him and for him. He is before all
> things, and in him all things hold together. (Colossians 1:16, 17)

Matter is not God, but God is in everything, and nothing works or exists except through his might.

Further, "to him are all things." Everything in the work of creation is *to* him. Because there was none but himself and none equal to himself, his motive and glory was of necessity himself. His own glory is his highest aim, and the day is coming when we shall see that all things are "to him." The new heavens and the new earth shall ring with his praise. "For from him and through him and to him are all things" (v.36).

As in creation, so is it in our salvation! Salvation is "from" him. God ordained the plan, the hour it was promised, the moment Jesus should come, when he should be born, what death he should die, and when he should rise and ascend. He elected the heirs of salvation and called them to eternal life. As Lewis said, "Amiable agnostics will talk cheerfully about 'man's search for God.' To me as I then was, they might as well have talked about the man's search for a cat."[5]

Salvation is also "through" him. Through him came the prophecies. Through him the Son was born. Through him came the atonement. Through him the word is preached.

And salvation is ultimately "to" him. Those who would give a single word of praise to man or angel will be silenced forever.

> Therefore God exalted him to the highest place and gave him the
> name that is above every name, that at the name of Jesus every knee
> should bow, in heaven and on earth and under the earth, and every
> tongue confess that Jesus Christ is Lord, to the glory of God the
> Father. (Philippians 2:9-11)

"To God alone be all the glory; from the first to the last let him who is the alpha and omega have all the praise; let his name be exalted. . . ."[6]

"For from him . . . are all things." What do we have that he has not given us? "And through him . . . are all things." What can we do without him? "And to him are all things." Who else deserves highest honor?

Finally, Paul reveals what is to be our ultimate devotion: "To him be the glory forever! Amen" (v. 36b). God's glory should be our sole and constant desire. To this end we should raise our families. To this we must focus all prosperity. To this end we ought to live our entire lives.

Praise the Lord!
   Praise God in His sanctuary;
Praise Him in His mighty expanse.
   Praise Him for His mighty deeds;
Praise Him according to His excellent greatness.
   Praise Him with trumpet sound;
Praise Him with harp and lyre.
   Praise Him with timbrel and dancing;
Praise Him with stringed instruments and pipe.
   Praise Him with loud cymbals;
Praise Him with resounding cymbals.
   Let everything that has breath praise the Lord.
Praise the Lord!

(Psalm 150, NASB)

How right life is when theology becomes doxology!

Therefore, I urge you, brothers, in view of God's mercy, to offer your bodies as living sacrifices, holy and pleasing to God — which is your spiritual worship. Do not conform any longer to the pattern of this world, but be transformed by the renewing of your mind. Then you will be able to test and approve what God's will is — his good, pleasing and perfect will. (12:1, 2)

23

Elements of Commitment

ROMANS 12:1, 2

Many of us associate certain Bible verses with specific events in our spiritual lives. I mentioned in an earlier chapter that as a twelve-year-old, with my eyes fixed on Romans 10:9, 10, I believed in Jesus Christ and my life was made new. Romans 10:9, 10 speaks new life to me still!

Another text that has been a benchmark in my spiritual life is Romans 12:1, 2. It happened exactly a year later at the same camp in the Sequoia National Forest as I sat astride a fallen sugar pine talking about my life with my pastor, the man who had led me to Christ. I was experiencing difficulties in living a Christian life at home and school and desperately wanted to get it together. My wise counselor knew exactly where to turn, and I was galvanized by another beautiful passage of God's Word.

Therefore, I urge you, brothers, in view of God's mercy, to offer your bodies as living sacrifices, holy and pleasing to God — which is your spiritual worship. Do not conform any longer to the pattern of this world, but be transformed by the renewing of your mind. Then you will be able to test and approve what God's will is — his good, pleasing and perfect will.

That passage states the call to commitment so clearly, the logic is so compelling, that it went straight to my heart.

At that time I understood nothing of its pivotal position in Romans, or its rich Greek words which make it even more compelling. I simply met it existentially, and it was food for my soul — a benchmark in my ongoing understanding of what the Christian life is all about.

We will consider the riches of this supreme expression of commitment under four headings:

I. The *Basis* of Commitment (v. 1a)
II. The *Character* of Commitment (v. 1b)
III. The *Demands* of Commitment (v. 2a)
IV The *Effects* of Commitment (v. 2b)

This passage can nourish us wherever we are in our spiritual pilgrimage. For those further along, it can serve as an affirmation and deepening of matters long settled. For those just beginning to seriously interact with the demands of Christ, it can be a spiritual benchmark.

THE BASIS OF COMMITMENT (v. 1a)

The basis of commitment is the mercies of God, as Paul so clearly states in the opening phrase of verse 1: "Therefore, I urge you, brothers, in view of God's mercy . . ." Specifically, Paul is talking about the mercy of God as spelled out in the eleven preceding chapters — God's mercy to the terribly fallen human race through the provision of his Son. Radically sinful man was radically lost. But God provided a radical righteouness through the radical person of his Son, which made a radical new life and view of history possible. In view of this mercy God calls us to commitment. Remember the massive theology of Romans 1 — 11 which burst into consummate doxology in the final verse of chapter 11: "For from him and through him and to him are all things. To him be the glory forever! Amen"? That very theology is the foundation for committed living.

The same pattern is discernible in Ephesians:

1 – 3, *Theology.*

3:20, 21, *Doxology* ("Now to him who is able to do immeasurably more than all we ask or imagine, according to his power that is at work within us, to him be glory in the church and in Christ Jesus throughout all generations, for ever and ever! Amen").

4:1, *Practicality* ("As a prisoner for the Lord, then, I urge you to live a life worthy of the calling you have received").

For the Christian there is a unity between theology, doxology, and practice—doctrine, doxology and duty.

The greater our comprehension of what God has done for us, the greater our commitment should be. Practically applied, Christ's gift, meditated on, accepted, taken to heart, is a magnet drawing us to deepest commitment to him. Immense vision will bring immense commitment. That is what Isaac Watts meant when he wrote:

> Love so amazing, so divine
> demands my soul, my life, my all.

Paul does not ask for a favor when he says, "Therefore, I urge you, brothers, in view of God's mercy . . ." but rather is stating an obligation. It is our obligation to think about what Christ has done and to make our commitment accordingly. There is scarcely anything more important for building our commitment than an increasing understanding of the greatness of God and his mercies to us.

THE CHARACTER OF COMMITMENT (v. 1b)

The *character* of the commitment is given in the last half of the verse: ". . . to offer your bodies as living sacrifices, holy and pleasing to God — which is your spiritual worship." This commitment has two prominent characteristics: it is *total* and it is *reasonable*.

The totality of the commitment comes dramatically to us through the language of sacrifice. The Greek translated "to offer" is a technical term used for the ritual presentation of a sacrifice. "Your bodies," referring to more than skin and bones, signifies everything we are — our totality. "Sacrifices" refers to the holocaust in which the offering is totally consumed. Old Testament sacrifices pervade the picture — total sacrifice.

Moreover, this sacrifice is described as "living . . . holy . . . pleasing." The believer isn't killed as the Old Testament sacrifices were, but remains alive. We are to be living sacrifices in the deep theological sense of "a new life" (cf. 6:4). We are also to be "holy" in that we have renounced sin and are set apart to God. Finally, we are to be "pleasing" sacrifices not because we deserve to be accepted, but because the offerings are true to God's specifications.

This is as bold a call to total commitment as there is anywhere in the sacred writings. It applies equally to all — to the professor, to the preacher, to the pianist, to high schoolers — to everyone! It is for the entire Church. We must put away the medieval thinking that makes a distinction between clergy and laity — the idea that ministers and missionaries should have 100 percent commitment, but the laity is permitted 75 percent, or 30, or . . . The truth is, *all believers* are called to be totally committed to Christ.

Not only is commitment to be total, it is also *logical*. I am glad I first memorized this in the King James Version which more accurately represents the last phrase of verse 1, ". . . which is your reasonable service," rather than the NIV's "which is your spiritual worship." Cranfield is correct in maintaining that the root idea of the word *logikos* is "logical."[1] For Paul, true worship in offering ourselves to God is reasonable or logical because it is consistent with a proper understanding of the truth of God as revealed in Jesus Christ. Total commitment is the only rational course to take when you really see who God is. Nothing else makes any sense. As Cranfield says:

> The intelligent understanding of worship, that is, the worship which is consonant with the truth of the gospel, is indeed nothing less than the offering of one's whole self in the course of one's concrete living, in one's inward thoughts, feelings and aspirations, but also in one's words and deeds.[2]

Halfway committment is irrational. To decide to give part of your life to God and keep other parts for yourself — to say "Everything is yours, Lord, but this relationship, this deal, this pleasure" — is beyond spiritual logic!

If we are worshiping apart from commitment to God, it is false worship. We are deceiving ourselves if we are doing "Christian things" but are not consecrated to Jesus Christ. Sam Shoemaker said it well: "To be a Christian means to give as much of myself as I can to as much of Jesus Christ as I know."[3] This is why as we grow in the knowledge of his mercy we should be more committed at age twenty-one than sixteen, and more so at thirty-five,forty-five, sixty and seventy!

Having seen the basis and character of commitment in verse 1, we turn to the demands of commitment in the first part of verse 2.

THE DEMANDS OF COMMITMENT (v. 2a)

Notice that in verse 2 there are two commands. The first is negative: "Do not conform any longer to the pattern of this world." The second is positive: ". . . but be transformed by the renewing of your mind." These are the two sides of commitment.

What does this *negative command*, "Do not conform any longer to the pattern of this world," mean? "Pattern" comes from the root word *schema*, from which we derive "scheme," and "world" should be translated "age," referring to the passing age (cf. 1 Corinthians 7:31; Galatians 1:4; and 1 John 2:17), which is dominated by Satan. Thus Paul's words can be paraphrased, "Don't be conformed to the schemes of this passing evil age."

The painful truth is, such conformity is common to many of us to a greater extent than we like to acknowledge. Sometimes it is difficult to know when we are conforming because there are many good things in the world. Moreover, we are not to write off our culture entirely. Yet we must think critically. As Harry Blamires says in *The Christian Mind*: "Because secularism is in the saddle, it follows that the Christian mind is suspicious of fashionable current conformities."[4]

We must be careful what we read and watch. We must not fear to challenge others' presuppositions. Above all, we must not be afraid to be different.

Then comes the *positive command:* " . . . but be transformed by the renewing of your mind." Again the language is graphic. "Transformed" sounds like "metamorphosed" in the original and is the word from which we get *metamorphosis*, the change from one form to another, as in the transformation of the tadpole to the frog or the caterpillar to the butterfly. But the full meaning is even richer, as the other three uses of the word in the New Testament indicate. In Matthew 17:2 and Mark 9:2 it is used to describe the transfiguration of Christ — when the Lord's glorious inner essence was allowed to show through his body so that his face radiated like the sun and his clothing was white with light. We experience such transfiguration in Christ. As Paul says in 2 Corinthians 3:18 (using the very same word):

> And we, who with unveiled faces all reflect the Lord's glory, are being transformed into his likeness with ever-increasing glory, which comes from the Lord, who is the Spirit.

How does this happen? Again the language in Romans is most expressive, because our text says we are to *"be* transformed" (passive imperative). This must be done by someone or something else, which is of course the Holy Spirit. We are to submit to the Holy Spirit who brings about "the renewing of your mind." We also understand from the present tense of the verb that this is a *process*, a gradual transformation. The Christian is to allow himself to be changed continually so that his life conforms more and more to that of Christ. Ultimately, as Romans 8:29 says, there will be the supreme metamorphosis when we will be transformed (*summorphos*) to the image of Christ in eternity.

As we answer the call to commitment, we are called to voice a monumental "no" to the schemes of this fleeting evil age and a determined "yes" to the transforming work of the Holy Spirit in renewing our minds. The "no" without the "yes" will lead to a life of futile negation. The "yes" without the "no" will lead to frustration because Christ will not dwell in Satan's house. These are not suggestions, but are rather imperial commands to be obeyed by all.

THE EFFECT OF COMMITMENT (v. 2b)

The final phrase of verse 2 reveals the effects of genuine commitment in our lives: "Then you will be able to test and approve what God's will is — his good, pleasing and perfect will." The *New English Bible* says it best: "Then you will be able to *discern* the will of God, and to *know* what is good, acceptable, and perfect" (italics added).

A committed life has the power to perceive what God's will is. Alexander Maclaren expressed it like this:

> To know beyond doubt what I ought to do, and knowing to do it, seems to me to be heaven on earth, and the man that has it needs but little more.[5]

The one who is committed to God sees life with a sure eye. While the careless and uncommitted are in confusion, he knows God's will. And he finds God's will to be "good, pleasing and perfect."

What is the *basis* of commitment? The mercies of God and his love for us.

What is the *character* of our commitment? "Therefore, I urge you, brothers, in view of God's mercy, to offer your bodies as living sacrifices, holy and pleasing to God."

What are the *demands* of commitment? There is the negative: "Do not conform any longer to the pattern of this world" and the positive: "be transformed by the renewing of your mind."

What is the *effect* of commitment? Knowing the will of God.

Nothing but total commitment of our lives to God makes any sense. He holds the universe together by the word of his power — "For from him and through him and to him are all things." And if this is not enough, he gave us his "mercies" through his Son, even while we were yet sinners.

Total commitment is the only logical way to live. Let us live under the logic of God.

For by the grace given me I say to every one of you: Do not think of yourself more highly than you ought, but rather think of yourself with sober judgment, in accordance with the measure of faith God has given you. Just as each of us has one body with many members, and these members do not all have the same function, so in Christ we who are many form one body, and each member belongs to all the others. We have different gifts, according to the grace given us. If a man's gift is prophesying, let him use it in proportion to his faith. If it is serving, let him serve; if it is teaching, let him teach; if it is encouraging, let him encourage; if it is contributing to the needs of others, let him give generously; if it is leadership, let him govern diligently; if it is showing mercy, let him do it cheerfully. (12:3-8)

24

Renewed Thinking

ROMANS 12:3-8

Assuming we are committed Christians according to the guidelines of Romans 12:1, 2, how do we who are having our minds renewed and our lives transfigured think about life as we live it? Specifically, how do we who have had our minds renewed think about ourselves? About fellow believers? About our spiritual gifts? Paul answers these question in verses 3-8:

> I. Thinking Rightly About Ourselves (v. 3)
> II. Thinking Rightly About Fellow Believers (vv. 4, 5)
> III. Thinking Rightly About Our Gifts (vv. 6-8)

THINKING RIGHTLY ABOUT OURSELVES (v. 3)

How are we to think about ourselves? In verse 3 Paul again advises us negatively and positively. First the negative:

> For by the grace given me I say to every one of you: Do not think
> of yourself more highly than you ought . . . .

The language here is alive. If we were very literal, we could render the phrase, "I say to everyone, do not super-think of yourself," or perhaps "Do not get hyper about yourself!" Perhaps Paul knew of some individuals in Rome who thought they were better than others. The opening verses of chapter 14 give a hint of this. Whatever the case, thinking more

219

highly of ourselves than we ought to think is a universal tendency of the human race. Our Adamic nature loves to over-think about itself.

This can take two classic forms. Primarily it is that of the self-elevating braggart — the person who tells you how smart he is, how much he has done, how strong he is, how rich he will be when he gets his big break — legends in their own mind. Walt Whitman expressed our universal tendency in these words: "I find no sweeter fat than sticks to my own bones."

The other form of overestimation is more subtle — that of self-deprecating Uriah Heeps, those who self-consciously talk about themselves as if they were nobodies. I remember Dr. Lloyd-Jones telling of being at a train station where a man met him and said, "Oh, Dr. Jones, I am just a chimney sweep in the house of the Lord. Let me carry your suitcase. I am a nobody, and you are a man of great gifts." Dr. Jones saw through the man immediately and did not deal too kindly with him. When a person acts like this, his expectation is that you will correct him. "No, no, you are really a great person." (The way to expose a Uriah Heep is to say, "You know, I think you're right!" But watch out!)

How then are we to think about ourselves? Paul gives us positive advice in verse 3b: "but rather think of yourself with sober judgment . . ." Instead of super-thought there is to be sober thought. Paul continues, "in accordance with the measure of faith God has given you." This most important phrase has often been given the misleading interpretation that sound judgment comes in proportion to the degree of *our* faith — if we have strong faith we will think rightly of ourselves. However, as Cranfield has shown from his research of classical sources and the Qumran, "measure" should really be translated "standard."[1] The idea is that God has allotted to each believer a standard of faith by which to measure himself — *and that standard is Christ.* Cranfield explains:

> . . . to estimate oneself according to the standard which consists of one's faith in Christ is really to recognize that Christ Himself in whom God's judgment and mercy are revealed is the One by whom alone one must measure oneself and also one's fellow-men.[2]

Paul is not asking the believer to estimate himself according to changing subjective feelings, but to estimate himself according to his relationship to Christ. When one sees that Christ is the standard of measurement, he will not think of himself more highly than he ought, but rather think of himself with sober judgment.

It is impossible to think more highly of ourselves than we ought if we are sound on this point. If we truly make Christ our standard, we will experience the reality of the opening beatitude, "Blessed are the poor in spirit, for theirs is the kingdom of heaven" (Matthew 5:3). This could be paraphrased, "How happy are those who realize that they have nothing within themselves to commend themselves to God, for theirs is the kingdom of God." Moreover, if Christ is our standard, the tendency to exalt ourselves by comparing ourselves with others will be curbed. Those who pride themselves because they are more gifted than another believer will cease their foolishness when they make Christ the standard of measurement. A clear focus on Christ, then, is the key to thinking rightly about ourselves and should be the goal of our spiritual practice. All of this is a call to profound humility.

The thought chain of Romans is compelling: 1:1 — 11:32, profound *theology*; 11:33-36, profound *doxology*; 12:1, 2, profound *dedication*; 12:3ff., profound *humility* resulting in action.

How are we thinking about ourselves today?

> For by the grace given me I say to every one of you: Do not think of yourself more highly than you ought, but rather think of yourself with sober judgment, in accordance with the measure of faith God has given you. (v. 3)

THINKING RIGHTLY ABOUT FELLOW BELIEVERS (vv. 4, 5)

From thinking rightly about ourselves, we move in verses 4 and 5 to thinking rightly about fellow believers. Here Paul, a master illustrator, gives us a wonderfully mystical conception based on the human anatomy:

> Just as each of us has one body with many members, and these members do not all have the same function, so in Christ we who are many form one body, and each member belongs to all the others. (vv. 4, 5)

The word "just" at the beginning of verse 4 links it closely with verse 3 because when we think rightly about ourselves, with Christ as the standard, we will be able to think accurately about others — the *Body* of Christ.

This illustration underscores three characteristics of the Body of Christ: its unity, diversity, and mutuality. First, we will view its *unity*. Both verses 4 and 5 stress the one Body of which we are all members. We must emphasize that while this unity is mysterious, it is real! This is not an illustration which serves only to suggest that we should try to live in a more close-knit manner. It describes the reality that all of us are part of Christ's Body if we trust in him for our salvation. We share the same nature.

> . . . he has given us his very great and precious promises, so that through them you may participate in the divine nature. . . . (2 Peter 1:4)

We derive our spiritual life from the same source: "I am the vine; you are the branches" (John 15:5).

Our unity is the subject of Christ's prayers to the Father. In his High Priestly prayer he prayed repeatedly:

> ". . . that all of them may be one, Father, just as you are in me and I am in you . . . that they may be one as we are one: I in them and you in me. May they be brought to complete unity." (John 17:21a, 22b, 23a)

Second, while there exists a profound, real unity, there is also a corresponding real *diversity*: ". . . these members do not all have the same function, so in Christ we who are many form one body . . ." (vv. 4b, 5a). I read of a youth pastor who painted a football to look like a huge human eye with a big, round pupil. He wrapped it in a blanket, put it under his arm, and showed it to his group, asking, "What do you think of my baby?" The typical response was, "Oh, gross!" Then he asked them, "What if your girlfriend was just an eye? Imagine taking her out on a date and having a giant eye sitting across from you in the booth!" Needless to say, he made his point. Without diversity the body would become a monstrosity.

F. F. Bruce writes:

> Diversity, not uniformity, is the mark of God's handiwork. It is so in nature; it is so in grace, too, and nowhere more so than in the Christian community. Here are many men and women with the most diverse kinds of parentage, environment, temperament, and capacity. Not only so, but since they became Christians they have been endowed by God with a great variety of spiritual gifts as well. Yet because and by means of that diversity, all can co-operate for the good of the whole.[3]

God's glory is revealed in the diversity of his people. This means that as we measure ourselves by Christ's standard we will be *ourselves*. Being in Christ's Body will maximize our uniqueness if we allow such.

Of course, we must also be careful to allow others to be themselves.

It is always a danger signal when members of a Christian organization or a church begin to all dress and act like the leader — combing their hair like him, standing like him, talking like him. *When the Spirit of God is free to work in a church, there is diversity.*

Finally, we must not stress this truth of diversity without grasping the balancing truth of our *mutuality*: "each member belongs to all the others" (v. 5b). First Corinthians 12 beautifully emphasizes this mutuality by pointing out that when one member rejoices, the others rejoice, and when one member hurts, the others hurt. When I was in college I broke my leg, and the rest of my body felt so bad that it stayed up all night to keep my leg company! Each of us belongs to and needs the others. The church is no place for lone rangers. If your life seems stuck even though you read your Bible and pray, it may be that you are neglecting getting together with other believers and are depriving yourself of the exchange necessary for spiritual growth (cf. the significance of "together with all the saints" in Ephesians 3:18).

How beautiful this all is. Those who think rightly about themselves, measuring themselves by the standard which God has given them in their faith, discern the one body and recognize that they do not exist for themselves. As a result, they are free to develop and use their gifts.

THINKING RIGHTLY ABOUT OUR GIFTS (vv. 6-8)

> We have different gifts, according to the grace given us. If a man's gift is prophesying, let him use it in proportion to his faith. If it is serving, let him serve; if it is teaching, let him teach; if it is encouraging, let him encourage; if it is contributing to the needs of others, let him give generously; if it is leadership, let him govern diligently; if it is showing mercy, let him do it cheerfully. (vv. 6-8)

In thinking rightly about our gifts, we must consider a few simple truths: 1) *We all have gifts.* No Christian is left out. You may not have one of those specifically mentioned here (though you probably do), but you do have at least one spiritual gift. 2) *This list is not exhaustive.* First Corinthians 12:27, 28 lists several others. Some tabulate fifteen gifts listed in Scripture, others nineteen. I personally think that the Scriptural lists do not purport to be exhaustive. 3) *Gifts are not to be utilized as a "Christian Zodiac."* "There's a Leo, there's a Pisces, there's an administrator, there's a teacher, there's an Aquarius." Such pigeon-holing can be spiritually stifling, especially when matched with an inaccurate understanding of the gifts. Many who have fallen to this type of thinking stumble by the wayside when they fail to measure up to false expectations. Instead, we must understand that spiritual "gifts" or "graces," as verse 6 calls them, are personally administered by the Holy Spirit in varying degrees and styles and should be simply, soberly, and unostentatiously exercised by the Spirit.

Paul tell us how to use seven of these graces. Verse 6b says, "If a man's gift is prophesying, let him use it in proportion to his faith." The gift of prophecy is sometimes predictive, but not necessarily or primarily. This gift is normally the communication of revealed truth in a manner that convicts and builds up its hearers. Oftentimes one who has this gift will have penetrating things to say about specific problems in society or life. One is to do this "in proportion to his faith" looking, as we saw in verse 3, to Christ as his standard or measure.

Next Paul says, "If it is serving, let him serve" (v. 7a)."Serving" is the same word from which we derive the word *deacon*, and it refers to the variety of services that deacons and deaconesses perform in the Church. The one who serves is to exercise his gift to the fullest — giving himself wholeheartedly to the work, just as Philip and his friends did in Acts 6.

Next is the grace of teaching: "If it is teaching, let him teach" (v. 7b). Teaching differs from prophecy in that it instructs the mind, whereas prophecy is addressed more to the heart and will. Teaching is more concerned with knowledge, prophecy with revelation. The teacher is to apply his all to the task. Dr. Barnhouse asks some piercing questions of those who have this calling:

> Have I listened to His voice? Have I laid my own reason in the dust before Him in order to take it again, enlightened by Him, for use in my work? Have I been spiritually alert and dependent upon the Holy Spirit? Have I gone again and again to the Word of God to refresh my own soul before speaking to others? Have I tried to live what I preach? Have I acknowledged my sins when the Lord showed them to me, and repented of them? Have I recognized moment by moment my utter dependence upon the Lord? Have I been lazy? Have I been diligent? Have I insulted the Lord by feeding His sheep with ill-prepared food?[4]

These are sobering questions — the kind we should ask ourselves in respect to all our gifts.

Then there is the grace of exhortation: "If it is encouraging, let him encourage" (v. 8a). The root idea is "to come alongside and encourage." I see this exemplified every time my church has a roller skating party, and the parents put their little ones on skates for the first time. Mom and Dad skate with their child, holding on to his or her hands, sometimes with the child's feet on the ground and sometimes in the air. But all the time the parents are alongside encouraging. Exhortation can take many forms — warning, advice, counsel, encouragement. It is a wonderful gift, and we are to place it at Christ's feet and be willing to be worn out in its use.

Next is the grace of giving: "If it is contributing to the needs of others, let him give generously" (v. 8b). "Generously" should be translated "with simplicity." This refers to our motive in giving. Those who have this gift are to exercise it without ulterior motives or hidden purposes, simply out of love. This is where Ananias and Sapphira failed. When we give, it is to be simply to the glory of God and to meet the needs of brothers and sisters in Christ in the world. A pastor under whom I served for years had a man in his congregation who gave only once a year — $10.00 which he placed in the pastor's hand saying, "This is for the church." He wanted to make sure he got credit for his generous gift!

Then there is the grace of leadership: "If it is leadership, let him govern diligently" (v. 8c). Those who exercise spiritual leadership in the church, whether pastors or elders or deacons or committee leaders, are not to "wing it." Leaders should not become casual and careless but should see their abilities as divinely granted gifts and their charges as from God.

Lastly, there is the grace of showing mercy: "If it is showing mercy, let him do it cheerfully" (v. 8d). This gift takes many forms — aiding the poor, working with the mentally handicapped, tending the ill. But whatever the function, it must be done with cheer. The English word *hilarious* originated from the Greek word translated "cheerfully." There is no room for a hangdog expression in the Church. Someone has written, "If you come with sympathy to sorrow, bring God's sunlight in your face."

Seven beautiful graces, are they not? Perfumes for the Body of Christ. If Paul's advice were followed, think how healthy the Church would be. Perhaps God is speaking to you about your gifts. Remember, the Church did not give you your gifts — God did. They are his. Use them for his glory!

How is our thinking today?

Are we thinking rightly about *ourselves* according to the standard we have learned in knowing Christ? Or are we thinking too highly of ourselves — comparing ourselves with others so we look good? If so, we need to look to Christ. "Blessed are the poor in spirit, for theirs is the kingdom of heaven" (Matthew 5:3).

Are we thinking rightly about *other believers*? Is the Body a reality to us? Its unity? Its diversity? Its mutuality?

Finally, how is our thinking about the *gifts* the Holy Spirit has given to us? Are we using them? If not, why not?

Love must be sincere. Hate what is evil; cling to what is good. Be devoted to one another in brotherly love. Honor one another above yourselves. Never be lacking in zeal, but keep your spiritual fervor, serving the Lord. Be joyful in hope, patient in affliction, faithful in prayer. Share with God's people who are in need. Practice hospitality. Bless those who persecute you; bless and do not curse. Rejoice with those who rejoice; mourn with those who mourn. Live in harmony with one another. Do not be proud, but be willing to associate with people of low position. Do not be conceited. Do not repay anyone evil for evil. Be careful to do what is right in the eyes of everybody. If it is possible, as far as it depends on you, live at peace with everyone. Do not take revenge, my friends, but leave room for God's wrath, for it is written: "It is mine to avenge; I will repay," says the Lord. On the contrary: "If your enemy is hungry, feed him; if he is thirsty, give him something to drink. In doing this, you will heap burning coals on his head." Do not be overcome by evil, but overcome evil with good. (12:9-21)

25

Love in Action

ROMANS 12:9-21

The thrust of the text discussed in this chapter suggests the question, how do we who are committed to Christ and have had our minds renewed love? Specifically, how do we love those in the Church and how do we love those in the world? These important questions must be considered together because we cannot love those in the Church without loving those in the world, and vice versa. The two loves complement and energize each other.

I saw this in the life of a man I became acquainted with when I first became a Christian. His obvious passion was service to God. He arranged his schedule so he could spend as much time as possible working behind the scenes of our summer youth camp and in his church. He projected a calm and loving spirit. And he was himself one of the most loved men of our denomination. In retrospect I see that he was a master at *loving the Church*.

At camp one summer some of us (we were then teenagers) were admiring this man, and one of the group began telling us that his daughter had been brutally murdered by a young man the family had taken into their home in an attempt to help him. Amazingly, this man repeatedly went to the prison to minister to his daughter's murderer, finally led him to Christ, and continued to visit him over the years. This Christian man was also a master at *loving the world*. No wonder we felt Christ's presence through him. The love of Christ had mastered him.

How are we to love the Church, and how are we to love the world? These are the questions our text addresses.

LOVE IN THE CHURCH (vv. 9-13)

Paul begins with an all-important statement about the quality of the love which is to be in the Church: "Love must be sincere" (v. 9). The word for "love" here is *agape*, which to this point had been used in Romans only for divine love (5:5; 8:35, 39), except in 8:28 where it is used for man's love for God. But here the word is used to indicate the kind of love Christians are to show *to others* — a Godlike love that loves regardless of the circumstances, a deliberate love that decides it will keep loving even if it is rebuffed. We are challenged to live out the highest love and to do so with the highest sincerity. Our love is to be genuine, not counterfeit.

This little statement, so simple and so straightforward — "Love must be sincere" — is foundational to Christian conduct. But despite its simplicity, it is not easy to put into practice because much of our lives is shot through with hypocrisy. Our culture encourages us to live an image. The media repeatedly present us with people pretending to be something they are not, and so tempt us to take up masks ourselves, to counterfeit a love we do not possess. Most of us can effect civilities which appear to be utterly sincere though they actually cover hostility — like the smiling face we present to a police officer as he hands us a ticket, while inside we are saying, "May all your days be filled with traffic jams!"

We even deceive ourselves into thinking we have love for people we neglect and, in fact, do not even like. Paul tells us that we must get beyond pretense — we must sincerely love. If we claim the commitment of Romans 12:1, 2, we must love without hypocrisy. This is not optional! The Scripture repeatedly sets this requirement before us. "Above all, love each other deeply" (1 Peter 4:8). "The goal of this command is love, which comes from a pure heart and a good conscience and a sincere faith" (1 Timothy 1:5). "All men will know that you are my disciples if you love one another" (John 13:35).

This is a call to honestly examine our own hearts, asking the question, "Do I love others, especially those in the Church, without hypocrisy?" If the answer is uncertain, we must go to God in prayer, because the Holy Spirit is the only One who can pour love into and through our hearts (5:5).

Having established that love is the foundation for Christian action, Paul now advances his thought in verses 9-13 with several challenging specifics. First, we see *love's morality*: "Hate what is evil; cling to what is good" (v. 9b). Some might suppose that love is soft on evil. Not so! Evil is to be hated. Sincere love demands God-honoring moral resolve regarding good and evil.

Next, Paul mentions *love's commitment in the Church*: "Be devoted to one another in brotherly love. Honor one another above yourselves" (v. 10). The words "Be devoted" are the translation of a Greek word which combines the words for friendship love and family love. A more helpful translation is, "Be devoted with warm family affection to one another in brotherly love." Family-type devotion to one another is more than friendship. Such love involves commitment like that experienced in good families.

The natural outcome will be then, as the last half of the verse commands, to "Honor one another above yourselves" (v. 10b). Healthy families have a mutual respect for one another. They defer to one another and take pleasure in the elevation of other family members.

This is the way it ought to be in the Church. Love heightens family commitment and family joy. But sometimes the Church fails. Some years ago a certain church in Dallas, Texas, divided. The split was so bad that one faction began a lawsuit to dispossess the other and claim the property. The newspapers picked up the story, and the locals followed what was happening with a great deal of interest. The judge finally stated it was not a matter for the civil courts until the church courts had made a ruling. After much discussion, the church court awarded the property to one of the two factions, and the losers withdrew and formed another church in the area.[1] How different things would have been had those in that church heeded Paul's call to mutual commitment: "Be devoted [with *warm family affection*] to one another in brotherly love. Honor one another above yourselves" (v. 10).

Next Paul challenges us with *love's energetic expression*: "Never be lacking in zeal, but keep your spiritual fervor, serving the Lord. Be joyful in hope, patient in affliction, faithful in prayer" (vv. 11, 12). The word "fervor" carries the idea of burning, and the *Revised Standard Version* better captures the energy of what Paul is saying here: "Never flag in zeal, *be aglow* with the Spirit, serve the Lord. Rejoice in your hope, be patient in tribulation, be constant in prayer" (italics added). Our love is to be dispensed with burning energy toward those around us!

Such fervent loving calls for our best and is costly. Luther said he worked so hard that when he went to bed he literally fell into bed. In fact, one account says he did not change his bed for a year! Now that is tired! Moody's bedtime prayer as he rolled his great bulk into bed on one occasion was, "Lord, I am tired. Amen." Calvin's biographers marvel at his output. John Wesley rode sixty to seventy miles a day and on average preached three sermons a day. When Alexander Maclaren went into his study, he would take off his slippers and put on working men's boots because he knew that a minister of God is to be a working man! True love labors.

Lastly, there is *love's care*: "Share with God's people who are in need. Practice hospitality" (v. 13). Our care for brothers and sisters in Christ should reach down right into our wallets and purses and cost us. Paul presents this as a privilege rather than a sacrifice because the word "share" is one of our great Christian words, *koinonia*, which suggests a common sharing or fellowship. Love's care is natural and right and joyful! When Christ's Church is living in love, the needs of its people are met through sharing and caring.

Love's care is exhibited when we "Practice hospitality." Here we must note something both beautiful and convicting: "practice" means "pursuing" or "chasing." The word sometimes even denotes strenuous pursuit. The idea is that the loving believer does not wait for the stranger to show up on the doorstep, but goes out and gets him. Of this, Origen wrote:

> How finely does he [Paul] sum up the generosity of the man who pursues hospitality in one word! For by saying that hospitality is to be pursued, he shows that we are not just to receive the stranger when he comes to us, but actually to inquire after, and look carefully for strangers, to pursue them and search them out everywhere. . . .[2]

Of course, this was terribly important during the early years of the Church when believers were disinherited. Today it is equally important in many parts of the world where similar situations exist. Moreover, it is important to the life of the Church anywhere. The benefits that mutual hospitality brings to the Church are incalculable: relationships enhanced, love disseminated, souls encouraged. All of us are to do this. Peter put it this way: "Offer hospitality to one another without grumbling" (1 Peter 4:9). And our text in Romans says we should aggressively pursue it. Genesis 18 gives us the example of Abraham, and Hebrews 13:2 tells us, "for by so doing some people have entertained angels without knowing it."

Let us review what we have seen about love. *Love's quality*: "love must be sincere." *Love's morality*: "Hate what is evil; cling to what is good." *Love's commitment*: "Be devoted [with warm family affection] to one another in brotherly love. Honor one another above yourselves." Think of what it would be like to see such family love in the Church.

Love's energetic expression: "Never be lacking in zeal, but keep your spiritual fervor, serving the Lord. Be joyful in hope, patient in affliction, faithful in prayer." Think of such blessed fire in the life of the Church. *Love's care*: "Share with God's people who are in need. Practice hospitality."

LOVE IN THE WORLD (vv. 14-21)

The apostle now switches his focus from love's actions in the Church to love's actions in the world. What we read here should be interpreted from the perspective of one who is under pressure from an unbelieving world. We will briefly consider some general principles of loving action in verses 14-16 and then, in verses 17-21, some specific principles for loving when wronged.

Loving in Action

We immediately know that a radical relationship with the world is in view from the supernatural injunction of verse 14: "Bless those who persecute you; bless and do not curse." This is the radical way of Jesus as given in his Sermon on the Mount. More than speaking well of one's enemies, it includes praying for their forgiveness and blessing. This is supremely radical. It is one thing not to curse your enemies, but entirely another to pray for their blessing. This is a life-changing call. The Arabs have a custom which (though practiced with differing levels of sincerity) symbolizes what is called for here. They touch the head, lips, and heart indicating, "I *think* highly of you, I *speak* well of you, my *heart* beats for you." What a way to love the world! "Bless those who persecute you; bless and do not curse."

Next Paul commands in verse 15, "Rejoice with those who rejoice; mourn with those who mourn." Believers are to identify with the world in the "ups and downs" of human life, to be a healing balm for a cold world. The world, says Chuck Swindoll, is characterized by

> Indifference, non-commitment, disengagement, no sharing or caring . . . meals eaten with hi-fi headsets turned up loud, even separate bedrooms, each with a personal telephone, TV, and turntable, private toilet, and an it's none-of-your-business attitude. No hassle . . . no conflict . . . no accountability. No need to share. Or reach out. Or give a rip. Just watch the numbers and look at nobody.[3]

Enter the loving believer — he who weeps with those who weep and rejoices with those who rejoice. He is a tonic for life — a light leading to Christ! George Fox, the great Quaker, recorded this prayer in his diary:

> I prayed to God that He would baptize my heart into all conditions so I might be able to enter the needs and conditions of all.[4]

The call to love is radical indeed! "Rejoice with those who rejoice; mourn with those who mourn" Put another way:

> *A sorrow shared is*
> *But half a trouble.*
> *A joy that's shared is*
> *A joy made double.*

How perfectly this leads to the next thought: "Live in harmony with one another. Do not be proud, but be willing to associate with people of low position. Do not be conceited" (v. 16).

A fitting illustration of this comes from the life of Chief Justice Charles Evans Hughes. When Mr. Hughes was appointed Chief Justice of the Supreme Court of the United States, he moved to Washington and transferred his letter to a Baptist church there. His father had been a Baptist minister, and Hughes had been a lifelong witness to his own faith in Christ. It was the custom in that Baptist church to have all new members come forward during the morning service and be introduced to the congregation. On this particular day the first to be called was a Chinese laundryman, Ah Sing, who had moved to Washington from San Francisco and kept a laundry near the church. He stood at the far side of the pulpit. As others were called, they took positions at the extreme opposite side. When a dozen people had gathered, Ah Sing still stood alone. Then Chief Justice Hughes was called, and he significantly stood next to the laundryman.[5] Christians are to associate with everyone — the ordinary people, the unimportant, the outcasts of society.

Verses 14-16 call for a caring heart which is vulnerable to the world. A Christian who is elitist, who only associates with people of the same intellectual or academic or professional interests, is not living up to what the Scripture mandates. We are to have a heart open to the world. We are to pray for those who persecute us, to enter others' joys and sorrows, to associate with everyone regardless of their station in life. What a way to go after the world!

Loving When Wronged

In the final verses we move into explicit counsel for loving a hostile world:

> Do not repay anyone evil for evil. Be careful to do what is right in the eyes of everybody. If it is possible, as far as it depends on you, live at peace with everyone. Do not take revenge, my friends, but leave room for God's wrath, for it is written: "It is mine to avenge; I will repay," says the Lord. On the contrary: "If your enemy is hungry, feed him; if he is thirsty, give him something to drink. In doing this, you will heap burning coals on his head." (vv. 17-20)

This is supremely radical because it is supremely unnatural. Our conditioned reflex is to hit back. The world says, "Common sense demands getting even." However, there is a better way, God's way, and it has two elements: First, *trust God*. The apostle says: "Do not take revenge, my friends, but leave room for God's wrath, for it is written: 'It is mine to avenge; I will repay,' says the Lord" (v. 19). We must trust God to work in the life of the one who wronged us. Leaving room for his wrath is to leave the vengeance to God, knowing also that he smites in order to heal (Isaiah 19:22). God's wrath may one day come in ultimate judgment to those who abuse us, but his wrath may also bring enemies to repentance in this life. Whatever happens, God will be perfectly equitable. We can trust him implicitly for this.

Second, we *do positive good*, as verse 20 exhorts us: "On the contrary: 'If your enemy is hungry, feed him; if he is thirsty, give him something to drink. In doing this, you will heap burning coals on his head.'" There has been much scholarly speculation as to what the final phrase regarding "burning coals" means, but I am confident that the oldest and simplest explanation is best: in doing good to our enemies, we will heap burning pangs of shame and contrition on their heads which hopefully (not surely) will lead them to God's grace. The best example of this in Scripture is the exchange between David and Saul after David had been so close to Saul in the cave that he cut off a corner of the king's robe, but for conscience's sake would not lift his hand against Saul even though the king was seeking David's life. Listen to David's words after the king had gone down from the cave:

> Then David went out of the cave and called to Saul, "My lord the king!" When Saul looked behind him, David bowed down and pros-

trated himself with his face to the ground. He said to Saul, "Why do you listen when men say, 'David is bent on harming you'? This day you have seen with your own eyes how the Lord delivered you into my hands in the cave. Some urged me to kill you, but I spared you; I said, 'I will not lift my hand against my master, because he is the Lord's anointed.' See, my father, look at this piece of your robe in my hand! I cut off the corner of your robe but did not kill you. Now understand and recognize that I am not guilty of wrongdoing or rebellion. I have not wronged you, but you are hunting me down to take my life. May the Lord judge between you and me. And may the Lord avenge the wrongs you have done to me, but my hand will not touch you. As the old saying goes, 'From evildoers come evil deeds,' so my hand will not touch you." (1 Samuel 24:8-13)

Coals of fire were heaped on Saul's head, and observe the magnificent effect:

When David finished saying this, Saul asked, "Is that your voice, David my son?" And he wept aloud. "You are more righteous than I," he said. "You have treated me well, but I have treated you badly. You have just now told me of the good you did to me; the Lord delivered me into your hands, but you did not kill me. When a man finds his enemy, does he let him get away unharmed? May the Lord reward you well for the way you treated me today." (1 Samuel 24:16-19)

Sadly, Saul never opened himself to God's grace, but he well could have. The coals were meant to be a prelude to blessing.

Toward the end of his life it is said that W. C. Fields was seen reading the Bible. A surprised friend asked him why he was doing so, and Fields answered, "Looking for loopholes, looking for loopholes." In relation to this text, there are no loopholes. We are never under any circumstances to avenge ourselves. Any plans we may have to the contrary are from the Devil.

Not only are we to not avenge ourselves, we are to do positive good to our enemies. Impossible? Not at all! Our Lord did it. And consider again the man I mentioned who was so Christlike that though his enemy had taken his daughter's life, he repaid him with good, and that good burned through to the man's heart, and God gave him a new one.

Our text closes with: "Do not be overcome by evil, but overcome evil with good" (v. 21). George MacDonald put it this way: "The dull world has gotten the wrong phrase, it is he who resents an affront who pockets it; he who takes no note of it lets it lie in the dirt."

Love in the Church and love in the world go together. They are the demands of commitment. Our minds have been renewed. Our lives have been transformed. And the Holy Spirit can do all this through us.

Are we loving the church?

Are we loving the world?

Everyone must submit himself to the governing authorities, for there is no authority except that which God has established. The authorities that exist have been established by God. Consequently, he who rebels against the authority is rebelling against what God has instituted, and those who do so will bring judgment on themselves. For rulers hold no terror for those who do right, but for those who do wrong. Do you want to be free from fear of the one in authority? Then do what is right and he will commend you. For he is God's servant to do you good. But if you do wrong, be afraid, for he does not bear the sword for nothing. He is God's servant, an agent of wrath to bring punishment on the wrongdoer. Therefore, it is necessary to submit to the authorities, not only because of possible punishment but also because of conscience. This is also why you pay taxes, for the authorities are God's servants, who give their full time to governing. Give everyone what you owe him: If you owe taxes, pay taxes; if revenue, then revenue; if respect, then respect; if honor, then honor. (13:1-7)

26

Heaven's Citizens and Human Government

ROMANS 13:1-7

It has been said that our Lord not only unites his friends, he also unites his enemies. I think this is proven from history. It certainly was true in his own time. Shortly after Jesus' Triumphal Entry into Jerusalem, the Pharisees sought out their enemies, the Herodians, to join them in an unholy alliance to "get him." There could hardly have been two more incompatible groups. The Herodians were not a religious sect or school, but a political party. Though they were Jews, or at least of mixed Jewish blood, they were Roman sympathizers and supporters who favored Roman occupation and taxation. Thus they were natural enemies of the Pharisees, who were extremely religious and anti-Caesar and loathed paying taxes.

These unlikely groups formulated a surefire plan to ensnare the Lord. They sent a combined delegation of young Pharisees (who would hopefully appear more guileless than the older ones) and Herodians to Jesus. Their instructions were to flatter him (which they did) and then ask this question: "Tell us then, what is your opinion? Is it right to pay taxes to Caesar or not?" (Matthew 22:17). The question was devilishly clever. If Jesus answered no he would be branded a traitor to Caesar. If he said yes he would be called anti-patriotic, and his ministry would be discredited. His enemies were sure they had him. But instead Jesus had them when he answered, "You hypocrites, why are you trying to trap me? Show me the coin used for paying the tax" (Matthew 22:18). A hush came over the crowd as Jesus held the coin for all to see. Then he asked them, "'Whose portrait is this? And whose inscription?' 'Caesar's,' they replied. Then he said to them, 'Give to Caesar what is Caesar's, and to God what is God's'" (Matthew 22:20, 21).

It was a brilliant answer, and all his critics could do was walk away shaking their heads in wonder.

With this single sentence our Lord established the validity of human government, while at the same time setting its limits. Caesar had his image on certain things, and they rightly belonged to him. There is a proper domain and function for human government. However, God has stamped his own image on man (the intellect, the will, and the soul bear the divine stamp). Thus, man may give outward things to Caesar, but the inner man belongs to God. Jesus was saying, "The coin is from the mint of the Roman Empire, but you are from God's mint. The coin's use is determined by its likeness, and your use is determined by the likeness you bear." Jesus' single sentence is certainly the most important political statement ever made!

Romans 13:1-7 is Paul's exposition of Jesus' remarkable saying. In fact, verse 7 bears some resemblance to it, beginning with, "give everyone what you owe him." Paul tells us how the citizens of Heaven are to relate to human government, how we can be the kind of citizens God wants us to be.

We must keep several things to in mind as we move through this passage. First, the political situation in Rome was explosive for the Early Church. Claudius had earlier expelled the Jews because of a dispute involving a certain "Chrestus" (i.e., Christ), and though the Jews had returned, the political situation was volatile.[1] Moreover, Paul was afraid some of the revolutionary attitudes of Jerusalem's Zealots might influence the Church. So Paul wrote to instruct the Church on how to behave properly toward the state. What he writes is not ivory-tower theory, but practical directions on how to live under an unfriendly government.

Secondly, we must realize what the passage does not tell us. It does not directly say what we ought to do when a government departs from the role God has given it. It does not specifically explain what to do when our government is committing a moral wrong. Neither are we told what to do in the midst of revolution. It also does not show us which form of government is best — it does not even commend democracy! I mention these things because many of the difficulties found in this chapter result from what is read into it rather than from what it actually teaches.

Lastly, we must keep in mind that understanding and living by what is taught here will not relieve the tension Jesus gave us when he said,

"Give to Caesar what is Caesar's, and to God what is God's" (Matthew 22:21). Paul begins by giving the basic rationale for a Christian's subjection to the state.

THE BELIEVER'S SUBMISSION TO HUMAN GOVERNMENT (vv. 1, 2)

> Everyone must submit himself to the governing authorities, for there is no authority except that which God has established. The authorities that exist have been established by God. Consequently, he who rebels against the authority is rebelling against what God has instituted, and those who do so will bring judgment on themselves. (vv. 1, 2)

The apostle gives us what we might call "the divine right of the state" as he says in the last half of verse 1, "for there is no authority except that which God has established. The authorities that exist have been established by God." Richard Halverson, present chaplain of the United States Senate, wrote:

> To be sure, men will abuse and misuse the institution of the State just as man because of sin has abused and misused every other institution in history including the Church of Jesus Christ, but this does not mean that the institution is bad or that it should be forsaken. It simply means that men are sinners and rebels in God's world, and this is the way they behave with good institutions. As a matter of fact, it is because of this very sin that there must be human government to maintain order in history until the final and ultimate rule of Jesus Christ is established. Human government is better than anarchy, and the Christian must recognize the "divine right" of the State.[2]

Despite the fact that almost every time we pick up a newspaper we read of corruption in government, we must still recognize the state as an essentially divine and moral institution. The Scriptures testify that it is God who sets up governments — even the bad ones — and he takes them down as well. When Daniel gave the prophecy of Nebuchadnezzar's fall, he began by saying:

"Praise be to the name of God for ever and ever; wisdom and power are his. He changes times and seasons; he sets up kings and deposes them." (Daniel 2:20, 21)

Later he summarized what Nebuchadnezzar had learned through his well-deserved humiliation: "he acknowledged that the Most High God is sovereign over the kingdoms of men and sets over them anyone he wishes" (Daniel 5:21).

Seeing that human government is created by God and that he takes an active interest in it, many Christians do not take it seriously enough. Christians too often ignore government or participate as little as possible in governmental affairs. Perhaps this tendency comes from the mistaken belief that when we become members of the Kingdom of Heaven we cease to be members of the secular community. This falsehood, coupled with the revulsion toward the corruption that permeates so much of government, wrongly leads believers to adopt a non-participatory mind-set. This should not be! God is the originator of government, and to ignore it is to dishonor him. Christians ought to be the best citizens.

The other major teaching of the first two verses is that believers are called to a profound obedience to secular government. In the opening command, "Everyone must submit himself to the governing authorities" (v. 1), "Everyone" is emphatic: *every believer*. So strong is the thought that verse 2 concludes, "Consequently, he who rebels against the authority is rebelling against what God has instituted." Resisting governmental authority is resisting God! Taken by itself, without any other Scriptural illumination, this statement can be wrongly interpreted to teach blind devotion to the state regardless of what it commands. Indeed this is how some Christians interpreted it in Nazi Germany despite Germany's treatment of the Jews. However, as we consider Christ's statement and parallel Scriptures, we see that the Christian's obedience to the state is always conditional, and sometimes disobedience is a duty.

There are at least three areas in which a Christian should resist authority. First, if he is asked to violate a command of God. The classic example of this is found in Acts 4, 5 when the authorities arrested the disciples for preaching and summoned them before the Sanhedrin, ordering them not to teach the name of Jesus (Acts 4:17-20). Of course, the disciples went right back to their preaching. Brought before the high priest, they were told, "We gave you strict orders not to teach in this name. . . . Yet you have filled Jerusalem with your teaching and are determined to make us guilty of this man's blood." Peter and the other apostles then told them, "We must obey God rather than men!" (Acts 5:28,

29). The command of God always takes precedence over the command of government. There are no exceptions.

Those who have followed in the footsteps of the apostles have sometimes paid a price for their obedience. For example, in 1962 Aida Skripnikova, a brand-new Christian, was arrested on the Nevski Prospect in Leningrad for handing out postcards proclaiming Christ — and spent most of her life in labor camps because she would not refrain from sharing her faith in Christ.[3] Christians can never violate a command of God, regardless of what the state says.

Secondly, Christians must resist when asked to do an immoral act. The sexual applications are obvious, but this also extends to ethical areas in which many are constantly asked to compromise — for example, falsifying records for "security reasons," perjury for the sake of the department, covering for subordinates by means of falsehoods. Christians must never think it is okay to commit immoral or unethical acts simply because the state has requested it.

Thirdly, believers must never go against their Christian conscience in order to obey the government. This could involve such diverse things as participation in licentious entertainment, or working in institutions that perform wholesale abortions, or working or not working on nuclear weapons. Believers must never sin against their conscience.

Here we must note that there are areas in which good Christians do not agree in matters of conscience — pacifism, for example. While I am not a pacifist myself, I come from a tradition which is, and I have witnessed the integrity of Christian pacifists who are convinced they must not kill. Some of these, if asked, "Suppose this country fell . . . would you resist soldiers coming into you home?" would answer, "No." "Suppose one threatened to harm your wife and daughter?" "I would try to stop them, but I would not kill him." "Suppose he killed you?" "I would go to Heaven." "What about your wife and children?" "God would provide for them."[4] Such a person must abide by his conscience, as must we all.

On the other hand, there are Christian military volunteers and professionals who might say, "I am devoting myself to the defense of my country, though I hate war and pray that I will never have to use my skills." Colonel Al Shine, who served as professor of military science at Wheaton College, writes of Romans 13:

> These verses are not in good repute in some circles today, through no fault of their own, but because some have taken them out of the context of the whole of Scripture to argue that disobedience to any government, under any circumstances, is unbiblical. But it is

nonetheless clear that these verses, supported and amplified by other portions of the Word, and contradicted by none, teach the legitimacy of human government. Bearing the sword, in order to execute justice, is a proper duty of human governments.. The soldier does not, of course, have a blanket license to hate or kill. As an individual sinner, prone to avenge and resist personal abuse, he must, like all other believers, restrain himself. He should, I believe, examine himself. He should, I believe, examine the cause for which his nation fights, and if he concludes that it is evil and unjust he should refuse to participate. Even when he finds the cause acceptable, he may at times feel led to disobey certain orders that he feels abuse the proper use of force.[5]

Again, such a man must obey his Christian conscience.

Our conclusion is this: a Christian must disobey his government when it asks him to 1) violate a commandment of God, 2) commit an immoral or unethical act, or 3) go against his Christian conscience (a conscience which is informed by Scripture and is in submission to the Spirit of God).

Verses 1 and 2 are a call to profound obedience. A profound subjection to the state is rooted in the realization of its "divine right." With right understanding and attitude, believers should be the best citizens. This requires a profound submission to God, which may involve obedience or disobedience to the state.

The committed Christian will continually experience tension in this matter.

THE ROLE OF HUMAN GOVERNMENT (vv. 3, 4)

Verses 3, 4 begin a new section which delineates the basic role of government:

> For rulers hold no terror for those who do right, but for those who do wrong. Do you want to be free from fear of the one in authority? Then do what is right and he will commend you. For he is God's servant to do you good. But if you do wrong, be afraid, for he does not bear the sword for nothing. He is God's servant, an agent of wrath to bring punishment on the wrongdoer.

The essential role of government is encapsulated in the designation it is twice given in verse 4: "God's servant." This is an apt expression of its function because the word for "servant" is *diakonos*, or "deacon." Government is the deacon of God, and as with any deacon, its job is to humbly serve. The teaching here, then, is that government either wittingly or unwittingly serves God. Think how it would be if those in places of political authority understood and believed this. Verse 6, which again says that "authorities are God's servants," emphasizes the servant aspect with even more force because the Greek wording has in view serving in a religious capacity, with an emphasis on solemnity and dignity.[6]

Notice that the servant function of government is to *do good* — "God's servant to do you good" (v. 4a) — and that is what government does, even the worst government. Even a Communist dictatorship is better than no state at all. The darkest days in Israel's history were those days described in Judges 17:6 when "everyone did as he saw fit." Just a few days (a few hours!) without law in today's world and all would be chaos, just as in the book of Judges. This is true both of dictatorships and democracies, although Paul does not have in mind a government which has lost its ability to rule or is at the whim of a madman.

At the end of verse 4 the apostle is most explicit about government's beneficial function: "He is God's servant, an agent of wrath to bring punishment on the wrongdoer." The state is given the responsibility of vengeance, a responsibility that is explicitly forbidden to the individual Christian (12:19). The state renders "evil for evil" (12:17), which the individual Christian must never do. God's way of dealing with evil is not by personal vengeance, but through justice dispensed by the state. Through the state comes an anticipatory display of God's wrath against sin. And as the state is faithful to its function, it does "good" to us (v. 4a). We should be thankful that it "does not bear the sword for nothing," even though it bears it imperfectly.

Paul tells us in verse 3 that if we "do right" we have nothing to fear. In today's terms, if you drive 55 in a 55 mph zone, you will have nothing to fear. But if you are doing 70, you will be looking in the rear-view mirror constantly.

Thus far Paul has shown us that we are called to a profound, intelligent obedience to government (vv. 1, 2) and that government is meant to serve us and do us good (vv. 3, 4). Now in verses 5-7 he describes the kind of obedience to which we are called.

THE DYNAMICS OF OBEDIENCE (vv. 5-7)

Verse 5 indicates the depth of obedience which is required of us: "Therefore, it is necessary to submit to the authorities, not only because of possible punishment but also because of conscience." We are to be in subjection not just because we are afraid of being punished, but because, unlike the world, we understand that the state is divinely instituted and that rulers are wittingly or unwittingly God's ministers.[7] Christians are able to see the big picture, and thus through their informed consciences they are able to live in profound subjection.

How does this work out practically? Verses 6 and 7 tell us: "This is also why you pay taxes, for the authorities are God's servants, who give their full time to governing" (v. 6). This is where the rubber meets the road for twentieth-century American Christians. And it was the same for the Romans. Taxes were exorbitant then too and were sometimes misspent. But the Roman Christians were to pay their taxes, understanding that government authorities are God's servants. That is, they were to pay them with a good attitude.

Ray Stedman comments:

> You have a right, of course, as does everyone, to protest injustice and to correct abuse, but don't forever be grumbling about the taxes that you have to pay. I have had to learn some lessons on this myself. The first time I had to pay an income tax was a few years ago. My income had been so low for a long time that I didn't have to pay any taxes. But gradually it caught up and I finally had to pay. I remember how I resented it. In fact, when I sent my tax form in I addressed it to "The Infernal Revenue Service." They never answered, although they did accept the money. The next year I had improved my attitude a bit. I addressed it to "The Eternal Revenue Service." But I have repented from all those sins, and I now hope to pay my taxes cheerfully.[8]

The believer is to fulfill his governmental obligations with a good attitude.

Verse 7 ties the bow on this matter of obligation: "Give everyone what you owe him: If you owe taxes, pay taxes; if revenue, then revenue; if respect, then respect; if honor, then honor." As Christians we may deplore the politics of a particular person in office. We may be repelled by his scandalous conduct. But that does not disallow us from respecting the office. The person is just a human, but the office exists at the discretion of God. Even in our dissent we must always be Christian gentlemen and gentlewomen.

In conclusion, it is the Christian's duty to obey those in political authority because: 1) government is divinely appointed, 2) it is a deacon to meet our needs, and 3) we see it for what it is. The question is, Is it possible to obey in this way?

The Apostle Peter wrote some relevant verses from Rome *on the eve of Nero's fiery persecution*:

> Submit yourselves for the Lord's sake to every authority instituted among men: whether to the king, as the supreme authority, or to governors, who are sent by him to punish those who do wrong and to commend those who do right. For it is God's will that by doing good you should silence the ignorant talk of foolish men. Live as free men, but do not use your freedom as a cover-up for evil; live as servants of God. Show proper respect to everyone: Love the brotherhood of believers, fear God, honor the king. (1 Peter 2:13-17)

The Church Fathers who lived amidst persecution faced this same challenge. Justin Martyr (A.D. 100-165) wrote:

> Everywhere, we, more readily than all men, endeavor to pay to those appointed by you the taxes, both ordinary and extraordinary, as we have been taught by Jesus. We worship only God, but in other things we will gladly serve you, acknowledging you as kings and rulers of men, and praying that, with your kingly power, you may be found to possess also sound judgment.[9]

Athenagoras (in the second century) wrote:

> We deserve favor because we pray for your government, that you may, as is most equitable, receive the kingdom, son from father, and that your empire may receive increase and addition, until all men become subject to your sway.[10]

Tertullian (A.D. 160-240) wrote:

> We offer prayer for the safety of our princes to the eternal, the true, the living God, whose favour, beyond all other things, they must themselves desire.... Without ceasing, for all our emperors we offer prayer. We pray for life prolonged; for security to the empire; for protection for the imperial house, for brave armies, a faithful senate, a virtuous people, the world at rest.[11]

Finally, listen to this remarkable prayer from one of the Apostolic Fathers, Clement of Alexandria:

Thou, Master, hast given the power of sovereignty to them through thy excellent and inexpressible might, that we may know the glory and honour given to them by thee, and be subject to them, in nothing resisting thy will. And to them, Lord, grant health, peace, concord, firmness that they may administer the government which thou hast given them without offence. For thou, heavenly Master, king of eternity, hast given to the sons of men glory and honour and power over the things which are on the earth; do thou, O Lord, direct their counsels according to that which is "good and pleasing" before thee, that they may administer with piety in peace and gentleness the power given to them by thee, and may find mercy in thine eyes.[12]

Through Jesus Christ we can live out our duty to obey as described in the Word of God. We can also fulfill our duty to disobey when it is the will of God to do so.

When it became clear that the Nazis were pursuing their terrible racist policies, Pastor Martin Niemoller continued to preach the truth and as a result was thrown into prison. The prison chaplain upon visiting Niemoller asked somewhat foolishly, "What brings you here? Why are you in prison?" To which Niemoller replied angrily, "And, brother, why are you *not* in prison?"[13]

"Give to Caesar what is Caesar's, and to God what is God's" (Matthew 22:21). This is a divine calling.

Let no debt remain outstanding, except the continuing debt to love one another, for he who loves his fellow man has fulfilled the law. The commandments, "Do not commit adultery," "Do not murder," "Do not steal," "Do not covet," and whatever other commandment there may be, are summed up in this one rule: "Love your neighbor as yourself." Love does no harm to its neighbor. Therefore love is the fulfillment of the law. And do this, understanding the present time. The hour has come for you to wake up from your slumber, because our salvation is nearer now than when we first believed. The night is nearly over; the day is almost here. So let us put aside the deeds of darkness and put on the armor of light. Let us behave decently, as in the daytime, not in orgies and drunkenness, not in sexual immorality and debauchery, not in dissension and jealousy. Rather, clothe yourselves with the Lord Jesus Christ, and do not think about how to gratify the desires of the sinful nature. (13:8-14)

27

Loving on the Level

ROMANS 13:8-14

One of the most eloquent and personally moving quotations I have come across in homiletical literature is from the great nineteenth-century preacher Alexander Maclaren of Manchester. It is a description of what happened when Jesus' followers lived out his *new commandment* to love one another as he loved them (John 13:34, 35). Says Maclaren:

> When the words were spoken, the then-known civilized Western world was cleft by great, deep gulfs of separation, like the crevasses in a glacier, by the side of which our racial animosities and class differences are merely superficial cracks on the surface. Language, religion, national animosities, differences of sex, split the world up into alien fragments. A "stranger" and an "enemy" were expressed in one language, by the same word. The learned and the unlearned, the slave and his master, the barbarian and the Greek, the man and the woman, stood on opposite sides of the gulf, flinging hostility across.[1]

Such was the world when Christ gave his new commandment to love. But as years sped by and the flame of Christianity spread around the Mediterranean, the world witnessed something unheard of before this time.

> Barbarian, Scythian, bond and free, male and female, Jew and Greek, learned and ignorant, clasped hands and sat at one table, and felt them-

selves "all one in Christ Jesus." They were ready to break all other bonds, and to yield to the uniting forces that streamed out from His cross. There never had been anything like it. No wonder that the world began to babble about sorcery, and conspiracies, and complicity in unnameable vices. It was only that the disciples were obeying the "new commandment," and a new thing had come into the world — a community held together by love and not by geographical accidents or linguistic affinities, or the iron fetters of the conqueror.[2]

Christ's radical command worked a profound commitment to love among his followers, and the world could not believe it! The truly radical nature of this love was that the Master's commandment called them to love *as Christ loved them*. It was a sacrificial love, the kind of love that even reaches out to those who wish us harm (as Jesus had done to Judas just moments before he gave the command). The reason Jesus' words, along with Maclaren's quotation, mean so much to me is, first, because they are so challenging. Who, even among those in the Early Church, fully lived up to the commandment? Probably very few. Who today? Perhaps even fewer. Second, the command is so promising, if the Church would just put it to work. The promise is, "All men will know that you are my disciples . . ." — will know that we are truly his — if we obey the command to love one another. The implication is that many will turn to Christ as a result.

Romans 13:8-14 contains a similarly profound call to love our fellowman, to develop a deep horizontal love, to love on the level.

THE CALL TO ONGOING HORIZONTAL LOVE (vv. 8-10)

Paul says in verse 8, "Let no debt remain outstanding, except the continuing debt to love one another." On the one hand he encourages us to get out of debt — "Let no debt remain outstanding," while on the other hand he tells us we have an ongoing debt of love — "except the continuing debt to love one another." Origen wrote in the second century, "So Paul desires that our debt of love should remain and never cease to be owed, for it is expedient that we should both pay this debt and always owe it."[3] The Christian is always a love-debtor, no matter how much love he gives.

Every time we meet someone we ought to say to ourselves, "I need to show him or her the love of Christ. I have a great and wonderful debt to pay." If you have ever had a personal debt, be it ever so small, you know that the first thing that enters your mind when you see that person is that you "owe" them. We need to truly see ourselves as spiritual debtors. When we go to church, town, work, shopping, school — wherever we go, whoever we meet, we owe love. This is our debt — loving on the level.

Paul concludes verse 8 with, "for he who loves his fellow man has fulfilled the law." How does loving one's neighbor fulfill the Law? The Ten Commandments contain two divisions, sometimes called the two tablets. The first division gives us vertical, Godward commands such as, "You shall have no other gods before me" (Exodus 20:3). The second division contains horizontal commands which pertain to human relationships. Each of the divisions can be summed up with a single comprehensive commandment, just as Christ explained in Matthew 22:37-40 when he was asked which is the great commandment:

> "'Love the Lord your God with all your heart and with all your soul and with all your mind.' This is the first and greatest commandment. And the second is like it: 'Love your neighbor as yourself.' All the Law and the Prophets hang on these two commandments." (cf. Deuteronomy 6:4, 5 and Leviticus 19:18)

Keep both the vertical and the horizontal commandments and you will keep the whole Law! Here in his letter to the Romans, Paul is assuming that his readers have a vertical love for God, but do they have a horizontal love for others? If so, they are fulfilling God's Law.

When we love our neighbors we will refrain from breaking the horizontal-relational commands. Paul gives some examples in verses 9, 10:

> The commandments, "Do not commit adultery," "Do not murder," "Do not steal," "Do not covet" and whatever other commandment there may be, are summed up in this one rule: "Love your neighbor as yourself." Love does no harm to its neighbor. Therefore love is the fulfillment of the law.

When you love your neighbor you will refrain from adultery. When you love your neighbor you will regard his life as inviolable. When you love your neighbor you will respect his ownership of property. There is a sense in which love for our neighbor is a more obvious measure of where we stand with God than our love for God himself. We can easily convince others that we love God, but it is far more difficult to feign love for our neighbors. They are not fooled as easily on that score, and neither are we. Thus our love for others provides a helpful measure of our spiritual state.

We live in a cold, uncaring world. The story of Mary Hannigan (told in the November 23, 1981 edition of the *Chicago Tribune*) is a case in point. The article was entitled "He Started Cutting . . . Nobody Stopped." Mary was assaulted on Chicago's Kennedy Expressway when a man purposely rammed her, then attacked her with a knife in her own car when she stopped to check the damage. As she struggled for her life, no one stopped to help. When she managed to move her car forward so it blocked an exit ramp, one car even drove around her without stopping — while she was being brutally attacked! Fortunately her assailant fell from the car when she was able to push on the accelerator again, and she escaped. In the hospital, after a plastic surgeon had worked six hours on her face, leaving some 100 stitches, her husband said, "That's what I can't believe. . . . It's as if people went out of the way not to help her." Sgt. James Marble commented, "The only ones who would have helped her would have been police officers driving by. . . . People just don't help other people, unfortunately."

Sgt. Marble's sad observation is generally true, though there are many notable exceptions. But the point I wish to make from this extreme story is this: how irresistible Christianity would be in everyday, uneventful life if Christians truly loved their "neighbors" ("others of a different kind," as the Greek literally says) as themselves. If we were to consistently see ourselves as love-debtors, just think how the gospel would spread! We would be living out the Law, and the authenticity of our inner spirits would sound wide the ring of truth to a needy world.

THE URGENT CALL TO
ONGOING HORIZONTAL LOVE (vv. 11, 12a)

Paul does not view this call to horizontal love as a casual matter. He sees it as having utmost urgency.

> And do this, understanding the present time. The hour has come for you to wake up from your slumber, because our salvation is nearer now than when we first believed. The night is nearly over; the day is almost here. (vv. 11, 12a)

Paul's sense of urgency is stressed by the word "time" in his opening phrase: "And do this, understanding the present *time*." Either of two Greek words could have been used. *Chronos* would emphasize chronological, calender time. *Kairos* emphasizes quality or kind of time. Paul uses *kairos*. "And this do, knowing the *kind* of time it is. . . ." What kind of time is it? The New Testament calls it "the last days" (Acts 2:17; 2

Timothy 3:1; Hebrews 1:2; 1 John 2:18) — not in the chronological sense but qualitatively. These "last days" began with Christ and could culminate in "*the day*" (v. 12a) of his return at any moment, but that is not the point here. Paul was telling his hearers, and us, that we are living in "the last days." C. E. B. Cranfield explains:

> . . . this present age, which Paul refers to as "the night," could never have a higher status than that of something "far spent." Henceforward "the day" would always be imminent, until it should finally break.

This brings an urgency to this matter of loving on the level. Believers are to wake up from spiritual lethargy and love their neighbors while they have opportunity to do so.

We ought to be like the little boy whose family clock malfunctioned and struck fifteen times, so that he rushed wide-eyed to his mother crying, "Mommy, it's later than it's ever been before!" What sanctifying logic! We should also keep in mind that if Christ does not return in our time, he will certainly come individually for us in death. Each ache, each pain, each gray hair, each new wrinkle, each funeral is a reminder that it is later than it has ever been before. It is time to love our neighbors as ourselves.

THE SPECIFICS OF THE CALL
TO HORIZONTAL LOVE (*vv. 12b-14*)

Paul next tells us there is something we must put off and something we must put on if we are going to succeed at loving on the level: "So let us put aside the deeds of darkness and put on the armor of light" (v. 12b). Paul is specific about "the deeds of darkness" we are to discard:

> Let us behave decently, as in the daytime, not in orgies and drunkenness, not in sexual immorality and debauchery, not in dissension and jealousy. (v. 13)

First, there must be no "orgies and drunkenness." These words used together picture drunken individuals having a so-called "good time" and disturbing the citizens of the town. The Christian who wants to love must set aside such pursuit of harmful pleasures.

Second, there is to be no "sexual immorality and debauchery." "Sexual immorality" is a Greek word which can simply be translated, "bed," and the word rendered "debauchery" is one of the ugliest words in the Greek language, describing one who is not only given to immorality, but is incapable of feeling shame. The Christian who wants to love must understand that one cannot both love people and live for sex.

The third specific is to abstain from "dissension and jealousy." This phrase describes someone who cannot stand being surpassed and grudges others their success and position. Tragically many believers act as if it is their holy duty to keep others in their place. Such behavior can never exist in a heart which truly loves a neighbor.

There is much that must go if we are to love on the level. May none of us be so naive as to think any of this is irrelevant. These evils are the precise reason there is too little love in the Church and in the world.

However, there is a gloriously positive side to this, given in verse 14: "Rather, clothe yourselves with the Lord Jesus Christ, and do not think about how to gratify the desires of the sinful nature." It is true that if we are Christians we have already put on the Lord Jesus Christ. Galatians 3:27 says, "for all of you who were baptized into Christ have been clothed with Christ." But our text here in Romans has reference to a practical day-to-day, repeated putting on of Christ. We are to embrace him again and again and again. Ray Stedman gives this illustration:

> When I get up in the morning I put on my clothes, intending them to be part of me all day, to go where I go and do what I do. They cover me and make me presentable to others. That is the purpose of clothes. In the same way, the apostle is saying to us, "Put on Jesus Christ when you get up in the morning. Make him a part of your life that day. Intend that he go with you everywhere you go, and that he act through you in everything you do. Call upon his resources. Live your life IN CHRIST."[4]

Paul emphasizes that it is "the *Lord* Jesus Christ" that we put on. We bow to his Lordship. He is King of all or he is not King at all. This is where we gain the capacity to love. Loving on the level comes from *the negative* — putting off the deeds of darkness, and *the positive* — putting on Jesus Christ day by day. We must constantly do this.

One other point here: our ability to love vertically and on the level comes from God's love to us. First John 4:19 says, "We love because he first loved us." His *agape* love reaches down to us in Christ, it is poured out in our hearts by the Holy Spirit (5:5), and we return it back to God and to those around us. *His great love is the source and motivation of our love.*

This principle was dramatically illustrated on the human level in the life of Kathryn Lawes.

When Louis Lawes became warden of Sing Sing Prison in 1920, the inmates existed in wretched conditions. This led him to introduce humanitarian reforms. He gave much of the credit to his wife, Kathryn, however, who always treated the prisoners as human beings. She would often take her three children and sit with the gangsters, the murderers, and the racketeers while they played basketball and baseball. Then in 1937, Kathryn was killed in a car accident. The next day her body lay in a casket in a house about a quarter of a mile from the institution. When the acting warden found hundreds of prisoners crowded around the main entrance, he knew what they wanted. Opening the gate, he said, "Men, I'm going to trust you. You can go to the house." No count was taken; no guards posted. Yet not one man was missing that night. Love for one who had loved them made them dependable.[5]

Of course this should be infinitely more true in relation to God's love for and through us. God's sacrifice for us, his love lavished upon us, ought to make us completely dependable in our showing love to the world.

How wonderful it would be if the majority of the Church began to do this. Surely such love would be so amazing that it would engulf whole continents. A second-century critic of Christianity said:

> Assuredly this confederacy should be rooted out and execrated for they know one another by secret marks and signs and they love one another almost before they know one another. Promiscuously they call one another brother and sister.

May God help us to love like that.

- Let us cultivate a sense of debt. Just as when we owe someone money and our debt is the first thing we think of when we see him, so may it be with our debt of love.
- Let us enlarge our definition of neighbor as, "My neighbor is not necessarily someone like me. It is any person God has put in my way whom I can help."
- Let us cultivate a sense of the time — "It is later than it has ever been before."
- Let us consciously put off the deeds of darkness (we individually know what these are) and put on Jesus — every day!

Accept him whose faith is weak, without passing judgment on disputable matters. One man's faith allows him to eat everything, but another man, whose faith is weak, eats only vegetables. The man who eats everything must not look down on him who does not, and the man who does not eat everything must not condemn the man who does, for God has accepted him. Who are you to judge someone else's servant? To his own master he stands or falls. And he will stand, for the Lord is able to make him stand. One man considers one day more sacred than another; another man considers every day alike. Each one should be fully convinced in his own mind. He who regards one day as special, does so to the Lord. He who eats meat, eats to the Lord, for he gives thanks to God; and he who abstains, does so to the Lord and gives thanks to God. For none of us lives to himself alone and none of us dies to himself alone. If we live, we live to the Lord; and if we die, we die to the Lord. So, whether we live or die, we belong to the Lord. For this very reason, Christ died and returned to life so that he might be the Lord of both the dead and the living. You, then, why do you judge your brother? Or why do you look down on your brother? For we will all stand before God's judgment seat. It is written: "'As surely as I live,' says the Lord, 'Every knee will bow before me; every tongue will confess to God.'" So then, each of us will give an account of himself to God. (14:1-12)

28

Unity and Diversity (I)

ROMANS 14:1-12

There is no doubt about the importance which God's Word places on the unity of his people. David wrote in Psalm 133:

How good and pleasant it is
    when brothers live together in unity!
It is like precious oil poured on the head,
    running down on the beard,
running down on Aaron's beard,
    down upon the collar of his robes.
It is as if the dew of Hermon
    were falling on Mount Zion.
For there the Lord bestows his blessing,
    even life forevermore.

Jesus, in his High Priestly prayer, prayed for unity not only for his disciples, but for us:

"My prayer is not for them alone. I pray also for those who will believe in me through their message, that all of them may be one, Father, just as you are in me and I am in you. May they also be in us so that the world may believe that you have sent me." (John 17:20, 21)

The propagation of the gospel of Christ is bound up for better or for worse with the degree of unity we display to the world. Our Christian unity is of the utmost importance.

At the same time diversity is characteristic of the Christian community. In fact, it is one of its principal glories. As Paul so beautifully explains in 1 Corinthians 12:

> If the whole body were an eye, where would the sense of hearing be?
> If the whole body were an ear, where would the sense of smell be?
> But in fact God has arranged the parts in the body, every one of them, just as he wanted them to be. (vv. 17, 18)

These two great realities — unity and diversity — are to coexist in the Body of Christ. Normally diversity does not make for unity. Because of our human tendency to judge those who do not conform to our customs or standards, the unity of Christ's Church is often imperiled by diversity, as church history repeatedly records.

This was precisely the situation at cosmopolitan Rome in Paul's day. Christ's love had brought together a remarkably heterogeneous group of Jewish and Gentile Christians. Their backgrounds had very little in common. The spiritually bankrupt paganism of the Gentiles required very little of them. On the other hand, the Roman Jews often outdid the Jerusalem Jews in their Jewishness. Now these Jews were Christians. As Cranfield says, they were not like the heretical Judaizers in Galatia who thought they could put God under obligation by obeying the Law — they knew it was all by grace.[1] However, though they understood this, they did not entirely escape the thought that observing the Law was pleasing to Christ. They felt this was an appropriate response to God's grace. Their position was understandable, but not Biblical.

Some had become vegetarians. Though the Old Testament Law did not command vegetarianism, these Jewish Christians came to the conclusion that a vegetarian diet was the safest because it was so difficult to be sure the meat was *kosher* in Rome. So they formed an anti-meat-eating, Law-observing segment in the Church of Rome. Still, the great majority in the church were meat-eaters.

As Paul writes to Rome, these two parties have been given labels. The Law-observing Jewish Christians are called "weak," and the liberated Gentile Christians are called "strong." Naturally the tension between the two groups was very intense at times.

Imagine a Gentile brother just returning from the corner store with an armload of meat, and he meets Boaz, a Jewish brother.

Boaz cheerfully greets him. "Grace and peace, friend! What have you got there?"

"Oh, we're having a barbecue tonight, so I've got some meat. Great prices — New York strip eleven cents a pound, T-bone nine cents, and pork is a steal! Why don't you bring the wife and kids and join us?"

Boaz assumes a grieved expression and leaves without speaking. The Gentile brother is taken aback, and then he realizes what is going on. He's angry at being judged!

The "easy" solution to this problem would have been to form two churches: "The Church of the Carnivores" (perhaps not a bad name for some churches I have heard of!) and "The First Church of the Vegetarians." Paul, fortunately, was committed to the nobler, though far more difficult, solution. In the first twelve verses of Romans 14, Paul tells us *what we need to know if we are to maintain unity amidst the diversity of the Church.*

There is no doubt about the relevance of this theme. Judging one another is one of the favorite indoor sports of Christians today. We are great grocery list makers — *for others!* Leslie Flynn writes in his book *Great Church Fights*:

> Wide disagreements exist today in our churches over certain practices. A Christian from the South may be repelled by a swimming party for both men and women, then offend his Northern brother by lighting up a cigarette. At an international conclave for missionaries, a woman from the Orient could not wear sandals with a clear conscience. A Christian from western Canada thought it worldly for a Christian acquaintance to wear a wedding ring, and a woman from Europe thought it almost immoral for a wife not to wear a ring that signaled her status. A man from Denmark was pained to even watch British Bible school students play football, while the British students shrank from his pipe smoking.[2]

Churches have been ripped apart by even smaller disagreements over which factions have polarized, the more broad-minded becoming openly contemptuous of their narrow brothers, and others becoming hardened in their criticism of their loose brethren.

> *Believe as I believe,*
> *No more, no less;*
> *That I am right,*
> *And no one else, confess;*

Feel as I feel,
  Think only as I think;
Eat what I eat,
  And drink but what I drink;
Look as I look,
  Do always as I do;
Then, and only then,
  Will I fellowship with you.

As Christians this should not be our attitude.

What do we need to know in order to maintain unity amidst the Church's diversity?

GENUINE ACCEPTANCE OF ONE ANOTHER IS THE ONLY OPTION (vv. 1-3)

Paul is explicit in verse 1: "Accept him whose faith is weak, without passing judgment on disputable matters." The one "whose faith is weak" is not weak in basic Christian faith, but is weak in assurance that his faith permits him to do certain things, such as eating meat. These "weak" are to be wholeheartedly accepted — they are not to be accepted with the ulterior motive of straightening them out. There is to be no phony condescension on the part of the "strong," no hidden agenda, but rather simple, unqualified acceptance.

Moreover, the acceptance is to be mutual on the part of both the strong and the weak.

> One man's faith allows him to eat everything, but another man, whose faith is weak, eats only vegetables. The man who eats everything must not look down on him who does not, and the man who does not eat everything must not condemn the man who does, for God has accepted him. (vv. 2, 3)

This call to mutual acceptance lays bare the psychology behind the rejection of the strong or the weak. The strong, Paul says, "look down on" those who do not eat, or as A. T. Robertson explains, *treats as nothing*[3] those who do not eat. The idea here is disdain. The human tendency is always to despise whatever or whoever we consider weak. The boy who can run faster, jump higher, or lift more despises the one who cannot. To despise the Christian who has a narrower morality as a mental midget or a cultural dinosaur — such an attitude is not Christian.

I experienced this in my own life on one occasion when I walked into a dining room for a meal and sat with a whole tableful of Russian brothers and sisters from the Soviet Union. We communicated as well as possible despite the language barrier, and when the meal was over a translator joined us. One of the brothers at the far end of the table asked me what I thought of playing cards. I responded that the Bible did not have anything to say about that, and he replied that some missionaries had been playing Pit the night before. I started to answer, but this brother launched into a ten-minute dialogue, and I could not get a word in edgewise. As I sat there, I felt judged and responded in my own sinful mind that he must be a "mental midget." I looked down on him, contrary to Paul's admonition.

On the other hand, because the weak are inclined toward judgmentalism, they are told not to "condemn" meat-eaters. The weak tend to be censorious, to pigeon-hole other believers according to their checklists. "That man cannot be a good Christian because he _____!"

How Paul's insights cut us to the quick. Too often you and I are guilty of both these errors. Whether we are "weak" or "strong" believers, there is to be mutual, wholehearted acceptance of one another.

But how are we to apply this to ourselves? After all, meat-eating is not an issue in the church today. No, but I can think of at least eleven issues on which Christians are divided today. Moreover, none of these items are listed as taboo or sinful in Scripture (although the Scriptures give guidelines in relation to each item). These issues are:

(1) *Theater.* Some Christians think they should never patronize a commercial theater. Others think they can, but that they should be selective, just as they are with the literature they read.

(2) *Cosmetics.* This is not the issue it used to be, but it is controversial in certain parts of the world.

(3) *Alcohol.* The e of alcohol is a major issue among American Christians today. Ironically, while there is growing medical evidence of its harmful physical and social effects, more Christians are exercising their freedom to partake. Hence rising tension.

(4) *Tobacco.* Traditionally, the Mason and Dixon Line has been the dividing line for the use and non-use of tobacco among many evangelical Christians.

(5) *Card playing.* Because of its association with gambling, Christians are ambivalent about the use of traditional cards. The controversy can also include similar games, as was mentioned above.

(6) *Dancing.* For some Christians this is a litmus test, especially among youth.

(7) *Fashion.*Trendiness is viewed by some Christians as worldliness. Withering judgments are sometimes made both ways on the basis of clothing and hair style.

(8) *Bible translation used.* In some Christian circles your translation can be a quick ticket for acceptance or rejection.

(9) *Sports.* I know of young Christians who consider competitive sports sinful and ego-exalting.

(10) *Music.* Today a heated controversy goes on regarding appropriate Christian music.

(11) *Material wealth.* This tension is manifested in such forms as: "Stop me if I'm wrong, George, but haven't you — uh, been spending a lot of money on a car?" "Nope." "No? You don't think the money could be better used, say, in the leprosy fund?"[4]

According to Romans 14, wherever you stand on these issues, you must accept your Christian brother and sister who differs. If you are an abstainer, you must not judge the participator. If you are a participator, you must not disdain the abstainer. This call to acceptance comes to us as a command of God. If we are to obey him, we have no choice.

Is this a call to become a bunch of wishy-washy Charlie Browns? Not at all! We are not talking about basic doctrines such as sin, the Deity of Christ, salvation by faith, or clear Scriptural commandments against adultery or lying. We are talking about non-essentials.

We are all called to a profound acceptance of one another. This is not optional. Verses 5, 6 give us the second element of understanding.

THE ACCEPTANCE OF NON-ESSENTIALS (vv. 5, 6)

Again Paul is very clear:

> One man considers one day more sacred than another; another man considers every day alike. Each one should be fully convinced in his own mind. He who regards one day as special, does so to the Lord. He who eats meat, eats to the Lord, for he gives thanks to God; and he who abstains, does so to the Lord and gives thanks to God. (vv. 5, 6)

This controversy over days probably involved Sabbath observance. The Christian Jews' conscience demanded that they observe it. The Christian Gentiles' conscience argued that every day is equally devoted to the service of God. Paul's advice to both is simply, "Each one should be fully convinced in his own mind." Each believer is to use his or her powers of reasoning which have at least begun to be renewed by the gospel under the authority of God's Word and act accordingly. The same is to be true of eating or abstaining from meat. The evidence that both the "weak" and the "strong" have right hearts is that they both give "thanks" to God. That is, both do what they do with the intention of serving the Lord.

Paul's indisputable point here is: people with opposing viewpoints on non-essentials can both be perfectly right with God. We need to take this to heart. Two of the most famous Christians in the Victorian Era in England were Charles Spurgeon and Joseph Parker, both mighty preachers of the gospel. Early in their ministries they fellowshiped and even exchanged pulpits. Then they had a disagreement, and the reports got into the newspapers. Spurgeon accused Parker of being unspiritual because he attended the theater. Interestingly enough, Spurgeon smoked cigars, a practice many believers would condemn. In fact, on one occasion someone asked Spurgeon about his cigars, and he said he did not smoke to excess. When asked what he meant by excess, he waggishly answered, "No more than two at a time."[5] Who was right? Perhaps neither, perhaps both! Better yet would be to realize that the two could disagree and both be in the will of God.

There is a reverse truth implicit here also, which is: If the Lord convicts you that something is wrong in your life, you had better not do it, even if other Christians are doing it!

THE ACCEPTANCE OF THE LORDSHIP OF CHRIST (vv. 7-12)

> For none of us lives to himself alone and none of us dies to himself alone. If we live, we live to the Lord; and if we die, we die to the Lord. So, whether we live or die, we belong to the Lord. (vv. 7, 8)

The Lordship of Christ is the foundational truth for the unity of the Church amidst diversity of opinion.

Verses 10-12 emphasize that we will all answer to him for our lives.

> You, then, why do you judge your brother? Or why do you look down on your brother? For we will all stand before God's judgment seat. It is written: "'As surely as I live,'" says the Lord, "'Every knee will bow before me; every tongue will confess to God.'" So then, each of us will give an account of himself to God.

Paul twice uses the term "brother" to emphasize the unity that "weak" and "strong" Christians have. He is saying in effect, "Stop trying to be God to one another. You 'weak,' why do you pass judgment on your brother? You 'strong,' why do you look down with contempt on your brother? Remember, all of us are going to stand before the *Bema*, the judgment-seat of Christ. There your works as believers will be judged. There God will judge your motives." As Paul wrote in 2 Corinthians 5:10, "For we must all appear before the judgment seat of Christ, that each one may receive what is due him for the things done while in the body, whether good or bad." And in 1 Corinthians 3:13-15 he says:

> . . . his work will be shown for what it is, because the Day will bring it to light. It will be revealed with fire, and the fire will test the quality of each man's work. If what he has built survives, he will receive his reward. If it is burned up, he will suffer loss; he himself will be saved, but only as one escaping through the flames.

What an inducement not to judge our brothers and sisters in things on which the Bible does not directly speak! "So then, each of us will give an account of himself [*not others*] to God" (v. 12). One thing we will certainly have to answer for will be our judgmental attitude. Is it not wonderful that final judgment is up to God, and his evaluation will be perfect? Our reward will be exactly what we deserve, as will our brother's and sister's.

This whole section is part of an extended commentary on the command of Jesus to love one another, and this has been the subject since Paul began the practical section of this letter. In chapter 12 we saw that the nature of love is to serve. In chapter 13 we discovered that love must be submissive. Now in chapter 14 we are learning that love must be patient and tolerant of other people's views.

Rupertus Meldenius understood this well and gave a motto to his followers (also the motto for the church which I serve): "In essentials, unity; in non-essentials, liberty; in all things, charity."[6]

There is room in Christ's Church for you whether you wear wingtips or sandals, whether you walk to church or ride in a Rolls, whether you powder your nose or not, whether you dance or not, whether you drink or refrain, whether you watch TV or abstain, whether you use *my* translation or not.

The pastor under whom I served for almost ten years liked to tell about a play he saw which portrayed an intense conflict between a father and a son. The point came when the father and son agreed to part. In the middle of the night the son had trouble sleeping, so he went down to the kitchen to fix himself a sandwich, and there was his father, who couldn't sleep either.

After they fixed their sandwiches they began to reminisce about the past — about the years in Little League, about their great hunting expeditions, about their swimming together, about their fishing trips.

As some needed healing was taking place, the son said, "Dad, do you remember the time we were out on the lake in that green boat?" His father said, "The boat was blue, son." The son said, "No, it was green." The father said, "You are mistaken — it was blue." "Green." "Blue." "Green." "Blue." And his son departed, never to return.

Some things just don't matter. May we allow God to give us the wisdom to see what is essential and what is not.

Therefore let us stop passing judgment on one another. Instead, make up your mind not to put any stumbling block or obstacle in your brother's way. As one who is in the Lord Jesus, I am fully convinced that no food is unclean in itself. But if anyone regards something as unclean, then for him it is unclean. If your brother is distressed because of what you eat, you are no longer acting in love. Do not by your eating destroy your brother for whom Christ died. Do not allow what you consider good to be spoken of as evil. For the kingdom of God is not a matter of eating and drinking, but of righteousness, peace and joy in the Holy Spirit, because anyone who serves Christ in this way is pleasing to God and approved by men. Let us therefore make every effort to do what leads to peace and to mutual edification. Do not destroy the work of God for the sake of food. All food is clean, but it is wrong for a man to eat anything that causes someone else to stumble. It is better not to eat meat or drink wine or to do anything else that will cause your brother to fall. So whatever you believe about these things keep between yourself and God. Blessed is the man who does not condemn himself by what he approves. But the man who has doubts is condemned if he eats, because his eating is not from faith; and everything that does not come from faith is sin. (14:13-23)

29

Unity and Diversity (II)

ROMANS 14:13-23

We have seen that the God-given diversity in the Body of Christ can conflict with our Lord's high call to unity. Diversity and unity are in natural antithesis because we humans tend to criticize and censor those who do things differently from us. Judging one another according to our little lists is one of the favorite sports of Christians today.

> *Look as I look,*
>   *Do always as I do . . .*
> *Then, and only then,*
>   *I'll fellowship with you.*

In answer to this problem, Romans 14 tells us three things we need to know if we are to maintain unity amidst diversity. First, genuine acceptance of one another is the only option available to believers. The tendency of the liberated Christian to look down on his less broad-minded brother and the tendency of that brother to judge his less restricted brother must be put away. Second, individual Christians can disagree over customs and social habits and both be perfectly right with God. Third, we must submit to the Lordship of Christ and refrain from judging others because we will all stand before the judgment-seat of Christ and give account of ourselves to him. These three elements are essential if we are to maintain Christian unity amidst our amazing diversity.

In this study we will see what we need to *do* in order to experience unity in diversity. Perhaps we have understood and accepted the logic of

Paul's argument against passing judgment. However, the extremely delicate conscience of the "weak" brother remains. What are we to do?

DETERMINE NOT TO BE A
SOURCE OF STUMBLING (vv. 13-15)

> Therefore let us stop passing judgment on one another. Instead, make up your mind not to put any stumbling block or obstacle in your brother's way. (v. 13)

The apostle's choice of words here calls for a complete determination not to be an obstruction because the word for "stumbling block" means something carelessly left about over which someone stumbles, whereas "obstacle" means something deliberately left to ensnare another. We must determine not to be a witting or unwitting cause of a weaker brother's stumbling as we exercise our Christian freedom. Our Christian lives must be salted with a refusal to do anything that will harm the spiritual life of weaker brothers.

Paul gives us the rationale behind this call to careful living in verse 14:

> As one who is in the Lord Jesus, I am fully convinced that no food is unclean in itself. But if anyone regards something as unclean, then for him it is unclean.

In averring that "no food is unclean in itself," the apostle was agreeing with Jesus' statement in Mark 7:14-19 that nothing that man eats defiles him. Inanimate things such as food and drink are morally neutral. Things have no moral qualities. However, "if anyone regards something as unclean, then for him it is unclean." So if a new Jewish believer feels (however wrongly) that certain meats are unclean and should not be eaten, they are truly unclean to him, and he would sin by partaking and would be in danger of moral shipwreck.

Paul views any behavior that distresses another's conscience as unconscionable: "If your brother is distressed because of what you eat," he says, "you are no longer acting in love. Do not by your eating destroy your brother for whom Christ died" (v. 15).

Some commentators suggest "your eating" alludes to one's petty insistence upon having meat regardless of the consequences to others. The idea is flaunting or deliberately shocking the weaker brother with a display of Christian freedom. Paul is horrified at the thought.

Rather, the key to exercising Christian freedom in all matters is "acting in love" (v. 15). Christian liberty does not mean flaunting your freedom and doing as you please. That would be license!

Exercising Christian liberty is very much like walking a tightrope. As you walk the rope with balancing pole in hand, at one end of the pole is *love for others* and at the other is *Christian liberty*. When these are in balance, your walk is as it should be. Martin Luther had it right when he began his treatise "On the Freedom of a Christian Man" by saying, "A Christian man is a most free lord of all, subject to none. A Christian man is a most dutiful servant of all, subject to all."[1] We are all immensely free in Christ. Our only bondage is the bond of love to our fellow believers.

It is our Christian duty, when exercising our freedom, not only to think about how our actions affect us but others. We must always remember that it is not our display of Christian freedom that commends our faith to the world, but our demonstration of *agape* love. Jesus said, "All men will know that you are my disciples if you love one another" (John 13:35). The strong, mature Christian voluntarily limits his freedom out of love for his weaker brothers and sisters.

How far should one go in applying this? If we fully apply what Paul says, will not our conduct be controlled by the narrowest Christian in the Church? It is indeed possible for disordered personalities to dominate the Church. I remember once having a self-consciously pious Christian grimly say to me that the Scripture nowhere records that Jesus smiled or laughed, and he wanted me to know that godly people like himself followed suit. The absurdity of this argument from silence is seen if you make a list of other things the Scriptures never mention Jesus doing! We are not called to an uncritical, indiscriminate limitation of our freedom.

In 1928 Dr. Donald Grey Barnhouse was speaking at a conference in Montrose, Pennsylvania where about 200 young people were present. One day two women came to him in horror because some girls were not wearing stockings! These women wanted him to rebuke the others. Barnhouse's reply is classic. As he tells it:

> Looking them straight in the eye, I said, "The Virgin Mary never wore stockings." They gasped and said, "She didn't?" I answered, "In Mary's time, stockings were unknown. So far as we know, they were first worn by prostitutes in Italy in the 15th century, when the Renaissance began. Later, a lady of the nobility wore stockings at a court ball, greatly to the scandal of many people. Before long, however, everyone in the upper classes was wearing stockings. . . ."
> These ladies, who were holdovers from the Victorian epoch, had no

more to say. I did not rebuke the girls for not wearing stockings. A year or two afterward, most girls in the United States were going without stockings in summer, and nobody thought anything about it. Nor do I believe that this led toward disintegration of moral standards in the United States. Times were changing, and the step away from Victorian legalism was all for the better.[2]

Voluntary limiting of our freedom is not meant to subject us to the prejudices of Christians who are well established in the faith but persistent in sub-Biblical legalism.

In Rome the believers were relatively young in the faith, and their scrupulous consciences had an ostensible Biblical base. We must remember to wisely apply Christian self-restraint and never to unknowingly or knowingly, by our exercise of liberty, cause another Christian to go against his conscience.

LIVE AS CITIZENS OF THE KINGDOM OF GOD (vv. 16-18)

Not only ought we to determine not to be stumbling blocks, we should also live as citizens of the Kingdom of God. Here Paul, with finely tuned pastoral insight, lifts the entire discussion to a higher level than mere eating and drinking.

> Do not allow what you consider good to be spoken of as evil. For the kingdom of God is not a matter of eating and drinking, but of righteousness, peace and joy in the Holy Spirit. . . . (vv. 16, 17)

We are prone to think that the Kingdom of God primarily involves what a person does or does not eat or drink, or what he wears, or what he does or does not do on the Lord's day, or how he combs his hair or does not. This is how the Pharisees lived, making a big deal of externals. But the Kingdom of God is not mainly a matter of *externals* but of *eternals* — "righteousness, peace and joy in the Holy Spirit." Paul's words and their inspired arrangement are supremely beautiful and truly spectacular.

The primary eternal element of God's Kingdom is "righteousness." The experience of God's righteousness in our lives produces an infinite longing for holiness, a driving desire to know him better, an intense thirsting in the inner parts. David's longing is expressed in Psalm 42:1, 2a:

> As the deer pants for streams of water, so my soul pants for you, O God. My soul thirsts for God, for the living God.

270

Jesus enjoined the pursuit of righteousness as the recommended pursuit for all humanity in Matthew 5:6 — "Blessed are those who hunger and thirst for righteousness, for they will be filled."

Properly following the eternal element of righteousness is "peace," that profound inner satisfaction which only God's presence can give. Peace with God is the secret of peace with one another. Kingdom peace is an inner unflappability which remains undisturbed by minor irritations, a quiet assurance that God is at work.

Lastly, there is the eternal element of "joy in the Holy Spirit." This joy is the outward mark of Christ's presence. Once when my wife and I were visiting London, we took a walk with a friend after dinner past St James Place, and he remarked that the Queen Mother was at home because her banner was flying. When joy flies as the flag over our lives, the world knows the King of Heaven is in residence in our hearts.

The Kingdom of God consists not of externals but of eternals. How wonderful it would be if we would concentrate on these things. How easy it is then to forego some external freedom for the sake of another believer.

Paul concludes this thought in verse 18: ". . . because anyone who serves Christ in this way is pleasing to God and approved by men." We are then acceptable to God who sees our hearts and approved by men who see our actions. The overall principle here is this: whether we be "weak" (limited in freedom) or "strong" (more liberated), we make a great mistake if we focus on externals. The weak shrivels his Christianity by seeing the externals as a road to greater righteousness. The strong trivializes his faith by insisting on his rights to the externals. If we flaunt our freedom, we are far less emancipated than we imagine.

The Kingdom of God is not operative in your life if your rights are so important to you that you are willing to separate from a brother who does not agree with you. The fact is, the man who feels he must demonstrate his emancipation on every possible occasion is a slave in spite of his apparent freedom, for the need to prove his liberty has become a tyranny. Whether we are strong or weak, we are to live as citizens of the Kingdom of God, focusing not on the externals, but on the elements of eternity — "righteousness, peace and joy in the Holy Spirit."

PURSUE THAT WHICH BRINGS
MUTUAL BENEFIT (vv. 19, 20)

Paul now reiterates much of what has been already said, but also introduces the idea that we are to pursue the benefit of others in the exercise of our Christian liberty:

Let us therefore make every effort to do what leads to peace and to
mutual edification. Do not destroy the work of God for the sake of
food. All food is clean, but it is wrong for a man to eat anything that
causes someone else to stumble. (vv. 19, 20)

In the exercise of our freedom, we must always ask ourselves if
what we are doing is building up others, especially those younger and less
experienced in the faith. If we cannot answer in the affirmative, we must
refrain. Paul concludes in verse 21, "It is better not to eat meat or drink
wine or to do anything else that will cause your brother to fall." This is a
fine summary statement, and even finer if we translate the word "good"
in its root sense of "beautiful": "It is *beautiful* not to eat meat or drink
wine or to do anything else that will cause your brother to fall."

Such behavior or thought is beautiful because it shows there is love
among the brethren. It is beautiful because arrogance is gone. It is beautiful because it is unselfish. It is beautiful because it means one has a
finely tuned sense of spiritual proportion, recognizing secondary issues
for what they are. It is especially beautiful because it puts others first.

During the war when vessels had to be convoyed across the Atlantic
because of the U-boats, all ships had to proceed at the speed of the slow-
est. This is something of what Paul has in mind here. The strong brother
could stride ahead, but his love will not permit it. The shepherd must pace
the flock to accommodate the weakest lamb. The Christian must regulate
his freedom to take into account the feeble conscience of a weaker
brother or sister.[3] We must actively pursue those things that make for
peace and mutual building up of one another. This is never easy, but it is
the way of love.

MAKE SURE ALL ACTIONS ARE DONE WITH A CLEAR CONSCIENCE (vv. 22, 23)

What else must we do to insure unity? Paul gives advice to the strong
regarding the use of his conscience in verse 22 and advice to the weak in
respect to his conscience in verse 23. First, *the advice to the strong*:

So whatever you believe about these things keep between yourself
and God. Blessed is the man who does not condemn himself by what
he approves. (v. 22)

Paul is saying, What you believe about neutral things is between you and
God. Keep it that way. Moreover, you are a happy (blessed) person if in

272

exercising your liberty you do not condemn yourself by harming another. You are blessed if your exercise of freedom is free from doubt. You are blessed if no one is being scandalized and led toward sin by you. You are blessed because you feel God's pleasure.

Charles Spurgeon, at the height of his fame, was one day walking down the street and saw a sign which read, "We sell the cigar that Charles Spurgeon smokes," whereupon Spurgeon gave up the habit. He came to see that what was for him a freedom might cause others to stumble. "Blessed is the man who does not condemn himself by what he approves."

Secondly, Paul gives *advice to the weak*:

> But the man who has doubts is condemned if he eats, because his eating is not from faith; and everything that does not come from faith is sin. (v. 23)

C. E. B. Cranfield, the peerless Romans commentator, gives the clearest explanation I know of:

> Paul has advice for the man who is weak in the faith, the man with the scrupulous conscience. It may be that this may disobey or silence his scruples. He may sometimes do something because everyone else is doing it. He may do it because he does not wish to stand in a minority of one. He may do it because he does not wish to be different. He may do it because he does not wish to court ridicule or unpopularity. Paul's answer is that if, for any of these reasons, a man defies his conscience he is guilty of sin. If a man in his heart of hearts believes a thing to be wrong, if he cannot rid himself of the ineradicable feeling that it is forbidden, then, if he does it, for him it is sin. A neutral thing only becomes a right thing when it is done out of faith, out of the real, reasoned conviction that it is the right thing to do. The only motive for doing anything is that a man believes it to be right. When a thing is done out of social convention, out of fear of unpopularity, to please men, then it is wrong.[4]

Conscience is not an infallible guide, but it is wrong to go against one's own conscience. We ought to never sin against our conscience, no matter who pressures us to do so.

The wise Apostle Paul has detailed four "dos" if we are to build unity amidst our diversity. First, we must determine never to be a source of stumbling. Second, we must live as citizens of the Kingdom of God, concentrating on the eternals rather than the externals. Third, we must actively pursue that which benefits other believers. Fourth, we must do all that we do with a clear conscience.

We are a diverse lot — there is no doubt about that. Diversity is one of the glories of the community of Christ. But our unity is supremely glorious. Let us seek to enhance it with all that we are!

We who are strong ought to bear with the failings of the weak and not to please ourselves. Each of us should please his neighbor for his good, to build him up. For even Christ did not please himself but, as it is written: "The insults of those who insult you have fallen on me." For everything that was written in the past was written to teach us, so that through endurance and the encouragement of the Scriptures we might have hope. May the God who gives endurance and encouragement give you a spirit of unity among yourselves as you follow Christ Jesus, so that with one heart and mouth you may glorify the God and Father of our Lord Jesus Christ. Accept one another, then, just as Christ accepted you, in order to bring praise to God. For I tell you that Christ has become a servant of the Jews on behalf of God's truth, to confirm the promises made to the patriarchs so that the Gentiles may glorify God for his mercy, as it is written: "Therefore I will praise you among the Gentiles; I will sing hymns to your name." Again, it says, "Rejoice, O Gentiles, with his people." And again, "Praise the Lord, all you Gentiles, and sing praises to him, all you peoples." And again, Isaiah says, "The root of Jesse will spring up, one who will arise to rule over the nations; the Gentiles will hope in him." May the God of hope fill you with all joy and peace as you trust in him, so that you may overflow with hope by the power of the Holy Spirit. (15:1-13)

30

Christ Our Example

ROMANS 15:1-13

Probably all of us have considered the question, "What would you do if you knew you had only twenty-four hours to live?" I remember discussing this in grade school with some other boys. We came up with crazy answers like ordering a filet mignon dinner (we didn't know what it was, but we were sure it was wonderful) or stealing a jet plane or calling Roy Rogers on the telephone.

If as adults we attempted to answer the same question, our answers would no doubt be more elevated but ultimately just as fatuous because it is impossible to perfectly foretell one's existential response in any situation. Moreover, none of us will know when the last twenty-four hours has arrived.

Yet there was one Man who knew exactly how long he had to live. Furthermore, he maintained absolute control over his actions and did exactly as he had determined beforehand. The Man was, of course, the Messiah, Jesus. What had he elected to do? First, he spent most of his time with his disciples instructing them in word and deed in the upper room. The remainder of his time was spent in prayer with God the Father. As the minutes ticked away, Jesus did exactly as he pleased. Moreover, he repeatedly prayed for what he considered to be of greatest importance: our oneness. John records in the seventeenth chapter that Jesus prayed for this at least three times:

> "Holy Father, protect them by the power of your name — the name you gave me — so that they may be one as we are one." (v. 11)

"My prayer is not for them alone. I pray also for those who will believe in me through their message, that all of them may be one, Father, just as you are in me and I am in you." (vv. 20, 21a)

"I have given them the glory that you gave me, that they may be one as we are one." (v. 22)

This is a remarkable prayer, especially when you consider the array of important things for which our Lord could have prayed. The oneness of his Church was of supreme importance to him. As he so perfectly said in verse 23:

. . . I in them and you in me. May they be brought to complete unity to let the world know that you sent me and have loved them even as you have loved me.

The quality of our unity either attracts or repels the world.

Unfortunately, while the Apostolic Church had some brilliant successes, regarding unity it failed miserably in many places. The church in Galatia was ravaged by legalism. The church in Corinth chose up sides as to what to do about one of its members who was committing incest (1 Corinthians 5:1-3). Pergamum was being divided and diluted by Christians' marriages to unbelievers (Revelation 2:14). And the Lord said in effect that the church at Laodicea made him sick (Revelation 3:16). The Apostolic Church sometimes fell far short of Christ's explicit teaching and prayer.

Some scholars believe that the church in Rome, to which Paul addressed this eloquent plea for unity in chapter 14 and the first thirteen verses of chapter 15, failed terribly. Theologians such as Oscar Cullmann believe that some of the early Christian martyrs (including Peter and Paul) were killed because of jealous strife among the members of the church in Rome! Rivalry was so bitter, they say, that some brethren turned in the names of their Christian opponents, naming them as traitors against the Empire. If this is true, envy among Christians helped feed saints to the lions in the Colosseum and light fires under Christians who burned in Nero's gardens.[1] But the fact is, if we do not take God's Word to heart, we will terribly fail too.

During my twenty-five years in the ministry I have seen my share of factiousness and division. I once had a conversation with a young man who let me know that he was deeply grieved because I wore clothing which contained mixed fibers (cotton and polyester as I remember) and I was thus in disobedience to Leviticus 19:19 which forbids wearing such a garment ("Do not wear clothing woven of two kinds of material"). As his delusions grew, he gathered devotees who were careful to make sure their fabrics were pure, their hair was cut in the same lock-step style, and their woman kept their ankles covered!

Churches have been known to divide over the smallest matters, such as one which split over a conflict as to where the piano ought to be placed. The story is told of two congregations that were located only a few blocks from each other in a small community. They thought it might be better if they would merge and become one united, larger, and more effective body rather than two struggling churches. Good idea . . . but they were not able to pull it off. The problem? They could not agree on how they would recite "The Lord's Prayer." One group preferred "forgive us our trespasses," while the other group demanded "forgive us our debts." So, as the local newspaper reported, "One church went back to its trespasses while the other returned to its debts."

As we have seen, Paul, so in tune with the mind of the Lord, recoils at such folly:

> The man who eats everything must not look down on him who does not, and the man who does not eat everything must not condemn the man who does, for God has accepted him. (14:3)

> Let us therefore make every effort to do what leads to peace and to mutual edification. (14:19)

Paul now turns to the supreme example, our Lord Jesus Christ.

CHRIST'S UNIFYING EXAMPLE: NOT SELF-SEEKING (vv. 1-6)

> We who are strong ought to bear with the failings of the weak and not to please ourselves. Each of us should please his neighbor for his good, to build him up. (vv. 1, 2)

If you are prone to judgmentalism and exclusiveness, this is a big pill to swallow. If you are the kind of person who is sure he is right and must have his way, you will not like this at all.

The call here to please others and not ourselves is directed to the "strong" — those who have a broader, more Biblical understanding of their freedom in Christ. This, of course, does not mean the "weak" are exempt from the responsibility of accepting and being patient with the strong, because verse 7 subsequently indicates that both strong and weak are to be accepting. Nevertheless, the greater burden is on the strong. In God's household strength denotes obligation. An unwillingness to forego our rights for others indicates we are not so "strong" after all.

What does Paul mean when he says the strong person is not to please himself, but rather ought "to please his neighbor for his good"? Paul does not mean we are never to please ourselves, as some have wrongly held. The "This is so much fun it must be sinful" school of thought is wrong. God wants us to have pleasure in life.

Moreover, there is a kind of pleasing others of which God does not approve. Galatians 1:10 says,

> Am I now trying to win the approval of men, or of God? Or am I
> trying to please men? If I were still trying to please men, I would not
> be a servant of Christ.

We are not to try to be "nice guys" who accommodate men's sinful ways. There are many who would be pleased if we would flatter and patronize their wrongdoing.

What is the pleasing others that Paul enjoins then? It is a determined adjustment of our lifestyle to whatever will contribute to the spiritual good of the other person. We are not to cater to the narrowest member of our fellowship, or to Christians who have over the years hardened themselves in sub-Biblical legalism, or to allow ourselves to be dominated by disordered persons. But there are times when for the sake of others we forego a course of action to which we are perfectly entitled. As F. F. Bruce says:

> It is so easy for a man whose conscience is quite clear about some
> course of action to snap his fingers at his critics and say, "I'll please
> myself." He has every right to do so, but that is not the way of Christ.[2]

We are to change our lifestyle if it will contribute to our brother's "good, to build him up" (v. 2). This is not to be done with a spirit of resignation or an air of condescension. It is to be done with humble love, sympathy, and patience.

Such a path is not optional. Our text says we "ought to bear with the failings of the weak" (v. 1). *Ought* was the past tense of *owe* in old English, and *owe* and *ought* have the same spiritual pronunciation. We *owe* this to our brothers and sisters in Christ. Perhaps God has been speaking to you about something you need to change in your lifestyle, and you are sensing it is your obligation. If so, do it by all means!

> *Love seeketh not itself to please,*
> *Nor for itself have any care,*
> *But for another gives its ease,*
> *And builds a Heaven in Hell's despair.*

(William Blake)

So intensely concerned is Paul that we be willing to forego our rights for the sake of unifying and building up our brothers and sisters that he does something he has not done in any of the preceding fourteen chapters of Romans. He holds up the example of Christ to enforce his argument: "For even Christ did not please himself but, as it is written: 'The insults of those who insult you have fallen on me'" (v. 3).

How was it that Christ did not please himself? Though Christ existed in indescribable glory from all eternity and was daily rejoicing in the fellowship of the Godhead in perfect holiness, he left all that for the sake of lost humanity. John 8:29 records Jesus as saying, "I always do what pleases him." And in John 4:34 he says, "My food . . . is to do the will of him who sent me." And in John 6:38 he tells us, "For I have come down from heaven not to do my will but to do the will of him who sent me."

Our Lord's earthly life culminated in reproach. "'The insults of those who insult you have fallen on me,'" says verse 3, quoting the prophecy of Psalm 69:9. He was rejected because he lived the life of God here on earth. Isaiah says:

> He was despised and rejected by men, a man of sorrows, and familiar with suffering. Like one from whom men hide their faces he was despised, and we esteemed him not. (53:3)

Could the whip and the nails and the weight of all our sin please any man? Whenever we crush the bread of Communion between our teeth and swallow the cup of his blood we cannot escape the fact that he did not please himself.

For Paul, the fact that Christ did not please himself has everything to do with our deferring to one another for the sake of Christian unity. Paul uses the example in an extended form in Philippians 2. First, he calls believers to humble deference:

281

... make my joy complete by being like-minded, having the same
love, being one in spirit and purpose. Do nothing out of selfish ambition or vain conceit, but in humility consider others better than yourselves. Each of you should look not only to your own interests, but
also to the interests of others. (vv. 2-4)

Then he eloquently puts forth Christ's supreme example as the rationale:

Your attitude should be the same as that of Christ Jesus: Who, being
in very nature God, did not consider equality with God something
to be grasped, but made himself nothing, taking the very nature of
a servant, being made in human likeness. And being found in
appearance as a man, he humbled himself and became obedient to
death — even death on a cross! (vv. 5-8)

For Paul, Christ's example carried immense power. The problem
for many of us is that we are victims of a "spectral theology" — Christ's
earthly actions are not quite real to us. But what Christ did is really true!
This is what Jesus was, and is, like! He really did not please himself. He
really did "please his neighbor for his good, to build him up" (v. 2). And
we are called to follow his example.

What is even more remarkable is that he is not only the pattern, but
the power. We *can* do this by Jesus' power. Thus if we say, "I cannot" we
are saying, "I will not." If God is calling us to change something in our
lives for the sake of Christian unity, we can do it through him.

Paul has made his point powerfully. But having mentioned Christ's
fulfillment of the Old Testament in Psalm 69:9, he cannot resist adding
parenthetically how helpful the Scriptures are:

For everything that was written in the past was written to teach us,
so that through endurance and the encouragement of the Scriptures
we might have hope. (v. 4)

The application is inescapable: believers are to be well acquainted with
the Old Testament Scriptures. The message to preachers is clear: preach
from both the Old and New Testaments. The ultimate result will be
"hope," that which most strikingly distinguishes the true Christian from
his pagan neighbor.

Then in verses 5, 6 Paul returns to his main theme with a prayer-
wish. First he prays for unity, and then for worship. Verse 5 contains his
desire for unity:

> May the God who gives endurance and encouragement give you a
> spirit of unity among yourselves as you follow Christ Jesus. . . .

The emphasis here is not that we see everything eye to eye, but rather that we regard one another with minds that are filled with and focused on the Lord as we "follow Jesus Christ." The fact is, most of us are nitpickers by nature. I flush with embarrassment when I remember that as a teenager I actually would wait in line to "share" with a speaker what I thought he should have included in his message! Conversely, how I thank God that the first ten years of my ministry were spent serving under a man who was *not* a divisive nitpicker. He followed so close to Christ that he was able to endure my youthful faults with a Christlike spirit of unity. Such a mind, filled with and focused on Christ, is able to control its actions and even deny itself for the sake of the unity of the Body of Christ.

Paul's concludes his prayer-wish by expressing his desire for *unified worship*: ". . . so that with one heart and mouth you may glorify the God and Father of our Lord Jesus Christ" (v. 6). The apostle understands that worship will not be what it is meant to be unless there is unity. Calvin put it this way:

> The unity of his servants is so much esteemed by God, that he will
> not have his glory sounded forth amidst discords and contentions.

We impoverish our worship and offer poor praise to God by stubbornness and lack of love to fellow believers. But, oh how beautiful the worship is when we worship together in unity (cf. Psalm 133).

It is no small thing to be asked to forego legitimate rights for the building up of brothers and sisters. This is demanding, but perfectly reasonable and possible, first, because Christ did it, and, second, because it is indispensable to true worship.

CHRIST'S UNIFYING EXAMPLE: ACCEPTING BOTH JEW AND GENTILE (vv. 7-13)

In concluding this long exhortation on Christian unity which began in chapter 14, Paul moves from the call to be willing to deny ourselves in order to please others to the call to accept one another. Again Christ is the example: "Accept one another, then," says Paul, "just as Christ accepted you, in order to bring praise to God" (v. 7).

The primary example here is Christ's acceptance of the Jews:

> For I tell you that Christ has become a servant of the Jews on behalf of
> God's truth, to confirm the promises made to the patriarchs. . . . (v. 8)

Christ's becoming a "servant" to Israel reveals the length to which he went to meet the Jews' needs.

But he also accepted Gentiles. In verses 9-12 Paul quotes four Old Testament Scriptures which predicted that the Gentiles would respond to God's grace and acceptance:

> . . . so that the *Gentiles* may glorify God for his mercy, as it is written: "Therefore I will praise you among the *Gentiles*; I will sing hymns to your name." [2 Samuel 22:50; Psalm 18:49] Again it says, "Rejoice, O *Gentiles*, with his people." [Deuteronomy 32:43] And again, "Praise the Lord, all you *Gentiles*, and sing praises to him, all you peoples." [Psalm 117:1] And again, Isaiah says, "The root of Jesse will spring up, one who will arise to rule over the nations; the *Gentiles* will hope in him." [Isaiah 11:10] (italics added)

Think of the amazing diversity of the Jews and Gentiles whom Christ has accepted!

Christ's astounding example gives mighty force to Paul's challenge to "Accept one another, then, just as Christ accepted you." How did Christ accept you and me? He accepted us with our many sins, prejudices, and innumerable blind spots. He accepted us with our psychological shortcomings and cultural naiveté. He accepted us with our provincialisms. He even accepted us with our stubbornness. This is how we are to accept one another.

No one knows when their last twenty-four hours will be. However, we do know how we should live our lives, whether we have twenty-four hours or twenty-four years or a hundred years. Jesus showed us what was important in his final hours when he prayed for our unity. And the example he set by his life backed it up. Christ made us one by his willingness not to please himself.

Are there some legitimate, good things, rightful things, that God is asking us to forego for the good of our brothers and sisters? Then by all means let us forego them. Are there some believers whom we have been unwilling to accept because they are not our type? God says we must accept them and love them. Let us each covenant to do this now.

I myself am convinced, my brothers, that you yourselves are full of goodness, complete in knowledge and competent to instruct one another. I have written you quite boldly on some points, as if to remind you of them again, because of the grace God gave me to be a minister of Christ Jesus to the Gentiles with the priestly duty of proclaiming the gospel of God, so that the Gentiles might become an offering acceptable to God, sanctified by the Holy Spirit. Therefore I glory in Christ Jesus in my service to God. I will not venture to speak of anything except what Christ has accomplished through me in leading the Gentiles to obey God by what I have said and done — by the power of signs and miracles, through the power of the Spirit. So from Jerusalem all the way around to Illyricum, I have fully proclaimed the gospel of Christ. It has always been my ambition to preach the gospel where Christ was not known, so that I would not be building on someone else's foundation. Rather, as it is written: "Those who were not told about him will see, and those who have not heard will understand." This is why I have often been hindered from coming to you. But now that there is no more place for me to work in these regions, and since I have been longing for many years to see you, I plan to do so when I go to Spain. I hope to visit you while passing through and to have you assist me on my journey there, after I have enjoyed your company for a while. Now, however, I am on my way to Jerusalem in the service of the saints there. For Macedonia and Achaia were pleased to make a contribution for the poor among the saints in Jerusalem. They were pleased to do it, and indeed they owe it to them. For if the Gentiles have shared in the Jews' spiritual blessings, they owe it to the Jews to share with them their material blessings. So after I have completed this task and have made sure that they have received this fruit, I will go to Spain and visit you on the way. I know that when I come to you, I will come in the full measure of the blessing of Christ. I urge you, brothers, by our Lord Jesus Christ and by the love of the Spirit, to join me in my struggle by praying to God for me. Pray that I may be rescued from the unbelievers in Judea and that my service in Jerusalem may be acceptable to the saints there, so that by God's will I may come to you with joy and together with you be refreshed. The God of peace be with you all. Amen. (15:14-33)

31

Paul's Missionary Heart (I)

ROMANS 15:14-33

Paul's life is cause for amazement and reflection. In the context of the times in which he lived, his situation appeared absurd. On one side there was Rome, metropolis of the world, heart of the Empire, insufferably proud on her seven hills, shaking the earth with the march of her fabled legions. On the other side was this little Jew, with scarred face and feeble body, ostensibly impotent amidst such power, armed only with something he called the "good news." Yet he changed the history of Rome, Western civilization, and indeed our own lives.

Obviously there was something about this little man that set him apart from the rest. What made him different is what makes our text so interesting, because now, having finished the argument of the book of Romans, Paul tells us why he wrote it and how he views his mission. Verses 14-33 of chapter 15 are an exposition of the anatomy of the greatest missionary heart ever.

Paul's heart has fascinated even secular minds. Michael Borodin, the American Communist who discipled Ho Chi Minh and Chou En-lai, once was heard to say in a reflective moment, "I used to read the New Testament. Again and again I read it. It is the most wonderful story ever told. That man Paul. He was a *real* revolutionary. I take my hat off to him."[1] Paul must be admired by all. But to the believing mind Paul's heart is even more impressive, for it sets the ideal for the missionary heart, an ideal which perhaps few attain. Nevertheless, it is the sublime example provided for us in the pages of Scripture by the infinite wisdom of the Holy Spirit.

PAUL'S LITURGICAL HEART (vv. 15, 16)

Paul's heart is first a heart that sees its mission as entirely sacred. Here Paul appropriates the vivid imagery of a Hebrew priest ministering at the altar in the Temple.

> I have written you quite boldly on some points, as if to remind you of them again, because of the grace God gave me to be a minister of Christ Jesus to the Gentiles with the priestly duty of proclaiming the gospel of God, so that the Gentiles might become an offering acceptable to God, sanctified by the Holy Spirit. (vv. 15, 16)

The imagery here is remarkably forceful because the word translated "minister" is the same root word from which we derive the word *liturgy*. The word even sounds like it — *lietourgon*. This is most significant, because Paul could have used other words to describe himself. For example, he could have used the common term *doulos* to indicate a servant of Jesus Christ, or he could have used *diakonos*, which means "servant" or "minister." But he chose *lietourgon* because he saw his missionary work like that of a priest offering sacred worship to God.

Consonant with this, he saw his priestly offering not as a lamb or a grain offering, but as Gentile converts. As he expresses it in verse 16: "that the Gentiles might become an offering acceptable to God, sanctified by the Holy Spirit." Here we are exposed to Paul's remarkable self-conception. Though he is involved in the dusty, mundane business of traveling the ancient world on foot, suffering from exposure, threats, beatings, and rejection, in his heart of hearts he sees himself in priestly garb in the Temple, lifting up the souls of men which then ascend as a sweet-smelling fragrance to Christ. Fully apprehended and appreciated, this is a dazzling picture.

It is common knowledge today that how we perceive ourselves greatly determines how we live our lives. Psychologists are constantly reminding us of the importance of self-image. Imagine, then, what this priestly self-perception did for Paul. His missionary life was to him intensely sacred. The most mundane daily occurrences were holy. However ignominious his treatment, he was garbed in imperturbable dignity as a servant of God. Everything was done to please God. All of life was a liturgy.

If only we could see our service as such, our lives would be transformed. A pie baked for a neighbor becomes an offering to God. A child held and loved is a liturgy, an employee treated with dignity a beatitude.

The gospel shared is a song in Heaven's courts, a Sunday school class well taught a fragrance to God. These are beautiful thoughts! Even better, they are true! This sacred view of life was a primary characteristic of the missionary heart of the Apostle Paul.

PAUL'S GLORIFYING HEART (vv. 17-19)

In verse 17-19 Paul does some sublime boasting, sublime because he is boasting about God.

> Therefore I glory in Christ Jesus in my service to God. I will not venture to speak of anything except what Christ has accomplished through me in leading the Gentiles to obey God by what I have said and done — by the power of signs and miracles, through the power of the Spirit. So from Jerusalem all the way around to Illyricum, I have fully proclaimed the gospel of Christ.

Paul mentions here at least three marvelous happenings in his life: 1) Gentiles came to belief, 2) signs and miracles accompanied his ministry, and 3) he himself preached the entire 1,400 miles from Jerusalem to Illyricum, which is in present-day Yugoslavia. Not bad — especially in sandals! But Paul takes no credit. Christ did it through him.

How contrary this is to the way things usually happen. More often we are like the Little Leaguer who put all his sixty pounds into a ferocious swing and barely connected. The ball scraped by the bottom of the bat, jiggled straight back to the pitcher, who groped and fumbled it. There was still plenty of time to nail the batter at first, but the pitcher's throw soared high over the first baseman's head. The slugger flew on toward second base. Somebody retrieved the ball. The next throw sailed wildly into left field. The hitter swaggered into third, puffing along with a man-sized grin, then continued on to cross home plate. "Oh, boy," he said, "that's the first home run I ever hit in my whole life!"

That is so like us! We step to the plate for Jesus, barely tip the ball, but he arranges for us to get home — and we take all the credit! If Paul had been someone else, he could have become insufferable: "Did I tell you about my Iconium escapade? Let me tell you . . . I was being stoned in Iconium because I stood tall for Jesus. I was always getting the stones — Barnabas always managed to save his pretty face. Well, I was really taking it, but I stood my ground and didn't flinch, and finally this guy threw a stone and put me down. It would have killed most men, but not me! So there I was, lying on a rubbish pile outside the city. Barnabas and

the saints had all gone to pieces, but I was awake, and I got to laughing
. . . What's a little stoning? The Lord needs more *men*, I guess."

That is just not the way Paul was. Paul made this very clear to the
Galatians: "May I never boast except in the cross of our Lord Jesus
Christ" (6:14). He also told the Colossians that Christ "is the beginning
and the firstborn from among the dead, so that in everything he might
have the supremacy" (1:18). God was everything to Paul.

That is the way it has been for the great missionary hearts that have
followed in Paul's footsteps as well. Raymond Lull, the brave missionary to the Moslems, lived by this famous refrain: "I have one passion —
it is He, it is He." Charles Wesley sang, "Thou, O Christ, art all I want,
more than all in Thee I find." It was said by Alexander Whyte of his long
Saturday walks with Marcus Dods, "Whatever we started off with in our
conversations, we soon made across country, somehow, to Jesus of
Nazareth." "We preach always Him," said Martin Luther; "this may seem
a limited and monotonous subject, likely to be soon exhausted, but we
are never at the end of it."[2] So it was with Paul. With Christ at the center, Paul could only boast of him.

If we are to have lives like Paul's, our hearts must not only see our
mission as entirely sacred, but they must give all glory to God. This is so
fitting, so right, the way we were designed to live.

PAUL'S VISIONARY HEART (vv. 20-29)

The third aspect of Paul's missionary heart is that it dreams. We must first
note that Paul had dreams and visions of incredibly large proportions.
Verses 20, 21 introduce them:

> It has always been my ambition to preach the gospel where Christ
> was not known, so that I would not be building on someone else's
> foundation. Rather, as it is written: "Those who were not told about
> him will see, and those who have not heard will understand." (cf.
> Isaiah 52:15)

Basic to Paul's dream was the obsession to preach where the gospel
had not been preached, wherever that might be. He voices this explicitly
in 2 Corinthians 10:16: ". . . so that we can preach the gospel in the
regions beyond you. For we do not want to boast about work already done
in another man's territory." This was an immense obsession. Other
Scriptures, such as verse 24 of our text, indicate that he even wanted to
go to Spain. No one really knows why — probably because Spain and

Britain were seen as the end of the world. William Barclay thinks it may be because Spain was the birthplace of many contemporary geniuses such as Lucan, Martial, Quintillian, and Seneca.[3] Maybe it was simply the lure of "untold millions still untold."

We do not know exactly what Paul hoped to do, but our text tells us he hoped to visit Rome (to have some fellowship with the church he had never seen) and then catch a ship for Iberia and begin his Spanish campaign. David Livingstone was cut out of the same mold as the Apostle Paul. When Livingstone volunteered as a missionary with the London Missionary Society and they asked him where he wanted to go, he replied, "Anywhere, so long as it is forward." Paul dreamed impossible dreams. This was fundamental to the greatness of Paul as a missionary, for dreams always precede action.

Verses 23-29 relate Paul's dreams to real life. The gist is this: if Paul had done as he wanted, he would have immediately set sail for Rome. However, he first had to complete the important business of taking an offering to the poor in Jerusalem which he had collected from the Gentile churches. His main motive in this was to cement the relationship between Jewish believers and new Gentile converts. The Book of Acts tells us that things did not go as planned, however. He did deliver the offering with great success, but he was almost killed by an unruly mob and escaped by night with Caesar's soldiers. Then he underwent shipwreck and deprivation before arriving in chains in Rome. As to his vision to go to Spain, we really cannot say for sure whether he ever got there. Modern scholarship inclines to say that he did not, though church tradition says he did.

I personally think it does not matter, and here is why: First, God knew Spain was in Paul's heart, just as much as it was in David's heart to build the Temple, though that king never saw a stone of it laid. Secondly, the value of a dream is not whether we achieve it or not, but in setting out to achieve it. This has been a great lesson for me personally. God is not so much interested in whether we reach our destination as in how we try to get there. To us arrival is everything, but to God the journey is most important, for it is in the journey that we are perfected, and it is in hardships that he is glorified as we trust him. Third, knowing Paul, I think we can safely surmise that in making his detour to Jerusalem and Rome Paul never felt that God had mocked him, or that if he never reached Spain his dream was misspent.

It is of greatest importance that we have hearts with dreams, great visions of what God can do with us. We need our "castles in the sky" — our Spains. We need to see "spires away on the world's rim,"[4] to dream of victories and accomplishments for God. Not all of us will meet our dream's end, but that is all right because God is more interested in the process than the prize, in the journey than the road's end.

May we learn to travel as Paul did. Someday we will stand before God and will possibly say, "God, this is the dream you gave me. I did not make it. I'm sorry." And he will say, "Yes, but that was in my hands. You were a magnificent traveler. Enter the joy that I have prepared for you before the foundation of the world!"

Paul concludes this section on a remarkably positive note: "I know that when I come to you, I will come in the full measure of the blessing of Christ" (v. 29). Such optimism! Paul was sure he would come to Rome in blessing. Little did he know his arrival would be in chains, and yet it was indeed in joy. What a way to go — "in the full measure of the blessing of Christ."

PAUL'S PRAYING HEART (vv. 30-33)

The final aspect of Paul's missionary heart is, he believes in prayer. Verses 30-32 contain his poignant call:

> I urge you, brothers, by our Lord Jesus Christ and by the love of the
> Spirit, to join me in my struggle by praying to God for me. Pray that
> I may be rescued from the unbelievers in Judea and that my service
> in Jerusalem may be acceptable to the saints there, so that by God's
> will I may come to you with joy and together with you be refreshed.

He asked for two things: 1) "that I may be rescued from the unbelievers in Judea" and, 2) that his service in Jerusalem "may be acceptable." Both prayers were answered.

Acts 21:17-20 records his offering's joyous reception and the resulting solidarity of the churches. In addition, Paul was granted a spectacular deliverance that could only be attributed to God, as Acts 21 — 23 makes so clear. The prayers of the Roman church brought great power to bear in Paul's life! Paul had called them "to join me in my struggle" in prayer — literally "to agonize together with me" — and that is what they did.

To those with Pauline hearts, the request, "Brother, pray for me," is not a cliché, and neither is the response, "I will pray for you." The missionary heart is, indeed, a heart that believes in prayer.

Now let us bring the pieces together. A missionary heart is *a heart that sees its mission as entirely sacred*. The sacredness of the work comes from seeing oneself as a priest offering up his or her service as a fragrant offering to Christ. Therefore, it regards its own life, however prosaic and mundane, as a liturgy. Let us ask God to help us see all of life as glorifying him.

A missionary heart is *a heart that gives God the credit for everything*. All home runs are God's home runs. Let us pause for a moment and give God the glory for what is happening through us.

A missionary heart is *a heart that is visionary*. Do we have a dream — a Spain? If not, let us ask God for one.

A missionary heart is *a heart that prays passionately*. Today it is not "in" to be passionate about anything except our favorite professional sports team. But in God's Kingdom the great heart passionately strives in prayer.

It is impossible to think of history without Paul. Nothing would be the same for any of us were it not for Paul's remarkable heart for God.

I commend to you our sister Phoebe, a servant of the church in Cenchrea. I ask you to receive her in the Lord in a way worthy of the saints and to give her any help she may need from you, for she has been a great help to many people, including me. Greet Priscilla and Aquila, my fellow workers in Christ Jesus. They risked their lives for me. Not only I but all the churches of the Gentiles are grateful to them. Greet also the church that meets at their house. Greet my dear friend Epenetus, who was the first convert to Christ in the province of Asia. Greet Mary, who worked very hard for you. Greet Andronicus and Junias, my relatives who have been in prison with me. They are outstanding among the apostles, and they were in Christ before I was. Greet Ampliatus, whom I love in the Lord. Greet Urbanus, our fellow worker in Christ, and my dear friend Stachys. Greet Apelles, tested and approved in Christ. Greet those who belong to the household of Aristobulus. Greet Herodion, my relative. Greet those in the household of Narcissus who are in the Lord. Greet Tryphena and Tryphosa, those women who work hard in the Lord. Greet my dear friend Persis, another woman who has worked very hard in the Lord. Greet Rufus, chosen in the Lord, and his mother, who has been a mother to me, too. Greet Asyncritus, Phlegon, Hermes, Patrobas, Hermas and the brothers with them. Greet Philologus, Julia, Nereus and his sister, and Olympas and all the saints with them. Greet one another with a holy kiss. All the churches of Christ send greetings. I urge you, brothers, to watch out for those who cause divisions and put obstacles in your way that are contrary to the teaching you have learned. Keep away from them. For such people are not serving our Lord Christ, but their own appetites. By smooth talk and flattery they deceive the minds of naive people. Everyone has heard about your obedience, so I am full of joy over you; but I want you to be wise about what is good, and innocent about what is evil. The God of peace will soon crush Satan under your feet. The grace of our Lord Jesus be with you. Timothy, my fellow worker, sends his greetings to you, as do Lucius, Jason and Sosipater, my relatives. I, Tertius, who wrote down this letter, greet you in the Lord. Gaius, whose hospitality I and the whole church here enjoy, sends you his greetings. Erastus, who is the city's director of public works, and our brother Quartus send you their greetings. (16:1-24)

32

Paul's Missionary Heart (II)

ROMANS 16:1-24

In the eyes of the world, Paul's frail frame was absurd, even comical, standing before the powers of Rome. Yet he changed the course of history. His heart effected a power greater than all the Roman Empire. None of our lives would be as they are today had it not been for the missionary heart of the Apostle Paul.

As we continue the study of Paul's great heart, we should bear in mind that the four qualities we have already considered (*Liturgical, Glorifying, Visionary,* and *Praying*) were essentially vertical, whereas in this chapter we will see the horizontal aspects of his missionary heart. And again they are galvanizing. I do not think that apart from the Lord himself there has ever been a heart as aflame as the Apostle Paul's. As we look at the horizontal anatomy of his great heart, my hope is that we all will be moved to some "sanctified envy" and imitation, so that our hearts will beat like Paul's heart, with Heaven's rhythm.

PAUL'S LOVING HEART (vv. 1-16)

The first characteristic of Paul's heart described in this chapter is that it overflowed with personal love. If the long list of names and greetings in these verses teaches us anything, it is that Paul had a diffusive love for people. The word "greet" appears nineteen times, and seventeen of them are by Paul. Our text features thirty-three names. Twenty-four were in Rome (seventeen men and seven women). In addition, the apostle mentions two households, the mother of Rufus, and the sister of Nereus. Nine of the people mentioned were with Paul in Corinth (eight men and one woman). Obviously Paul maintained a remarkable amount of affectionate relationships.

We do not perhaps normally think of Paul this way. We may naturally assume that though he was a great man, his greatness made him a forbidding companion. Having read through Romans, and knowing of his massive intellect, most of us would feel somewhat intimidated if we knew we were to spend an evening alone with him. We probably would spend the day brushing up on our memory work, wading through the Minor Prophets, or clarifying some points in theology. No doubt such time would be well spent, but our fears unfounded, for Paul was a "people person" *par excellence*. Moreover, he did not determine his friendships on the basis of intellectual capability or theological literacy.

What makes this list of those he knew in the church of Rome so amazing is the fact that *he had never been to Rome*! Most of the people he mentions are those whom he had met on his journeys and who had subsequently taken up residence in Rome. In a recent America's Cup Race the tradition-conscious New York Yacht Club allowed no TV or radio on the premises. Rather, they used a tracking board on which someone in contact with the yachts moved by hand the ships on the board throughout the course of the race. Paul's "tracking-board" heart knew where each friend was geographically and spiritually.

Think of the energy such "keeping in touch" involved! Imagine Paul on ship and in port beseeching travelers for information: "What about Patrobas? Where is Hermes now? Is he still walking in faith? What can I pray for?" We know from the testimony of other Scriptures that this is the way Paul was. He routed his journeys and scheduled his disciples' travels so as to obtain as much information as possible. Paul, one of the greatest of intellects, a true master of theology, was also a caring man who loved people.

Names were very important to Paul. I am told that if you visit the old Natural Bridge of Virginia you will see hundreds of names scrawled on the rocks. But high on the side of it, above almost all the names, is scratched, "George Washington." Even "The Father of Our Country" could not resist imposing his personal graffiti on nature! Our own names are music to our ears. Certainly Paul knew this. But it is also true that you learn the names of those for whom you really care. Some perceptively suggest that the reason Paul could so readily recite all these names in dictation was because of their frequent mention in his personal prayer list.

We should also note the abundance of women the apostle mentions with obvious affection. There are far more women mentioned here than in the typical literature of the day. Paul was no misogynist! As we look at the list of greetings and kind words in the first sixteen verses, we cannot escape the sense of genuine affection contained there.

It would take more space than we have to fully treat all the names, but a few selective comments will give the idea. In verses 1, 2 Paul mentions Phoebe, whom he gives four endearing names: "sister," "servant," "saint," and "a great help." In verses 3, 4 he greets Priscilla and Aquila, who had "risked their lives" for him in Ephesus. This graphic phrase undoubtedly recalled a warm flood of memories in Priscilla and Aquila. In verse 5 he greets Epenetus, his first convert in Asia. What Christian worker can forget his first convert? The first person I directed to Christ was a man about my same age whom I have carefully tracked now for over thirty years.

In verse 7 the apostle says,

> Greet Andronicus and Junias, my relatives who have been in prison
> with me. They are outstanding among the apostles, and they were in
> Christ before I was.

"These men are brother Jews," says Paul, "but they are even closer because they have done time with me in the slammer. They are outstanding apostolic types." In verse 10 he greets "Apelles, tested and approved in Christ." Bengel calls this "an incomparable epithet."[1] What a loving bouquet from the old soldier!

"Tryphena and Tryphosa" (v. 12) were probably twins who were given names that go together. Their names mean "dainty" and "delicate." Paul employs some playful irony here because he calls them "women who work hard in the Lord," using a word that means to labor to the point of exhaustion. Dainty and delicate, yes — but "dynamite comes in small packages."

Who was the "Rufus" of verse 13? Mark 15:21 identifies Simon of Cyrene as the father of Alexander and Rufus. Couple this with the fact that Mark wrote his Gospel to Rome and we conclude that Rufus was the son of Simon of Cyrene who carried Jesus' cross.

How alive were Paul's remembrances and *bon mots* to Rome. William Barclay writes:

> Now if a man is identified by the names of his sons, it means that,
> although he himself may not be personally known to the community
> to whom the story is being told, the sons are. To what Church did

Mark write this gospel? Almost certainly he wrote it for the Church of Rome, and he knew that the Church would know who Alexander and Rufus were. . . . He was the son of that Simon who carried the cross of Jesus.[2]

The parade of names in this closing chapter of Romans repeatedly affirms Paul's affection for his Christian brothers and sisters in Rome. The best exposition of this horizontal affection was given by Paul himself in 1 Thessalonians 2:7, 8:

> . . . but we were gentle among you, like a mother caring for her little children. We loved you so much that we were delighted to share with you not only the gospel of God but our lives as well, because you had become so dear to us.

"Our lives" equals *our souls*! How Paul loved the Church!

Warmhearted Paul's loving example challenges us. If our hearts beat with something of the pulse of the Apostle Paul, we will be "people persons" who are affectionate to each other. This is the very plain meaning of verse 16, which completes Paul's individual greetings to Rome: "Greet one another with a holy kiss." It is Biblical to express love and affection, even to the point of an embrace and a kiss. What a difference authentic Christian affection can make in a cold, indifferent world.

Not long ago, an eighty-seven-year-old widow in Grand Rapids appealed to the state to place her in a nursing home. "I don't blame people for not taking the time to see me. I'm not very interesting," she said. "Everybody I knew is dead or moved away. I'd like to talk to somebody who's alive. I'd like some company." The newspaper article reporting on her situation went on to state that except for a shopping trip once or twice a month this widow rarely left her apartment. Her typical day began at 6:30 with a breakfast of toast and coffee. Then she would water her "garden in the kitchen," which consisted of five small potted plants. After tidying up the place, she would spend the rest of the day looking out the window. Her day ended at 8:30. After a light supper she went to bed.

Perhaps we may regard this story as sensational, but listen to what an eminently astute observer (Charles Reich) writes in his book *The Greening of America*:

> America is one vast terrifying anticommunity. The great organizations to which most people give their working day, and the apartments and suburbs to which they return at night, are equally places

of loneliness and alienation. . . . Protocol, competition, hostility and fear have replaced the warmth of the circle of affection which might sustain man against a hostile universe.[3]

The problem, of course, is that the Church is often as cold as or even colder than the world. Sometimes strangers cannot pry a grin from regular attenders. It is imperative that we remember that people are important. The absence of *agape* love in the typical church should burden our hearts. We must reach out in love to those around us.

The answer to this dilemma? First, *we must be "people persons."* If we are businessmen and business keeps us going so fast that people are ciphers, something is wrong. If we are scholars devoted to our books, we must remember that our books should not be ends in themselves, but platforms to launch us up to God and out toward others. The names of people around us must be important to us. We should remember them because we care.

Secondly, *we are to be affectionate.* Charles Swindoll tells about one time after a Wednesday evening prayer meeting when a big, burly six-footer, holding a motorcycle helmet in one hand, came up to him and said, "There's something I've always wanted to do to you." Swindoll wondered what was coming next. The man put down his helmet and gave Swindoll a big, full-bodied hug. We are not suggesting a self-conscious affectionate love where hugging becomes the "in thing" — a sign of truly spiritual people. Paul's example challenges us to a deep heart affection that shows itself in sincere eye contact, perhaps a touch, and sometimes an embrace.

We must note before we move on to the next section that though Paul was the great giver, it all came back to him! In Galatians 4:15 Paul testifies that there were some in the Church who loved him so much they would have plucked out their eyes for him. Here in verse 13 of our text, when he greets Rufus he also greets Rufus' mother, who he says "has been a mother to me, too." When did she "mother" Paul? In Antioch when he was getting started? In some small town after a beating? At times Paul no doubt felt he could use a little mothering. Paul received back more than he gave. Jesus said:

> "I tell you the truth . . . no one who has left home or brothers or sisters or mother or father or children or fields for me and the gospel will fail to receive a hundred times as much in this present age (homes, brothers, sisters, mothers, children and fields)." (Mark 10:29, 30)

The "hundred times" principle was alive in Paul's life. He had a hundred mothers, a hundred farms, a thousand brothers and sisters and children. He was the richest man in Rome!

The richest people in town are always those who love the most. "People persons" — the affectionate — those who remember names and pray for them — receive the most.

So we see from the list in verses 1-16 that Paul's heart overflowed with a *diffusive* love.

PAUL'S PROTECTIVE HEART (vv. 17-20)

This section is forceful and lacks the careful restraint that has thus far marked Paul's approach to the Romans.

> I urge you, brothers, to watch out for those who cause divisions and put obstacles in your way that are contrary to the teaching you have learned. Keep away from them. For such people are not serving our Lord Christ, but their own appetites. By smooth talk and flattery they deceive the minds of naive people. Everyone has heard about your obedience, so I am full of joy over you; but I want you to be wise about what is good, and innocent about what is evil. (vv. 17-19)

Paul briefly suggests three protective measures that need to be taken by a Christian church. First, in verse 17a, he says, "watch out for those who cause divisions." Paul has no sympathy with theological sleepiness. Christians are to make a mental note of those who are off-base. Second: "Keep away from them" (v. 17b). Heretics are to be spurned. Third: "be wise about what is good, and innocent about what is evil" (v. 19b). This is an echo of Jesus' saying in Matthew 10:16: "be as shrewd as snakes and as innocent as doves." This is good advice because our tendency is to be as wise as doves and innocent as serpents.

This no-nonsense advice eloquently demonstrates the second aspect of Paul's horizontal love: it is *protective*. The connection is clear: When you really love people as much as Paul loved the Romans, you protect them. This is a great example for all of us. We need to love in such a way that we really put it on the line for others and speak the truth in love. Paul's heart is *loving*, protective, and, furthermore, *contagious*.

PAUL'S CONTAGIOUS HEART (vv. 21-23)

I picture the scene in chapter 16 like this: As Paul nears the end of dictating his letter to the Romans, his friends gather around him in the home of his gracious host, Gaius. Tertius is writing down Paul's words, and Timothy, Jason, Lucius, and Sosipater really get into the long recitation of greetings to real flesh-and-blood people. Their hearts are warmed, and all three interrupt: "Say hi for me." "Me too!" So Tertius writes:

> Timothy, my fellow worker, sends his greetings to you, as do Lucius, Jason and Sosipater, my relatives. I, Tertius, who wrote down this letter, greet you in the Lord. Gaius, whose hospitality I and the whole church here enjoy, sends you his greetings. Erastus, who is the city's director of public works, and our brother Quartus send you their greetings. (vv. 21-23)

We see here that a heart that is filled with love is by nature contagious. I personally cannot think of a better human example in all the world than Evan Welsh, the former alumni chaplain of Wheaton College. When he looked you in the eye, you knew he was there and that you were important to him and to God. Just to be with him for a few minutes was a great blessing.

We live in a heartless world. The recent United States census missed at least 5.7 million people who were anonymous even to the census takers. Every year thousands of unidentified and even unidentifiable bodies are found across North America. And only one out of twenty such bodies ever has a name attached to it! Our society has become a breeding ground for lonely people. Life in today's world is very much like the unwritten rule in elevators: "No talking, smiling, or eye contact allowed without written consent of the management."

A survey was taken recently in a suburban area of Houston to find out what had motivated people to choose the particular church where they were members. Some surprising answers were given: 12 percent chose their church because of prior denominational affiliation, 8 percent on the basis of the architectural beauty of the structure, 3 percent because of the person in the pulpit, 18 percent because of convenience of location, 21 percent because of people in the congregation whom they respected. But a whopping 37 percent were influenced by the fact that friends and neighbors took an interest in them and invited them. Take Paul's heart to heart. It can make all the difference in the world — and for eternity.

Though Paul was the supreme intellect of the Early Church, and though Paul had a heart that burned for the glory of God, as few have in the history of the world, he would not have been used like he was if he had not had a heart for people. The truly revolutionary heart is not just a visionary heart with great dreams, but a heart which loves people, a heart which remembers names, a heart with a good word for its brothers and sisters, a protective heart, and finally a contagious heart.

The beautiful Greek and Latin names in Romans 16 were the names of real people. Each name had its joys and sorrows, its cares, its hope, its trials. All drank of the common cup of human experience. These were, and are, our brothers and sisters in Christ. Someday we will walk with them in radiant white.

One of the primary human reasons this is so is that *Paul loved them.* May we have such a heart so that future generations may sing:

> *For all the saints who from their labors rest,*
> *Who Thee by faith before the world confessed,*
> *Thy name, O Jesus, be forever blest,*
> *Alleluia! Alleluia!*

William W. How

Now to him who is able to establish you by my gospel and the proclamation of Jesus Christ, according to the revelation of the mystery hidden for long ages past, but now revealed and made known through the prophetic writings by the command of the eternal God, so that all nations might believe and obey him — to the only wise God be glory forever through Jesus Christ! Amen. (16:25-27)

33

The End Is Praise

ROMANS 16:25-27

Villiam Tyndale, the pioneer English Bible translator, wrote these famous words in his prologue to Romans (1534 edition of the English New Testament):

> Forasmuch as this epistle is the principal and most excellent part of the New Testament, and most pure [gospel] . . . and also a light and a way in unto the whole scripture, I think it meet that every Christian man not only know it by rote but also exercise himself therein evermore continually as with the daily bread of the soul. No man verily can read it too oft or study it too well: for the more it is studied the easier it is, the more it is searched the more precious things are found in it, so great treasure of spiritual things lieth hid therein.[1]

Such was Tyndale's opinion some 450 years ago, and it remains ours today. Paul's letter to the Romans is the most closely reasoned and compelling book of the New Testament. Its massive theology, so ably argued in the first eleven chapters, logically proceeds from the statement of the gospel in the opening verses of chapter 1 to the need for the gospel because of man's sin in chapters 1 — 3. Next it describes the provision of the righteousness which comes by faith in chapters 3, 4. Then our position in Christ is beautifully described in chapter 5. The secret of spiritual victory is mapped out in chapters 6 — 8. And finally, in chapters 9 — 11, a vindication of God's work in history is provided. As Paul concludes his argument, his foundational theology gives way to an appropriately rousing doxology in 11:36 — "For from him and through him and to him are all things. To him be the glory forever! Amen." There is simply nothing like the first eleven chapters of Romans.

Then follows the properly compelling call to practical Christian living in chapters 12 — 15, which begins with these words:

> Therefore, I urge you, brothers, in view of God's mercy, to offer your bodies as living sacrifices, holy and pleasing to God — which is your spiritual worship. Do not conform any longer to the pattern of this world, but be transformed by the renewing of your mind. Then you will be able to test and approve what God's will is — his good, pleasing and perfect will. (12:1, 2)

In logical succession Paul encourages us to practice our theology by using our gifts to serve one another in love. We are to subject ourselves to the authority over us, living by the law of love in the Church, offering all of life to God. This section also concludes with a doxology: "The God of peace be with you all. Amen" (15:33). Then, as we saw in the last chapter, Paul gives his greetings to all the saints in Rome and closes with another doxology: "The grace of our Lord Jesus be with you" (16:20b).

These are the magnificent structures of the greatest theological treatise ever written. The word "God" is used no less than 153 times (even more than the verb "to be," which occurs in its various forms only 113 times). There is nothing like the book of Romans!

Now comes the end. His friends have chimed in with their greetings, and Paul takes the pen in his own hand and writes the last few lines. We know this because in 2 Thessalonians 3:17, 18 he mentions that he does this in every letter, presumably so the readers will know the letter is not a forgery. Perhaps with pen poised he hesitated for a moment, and then began to write. What did he write? Another doxology, of course, the longest of all his doxologies, and one of the most beautiful. I have entitled it, "The End Is Praise." Logically there is no other way he could have ended the monumental argument of Romans, and there is no other way we can properly end its study. Paul's final praise is a model for all times, a model for our song in the Lord. Let us study it with an eye to the kind of praise the truths of Romans should call from us. Essentially there are two broad categories of praise: 1) praise for God's *work* (vv. 25, 26) and 2) praise for God's *wisdom* (v. 27).

PRAISE FOR GOD'S WORK (vv. 25, 26)

Paul begins by praising God for his work in establishing his children: "Now to him who is able to establish you . . ." (v. 25a). We see the idea more fully when we understand that the root from which the word "establish" comes from is the word "prop," as with a prop which holds something up. God is able to make us stand, thereby establishing us.[2] The same word is used in 1 Thessalonians 3:13, which says God is able to "establish" (NASB) our hearts in blameless holiness. The thrust here at the end of the great theological foundation of Romans is that spiritually God is able to make us stand strong and steadfast. He props his people up so they will not fall. Perhaps Paul is considering his readers' life in Rome now and in the future, seeing their struggles. Though he cannot do anything for them, he knows God is able to make them stand, and for this he offers doxology.

God can establish us and make us strong and steadfast in any circumstance. When he so chooses, he demonstrates this in the physical realm as well. Years ago when Ira Sankey was at the height of his ministry and traveling on a steamer in the Delaware River, he was recognized by some of the people on board. They had seen his picture in the newspaper and knew he was associated with evangelist D. L. Moody. When he was asked to sing one of his own compositions, Sankey said he preferred the hymn by William Bradbury, "Savior, Like a Shepherd Lead Us." He suggested that everyone should join in the singing. One of the stanzas begins, "We are Thine, do Thou befriend us; be the guardian of our way." When he finished, a man stepped out of the shadows and inquired, "Were you in the army, Mr. Sankey?" "Yes, I joined up in 1860." "Did you ever do guard duty at night in Maryland, about 1862?" "Yes, I did." "Well, I was in the Confederate Army," said the stranger, "and I saw you one night at Sharpsburg. You were wearing your blue uniform, and I had you in my gun sight as you stood there in the light of the full moon. Then just as I was about to pull the trigger, you began to sing." Sankey was astounded as he recalled the incident. "It was the same hymn you sang tonight," continued the man. "I couldn't shoot you."[3] There is no doubt about it — God can make us stand firm under his protection!

We do not have to go back 120 years for a story like that. A missionary, Thomas Young, served for many years in the deep Amazon with the South America Mission. The natives there were big men who carried sixty-pound bows with arrows over six feet long. One day Tom and his friends were headed down the Amazon in canoes when they came to a narrow place. As they looked up at the cliffs above them, a group of

Indians were poisedwith their bows drawn . The water was going too fast for the missionaries to pull to one side or the other. But as the natives let fly their arrows at almost point-blank range, a miracle happened. A great gust of wind arose, causing the arrows to fall into the river behind the missionaries! Some time later one of the natives came to see Tom, and the first thing he did was to take his pulse to see if he was human. God establishes and protects his people!

However, the principal thrust in verse 25 is on God establishing his people in salvation. Since our salvation is all of God, God can certainly make his people stand. Paul phrased it this way in Philippians 1:6: "being confident of this, that he who began a good work in you will carry it on to completion until the day of Christ Jesus." There is no fear he cannot allay, no danger from which he cannot deliver, no anxiety he cannot quiet, no despair he cannot lift. This is good news! Because of the ineluctable logic of Romans, because everything is of God, we are *established*. And for this Paul offers doxology at the end of the book of Romans. Believe it! God is able to make us stand. Let us praise him for this now!

As Paul further expresses his thought in verse 25, he tells us how God establishes us: "by my gospel and the proclamation of Jesus Christ" — that is, according to the gospel, the preaching about Jesus Christ. We were established initially through Jesus Christ, and we are maintained continually by him.

John 1:1 tells us that Jesus existed from the very beginning as the Word. He was the ultimate communication of God, and he longed to communicate to us. So he came into the world, and the Apostle John was able to rejoice with these words: "No one has ever seen God, but God the only Son, who is at the Father's side, has made him known" (John 1:18). In the Greek this literally reads, "He has exegeted him." Jesus is the exegesis, the explanation of the Godhead. Therefore, our knowledge of Jesus is the key to knowing God and to standing or being established. That is why Jesus prayed, "Now this is eternal life: that they may know you, the only true God, and Jesus Christ, whom you have sent" (John 17:3). The key to standing is making Jesus the center of everything. Moreover, the story of Jesus should be our constant meditation, as it was for Paul. Then we will be able to stand, for it is Jesus who establishes us.

If you have been tottering, focus on Jesus, read about him, think about him, make the Gospels your spiritual meat and potatoes, the sustenance of your life.

The second aspect of our being established is given in the last half of verse 25 where Paul says, "according to the revelation of the mystery hidden for long ages past." In other words, we are established when and as the ancient mystery is opened to us. How is this so? Part of the answer lies in the word "mystery" (*mysterion*), which in the New Testament does not mean mysterious (as the English word suggests) but rather *a secret which was once kept dark but is now revealed.*

Dr. Barnhouse illustrated this idea when he recounted how he once employed a single woman as his private secretary who was terrific and so far as he knew never dated anyone. This was fine with him because he did not want to lose her. However, one Sunday morning as he parked his car someone approached him saying, "Max and Elizabeth are engaged." He did not believe it. However, when he got to the church door someone else said the same thing. When he stepped into his office there stood his secretary beaming radiantly. In answer to his question she affirmed it to be true. She and her new husband planned to serve with Wycliffe Bible Translators in Mexico. Barnhouse reflected:

> Here was a true *mysterion* in the New Testament sense. It had been completely hidden, absolutely unknown, totally unsuspected. Then suddenly it was whispered to one person, and the news spread like leaves in the wind. . . . True, after we knew that the young couple were engaged, we could look back and remember certain circumstances which might have led us to suspect if we had only been thinking in that direction.[4]

Here in Romans a great and ancient secret has been thrown wide-open to believers by the work of the Holy Spirit. It is the mystery of Jesus, which Paul calls the "mystery, which is Christ" in Colossians 1:27. God has given Jesus to us through the virgin birth, through his absolutely perfect earthly life, through his vicarious death for us, through his breaking the bonds of death and ascending to the right hand of the Father. Thus the *mysterion* has been opened to us. We cannot understand everything, for even in eternity the wonder of it will continue to unfold. Yet now, in time, we understand what was in ages past darkly veiled.

There follows from this the grand mystery of the Church, which is like a marriage. Ephesians 5:32 says, "This is a profound mystery — but I am talking about Christ and the church." The marriage relationship illustrates the great mystery of the personal relationship which exists between each believer and Jesus.

The spiritual understanding of the mystery of the Church, the inner secret which was hidden and now is made known, can be more fully apprehended by meditating on the tiny word "in." Paul uses this word fifteen times in the first fifteen verses of Ephesians concerning us and

Jesus Christ: "in Christ Jesus" (v. 1), "in Christ" (v. 3), "in him" and "in his sight" (v. 4), "in accordance with his pleasure and will" (v. 5), "in the One he loves" (v. 6), "in him" and "in accordance with the riches of God's grace" (v. 7), "in Christ," (v. 9), "in him" and "in conformity with the purpose of his will" (v. 11), "in Christ" (v. 12), "in Christ" and "in him" (v. 13), "in the Lord Jesus" (v. 15). This amazing reciprocal truth is the signature of the Christian life: I am in Christ, and he is in me. No other religion knows anything of this. It is our *mysterion*.

Moreover, one day our union will bring such a bloom that were we to see it now, we would not believe it — *we shall be like him* (cf. 1 John 3:1-3). John Donne said of this :

> I shall be so like God, as that the devil himself shall not know me from God, so farre as to finde any more place to fasten a temptation upon me, then upon God; not to conceive any more hope of my falling from that kingdome, then of God's being driven out of it.[5]

To quote Ephesians 5:32 again, "This is a profound mystery — but I am talking about Christ and the church." Brothers and sisters, this is cause to praise. Our theology must become doxology!

The extent of the mystery is underlined by the fact that it includes both Jews and Gentiles. Paul explains in Ephesians 3:2-6:

> Surely you have heard about the administration of God's grace that was given to me for you, that is, the mystery made known to me by revelation, as I have already written briefly. In reading this, then, you will be able to understand my insight into the mystery of Christ, which was not made known to men in other generations as it has now been revealed by the Spirit to God's holy apostles and prophets. This mystery is that through the gospel the Gentiles are heirs together with Israel, members together of one body, and sharers together in the promise in Christ Jesus.

There were explicit hints of this in the Old Testament. Consider, for example, God's word to Abraham in Genesis 12:3, "and all peoples on earth will be blessed through you." Similar promises occur in Genesis 18:18 and 22:18. The very bloodline of Christ had a number of Gentile women in it. However, it was a dim secret in Old Testament times. But verse 26 of our text emphasizes the opening of the mystery to the Gentiles, which is "now revealed and made known through the prophetic writings by the command of the eternal God, so that all nations might believe and obey him."

The Old Testament Scriptures now can clearly be seen to teach this truth, and the nations (the Gentiles, the *goyim*) are learning the obedience of faith. This mystery is nothing less than a miracle. God's salvation extends to all races, and those who receive it are "in" Christ and he is "in" them. Moreover, all Jewish and Gentile believers are brothers and sisters together.

What a *mysterion*, what a miracle, and what a call to praise God! God is able to prop us up. Actually, he is able to do even more. He is able to *establish* us. His way of doing this is Jesus! When Jesus is the subject of our proclamation, our conversation, our meditation, we stand! And as we live and grow in Jesus, the *mysterion* opens wider and wider, and we become more firmly established. The unfolding mystery of God Incarnate assaults our souls and draws us up to glory:

> *O the deep, deep love of Jesus,*
> *'Tis a Heaven of Heavens to me,*
> *And it lifts me up to glory,*
> *For it lifts me up to Thee.*

Thus we stand strong! The mystery of our union in the Lord Jesus Christ as bride and groom opens wider and wider. This is not hopeful thinking. This is no pious rhetoric. It is true! Jesus is in me and you, and we are in him. And this *mysterion* which makes us stand is for all the world. Through Christ, believing Jews and Gentiles stand together and will be established for eternity. This is Paul's doxology!

Perhaps if he had not already said it, he would have now said, "For from him and through him and to him are all things. To him be the glory forever! Amen" (11:36). Praise is to be our constant occupation and preoccupation.

All the angels were standing around the throne and around the elders and the four living creatures. They fell down on their faces before the throne and worshiped God, saying: "Amen! Praise and glory and wisdom and thanks and honor and power and strength be to our God for ever and ever. Amen!" (Revelation 7:11, 12)

PRAISE FOR GOD'S WISDOM (v. 27)

Paul fittingly ends Romans with praise to God for his wisdom: ". . . to the only wise God be glory forever through Jesus Christ! Amen" (v. 27). Our God is the *only God*. There is none but him. He is incomprehensible. One day a little boy was drawing for his teacher. "What are you drawing?" asked the teacher. "I'm drawing God." "You cannot do that. No one knows what God looks like." "They will when I am through," the boy said confidently.

The little boy did not quite have the idea, unless by "when I am through" he meant through with this life. Then we will all have a clearer idea of God, though we will also keep learning more about him for all eternity.

Our God is also the *only wise* God. In affirming this, I am reminded that whatever God is he is infinitely. Therefore, God is infinite wisdom. Wisdom, among other things, is the ability to devise perfect ends and to achieve those ends by perfect means. This our God does without limit.

In his wisdom he has made it possible for those who were once bound to earth by their own sinful depravity to be loosed from their sins and to know the throne of God as eternal home. He has made it possible for men who were made lower than the angels to rise higher than the angels. He has made it possible for us to become his own sons and daughters.

For all this there can only be doxology — "to the only wise God be glory forever through Jesus Christ! Amen."

Soli Deo Gloria!

Notes

CHAPTER ONE: *INTRODUCING PAUL TO ROME*

1. Karl Barth, *The Epistle to the Romans*, trans. Edwyn C. Hoskyns (London: Oxford University Press, 1976), p. 27.
2. James Ford, *St. Paul's Epistle to the Romans, Illustrated from Divines of the Church of England* (London: Joseph Masters, 1862), p. 25.
3. Alan F. Johnson, *The Freedom Letter* (Chicago: Moody Press, 1974), p. 26.
4. W. Robertson Nicoll, ed., *The Expositors Greek Testament*, Volume 2, James Denney, *St. Paul's Epistle to the Romans* (Grand Rapids, MI: Eerdmans, 1970), p. 586.
5. Barth, *The Epistle to the Romans*, p. 31.
6. George MacDonald, *Diary of an Old Soul* (Minneapolis: Augsburg, 1975), p. 11.

CHAPTER TWO: *PAUL'S MOTIVATION FOR MINISTRY*

1. Allan C. Emery, *A Turtle on a Fencepost* (Waco, TX: Word, 1979), pp. 59-63.
2. John Phillips, *Exploring Romans* (Chicago: Moody Press, 1969), p. 19, who quotes Sir H. Rider Haggard, *Pearl Maiden* (London: Longmans, Green and Company, 1901), p. 15.
3. Anders Nygren, *Commentary on Romans* (Philadelphia: Fortress Press, 1978), p. 76.
4. C. E. B. Cranfield, *A Critical and Exegetical Commentary on the Epistle to the Romans*, Volume 1 (Edinburgh: T. & T. Clark Limited, 1975), p. 100 says:

   The sense of the whole sentence may be set out as follows: For in it (i.e. in the Gospel as it is being preached) a righteous status which is God's gift is being revealed (and so offered to men) — a righteous status which is altogether by faith.

   See also Nygren, *Commentary on Romans*, p. 78:

   Faith is both the beginning and the culmination. The manner of expression suggests something like *sola fide*. When the righteousness of God is revealed in the gospel, it is to faith and faith alone.

5. F.W. Boreham, *A Bunch of Everlastings* (New York: Abingdon, 1920), pp. 19, 20.

CHAPTER THREE: *UNDERSTANDING UNBELIEF (I)*

1. Harry Emerson Fosdick, *A Guide to Understanding the Bible* (New York and London: Harper & Bros., 1938), pp. 1-54.
2. Bertrand Russell, *Why I Am Not a Christian* (New York: Simon and Schuster, 1964), p. 17.
3. Henry Wadsworth Longfellow, "The Fiftieth Birthday of Agassiz," *An Oxford Book*

of American Verse, ed. Bliss Carmon (New York: Oxford University Press, 1927), pp. 90, 91.

4. Alan F. Johnson, *The Freedom Letter* (Chicago: Moody Press, 1974), p. 41.

CHAPTER FOUR: *UNDERSTANDING UNBELIEF (II)*

1. Richard C. Halverson, *Prologue to Prison* (Los Angeles: Cowman Publishing Company, 1964), p. 52.
2. Archibald Thomas Robertson, *Word Pictures in the New Testament*, Volume 4 (Nashville: n.p., 1931), p. 331.
3. C. S. Lewis, *Mere Christianity* (New York: Macmillan, 1976), pp. 94, 95.
4. It should be noted here that there is a distinction between homosexual practice and homosexual orientation. Homosexual practice is *sin*. Homosexual orientation is a result of sin, both individual and societal. A homosexual who lives a chaste life, but has not been delivered from his or her orientation must receive the same love and understanding as others working through their besetting sins. Through God's grace many homosexuals have forsaken homosexual practices, and some have been delivered from their orientation. Further information may be found in Don Williams, *The Bond That Breaks: Will Homosexuality Split the Church?* (Los Angeles: BIM, Inc., 1978), pp. 123-132, and Richard Lovelace, *Homosexuality and the Church* (Old Tappan, NJ: Revell, 1978), pp. 117-142.
5. *Time* Magazine, December 13, 1982, Volume 120, Number 24, "And Now Gay Family Rights?," p. 74.
6. *Time* Magazine, August 21, 1972, Volume 100, Number 8, "Teenage Sex: Letting the Pendulum Swing," pp. 34-40.
7. John Leo, *Time* Magazine, August 2, 1982, Volume 120, Number 5, "The New Scarlet Letter (Herpes)", pp. 82-86.
8. C. E. B. Cranfield, *A Critical and Exegetical Commentary on the Epistle to the Romans*, Volume 1 (Edinburgh: T. & T. Clark Limited, 1975), p. 128.
9. Ray C. Stedman, *From Guilt to Glory*, Volume 1 (Waco, TX: Word, 1981), p. 34. Note that the thoughts in this paragraph come from Stedman, though they are not quoted exactly.

CHAPTER FIVE: *GOD'S PERFECT JUDGMENT*

1. William Barclay, *The Letter to the Romans* (Philadelphia: Westminster Press, 1957), p. 35.
2. Ray C. Stedman, *From Guilt to Glory*, Volume 1 (Waco TX: Word, 1981), p. 39.
3. Anders Nygren, *Commentary on Romans* (Philadelphia: Fortress Press, 1978), p. 125.
4. *Christian Life* Magazine, Volume 31 (January 1970), p. 64.

CHAPTER SIX: *THE HEART OF THE MATTER*

1. C. S. Lewis, *The Great Divorce* (New York: Macmillan, 1966), pp. 38, 39.
2. William Barclay, *The Letter to the Romans* (Philadelphia: Westminster Press, 1957), p. 45.
3. Archibald Thomas Robertson, *Word Pictures in the New Testament*, Volume 4 (Nashville: n.p., 1931), p. 339.
4. C. E. B. Cranfield, *A Critical and Exegetical Commentary on the Epistle to the Romans*, Volume 1 (Edinburgh: T. & T. Clark Limited, 1975), p. 170.
5. D. Stuart Briscoe, *Romans*, Volume 6 in the Communicators' Commentary, ed. Lloyd J. Ogilvie (Waco, TX: Word, 1982), pp. 69, 70.

6. Charles Hodge, *Commentary on the Epistle to the Romans* (Grand Rapids, MI: n.p., 1965), p. 63.
7. *Ibid.*
8. Donald Grey Barnhouse, *Man's Ruin, God's Wrath*, Volume 1 (Fincastle, VA: Scripture Truth Book Co., n.d.), pp. 127, 128.

CHAPTER SEVEN: THE RELIGIOUS ADVANTAGE

1. William Barclay, *The Letter to the Romans* (Philadelphia: Westminster Press, 1957), p. 51.
2. Kenneth S. Wuest, *Wuest's Word Studies*, Volume 1 (Grand Rapids, MI: Eerdmans, 1973), p. 55.
3. Will and Ariel Durant, *Lessons from History* (New York: Simon and Schuster, 1968), p. 81.

CHAPTER EIGHT: THE MIRACLE OF RIGHTEOUSNESS

1. Donald Grey Barnhouse, *God's Remedy, God's River*, Volume 2 (Fincastle, VA: Scripture Truth Book Co., n.d.), p. 6.
2. F. F. Bruce, *The Epistle of Paul to the Romans* (London: The Tyndale Press, 1966), pp. 104, 105.
3. Anders Nygren, *Commentary on Romans* (Philadelphia: Fortress Press, 1978), p. 159.
4. C E. B. Canfield, *A Critical and Exegetical Commentary on the Epistle to the Romans*, Volume 1 (Edinburgh: T. & T. Clark Limited, 1975), p. 214, italics mine.

CHAPTER NINE: SOLA FIDE

1. Herbert Danby, *The Mishnah* (London: Oxford University Press, 1974), p. 329.
2. R. H. Charles, *The Apocrypha and Pseudepigrapha of the Old Testament*, Volume 2 (London: Oxford University Press, 1968), p. 48.
3. *Ibid.,*, p. 622.
4. F. F. Bruce, *The Epistle of Paul to the Romans* (London: The Tyndale Press, 1966), p. 114.
5. C. E. B. Cranfield, *A Critical and Exegetical Commentary on the Epistle to the Romans*, Volume 1 (Edinburgh: T. & Clark Limited, 1975), p. 323.
6. A. A. Anderson, *The Book of Psalms*, Volume 1 (Grand Rapids, MI: Eerdmans, 1981), p. 401 writes regarding Psalm 51:

In verse 16 the underlying thought is, so it seems, that the Law simply does not prescribe any atoning sacrifices for such things as murder and adultery, and since these or similar grave offences may have been the cause of the Psalmist's downfall, it is clear that the only alternative was penitence (see verse 17; 2 Sam. 12:13ff.). Even so, the cleansing is not the inevitable end-product of man's contrition, but it depends upon the faithfulness of God. Sacrifice, as a God-given means, functions only within the setting of the Covenant; if the Covenant relationship is broken by man, then also sacrifice and any other cultic means have lost their significance (cf. Eichrodt, TOT, 1, p. 168).

7. Bruce, *The Epistle of Paul to the Romans*, p. 111.
8. Cranfield, p. 235, which references *Seder Olam* R.1 in Strack Billerbeck 3, p. 203.

CHAPTER TEN: THE FAITH OF ABRAHAM

1. Norris and Ross McWhirter, *Guinness Book of World Records* (New York: Sterling, 1971), pp. 10, 11, 23.
2. John Huffman, Jr., *Who's in Charge Here?* (Chappaqua, NY: Christian Herald Books, 1981), p. 63.
3. F. F. Bruce, *The Epistle of Paul to the Romans* (London: The Tyndale Press, 1966), p. 118.
4. Ray C. Stedman, *From Guilt to Glory*, Volume 1 (Waco, TX: Word, 1981), p. 10.
5. Anders Nygren, *Commentary on Romans* (Philadelphia: Fortress Press, 1978), p. 183.

CHAPTER ELEVEN: JUSTIFICATION – EXULTATION

1. Lloyd John Ogilvie, *Drumbeat of Love* (Waco, TX: Word, 1978), pp. 176, 177.
2. Vance Havner, *It Is Toward Evening* (Old Tappan, NJ: Revell, 1968), pp. 39-41.
3. Charles Hodge, *Commentary on the Epistle to the Romans* (Grand Rapids, MI: n.p., 1965), p. 135.
4. Anders Nygren, *Commentary on Romans* (Philadelphia: Fortress Press, 1978), p. 183.
5. C. E. B. Cranfield, *A Critical and Exegetical Commentary on the Epistle to the Romans*, Volume 1 (Edinburgh: T. & T. Clark Limited, 1975), p. 263.
6. *Ibid.*, p. 265.
7. John W. Alexander, ed., *Believing and Obeying Jesus Christ* (Downers Grove, IL: InterVarsity Press, 1980), pp. 106, 107.

CHAPTER TWELVE: GRACE ABOUNDING

1. Anders Nygren, *Commentary on Romans* (Philadelphia: Fortress Press, 1978), p. 207.
2. F. F. Bruce, *The Epistle of Paul to the Romans* (London: The Tyndale Press, 1966), p. 130.
3. Charles M. Coffin, ed., *The Complete Poetry and Selected Prose of John Donne* (New York: Random House, 1952), p. 441, *Devotions Upon Emergent Occasions*, XVII, *Meditation*.
4. Ray C. Stedman, *From Guilt to Glory*, Volume 1 (Waco, TX: Word, 1981), p. 135.
5. Elgin Moyer, *Wycliffe Biographical Dictionary of the Church*, rev. Earle E. Cairns (Chicago: Moody Press, 1982), p. 406.
6. John Phillips, *Exploring Romans* (Chicago: Moody Press, 1969), p. 98 quotes the full text of this Ira Sankey hymn.

CHAPTER THIRTEEN: FREEDOM FROM SIN

1. James Hogg, *Private Memoirs and Confessions of a Justified Sinner* (New York: Grove Press, 1959), p. xiii where Andre Gide in his introduction summarizes the process which made the novelist's main character, Robert Wringham, an "antinomian" — a man who believed a child of God cannot sin and that those things which are sins in the wicked are *not sins in him!*
2. Ray C. Stedman, *From Guilt to Glory*, Volume 1 (Waco, TX: Word, 1981), pp. 152, 153.
3. Frank E. Gaebelein, *The Expositor's Bible Commentary*, Volume 10, *Romans — Galatians* (Grand Rapids, MI: Zondervan, 1976), p. 70.
4. D. Stuart Briscoe, *Romans*, Volume 6 in the Communicators' Commentary, ed. Lloyd J. Ogilvie (Waco, TX: Word, 1982), p. 138.

CHAPTER FOURTEEN: FREEDOM IN SLAVERY

1. F. F. Bruce, *The Epistle of Paul to the Romans* (London: The Tyndale Press, 1966), p. 141.
2. N. G. L. Hammond and H. H. Scullard, eds., *The Oxford Classical Dictionary* (Oxford: Oxford University Press, 1978), p. 995. See also James Hastings, ed., *Dictionary of the Apostolic Church*, Volume 2 (Grand Rapids, MI: Baker, 1973), p. 509.
3. C. E. B. Cranfield, *A Critical and Exegetical Commentary on the Epistle to the Romans*, Volume 1 (Edinburgh: T. & T. Clark Limited, 1975), p. 322, says the fact that *righteousness* "has here its forensic, rather than its moral, sense is clear from the contrast with" *death*.
4. Elisabeth Elliot, "The Glory of God's Will," *World Vision* (April 1977), pp. 12-14. Also available in booklet form, same title (Westchester, IL: Good News Publishers, 1982).
5. Bruce, *The Epistle of Paul to the Romans*, p. 142.
6. Cranfield, *A Critical and Exegetical Commentary on the Epistle to the Romans*, p. 324.
7. *Ibid.*, p. 326.
8. Dietrich Bonhoeffer, *The Cost of Discipleship* (New York: Macmillan, 1977), p. 47.

CHAPTER FIFTEEN: FREEDOM IN CHRIST

1. F. F. Bruce, *The Epistle of Paul to the Romans* (London: The Tyndale Press, 1966), p. 145.
2. John Huffman, Jr., *Who's in Charge Here?* (Chappaqua, NY: Christian Herald Books, 1981), pp. 116, 117.
3. Alan F. Johnson, *The Freedom Letter* (Chicago: Moody Press, 1974), p. 112.
4. Ray C. Stedman, *From Guilt to Glory*, Volume 1 (Waco, TX: Word, 1981), p. 190.
5. Edward Hastings, ed., *The Speakers Bible*, Volume 13 (Grand Rapids, MI: Baker, 1971), p. 105.
6. Colin Brown, ed., *Dictionary of New Testament Theology*, Volume 3 (Grand Rapids, MI: Zondervan, 1971), p. 858.
7. Stedman, *From Guilt to Glory*, p. 195.

CHAPTER SIXTEEN: LIBERATION BY THE SPIRIT

1. F. F. Bruce, *The Epistle of Paul to the Romans* (London: The Tyndale Press, 1966), p. 151.
2. *Ibid.*, p. 159.
3. C. E. B. Cranfield, *A Critical and Exegetical Commentary on the Epistle to the Romans*, Volume 1 (Edinburgh: T. & T. Clark Limited, 1975), p. 382.
4. Bruce, *The Epistle of Paul to the Romans,* p. 162.
5. Wesley H. Hager, *Conquering* (Grand Rapids, MI: Eerdmans, 1965), p. 65.
6. Bruce, *The Epistle of Paul to the Romans*, p. 164.
7. Warren W. Wiersbe, *Be Right, An Expository Study of Romans* (Wheaton, IL: Victor Books, 1977), p. 164.
8. Carlos Baker, *Ernest Hemingway, A Life Story* (New York: Charles Scribner's, Inc., 1969), p. 555.
9. Bruce, *The Epistle of Paul to the Romans*, p. 166.

CHAPTER SEVENTEEN: *THREE GROANS AND ONE GLORY*

1. C. S. Lewis, *The Weight of Glory* (Grand Rapids, MI: Eerdmans, 1965), p.13.
2. *Ibid.*, pp. 1, 2.
3. C. E. B. Cranfield, *A Critical and Exegetical Commentary on the Epistle to the Romans*, Volume 1 (Edinburgh: T. & T. Clark Limited, 1975), p. 410.
4. F. Godet, *Commentary on the Epistle to the Romans*, trans. A. Cusin (Grand Rapids, MI: Zondervan, 1956), p. 314.
5. Ray C. Stedman, *From Guilt to Glory*, Volume 1 (Waco, TX: Word, 1981), p. 241.
6. Alan F. Johnson, *The Freedom Letter* (Chicago: Moody Press, 1974), p. 131.

CHAPTER EIGHTEEN: *SUPER CONQUERORS*

1. James McGraw, *Great Evangelical Preachers of Yesterday* (New York: Abingdon Press, 1961), p. 37.
2. *Ibid.*, p. 35.
3. *Ibid.*, p. 37.
4. F. W. Boreham, *A Casket of Cameos* (New York: Abingdon Press, 1924), p. 92.
5. McGraw, *Great Evangelical Preachers of Yesterday*, p. 35.
6. Boreham, *A Casket of Cameos*, p. 92ff.
7. Anders Nygren, *Commentary on Romans* (Philadelphia: Fortress Press, 1978), pp. 337, 338.
8. W. Robertson Nicoll, ed., *The Expositor's Greek Testament*, Volume 2, James Denney, *St. Paul's Epistle to the Romans* (Grand Rapids, MI: Eerdmans, 1970), p. 652.
9. Logan Pearsall Smith, *Donne's Sermons* (Oxford: The Clarendon Press, 1916, 1968), p. 228.
10. Alan F. Johnson, *The Freedom Letter* (Chicago: Moody Press, 1974), p. 136, who quotes from Henry Hart Milman, *History of Christianity*, Volume 4 (New York: Crowell, 1881), p. 144.
11. Boreham, *A Casket of Cameos*, pp. 96, 97.

CHAPTER NINETEEN: *SOVEREIGN ELECTIONS*

1. Martin Luther, *Commentary on the Epistle to the Romans*, trans. J. Theodore Mueller (Grand Rapids, MI: Kregel, 1976), p. 136.
2. *Ibid.*, p. 139.
3. A. W. Tozer, *The Knowledge of the Holy* (New York: Harper & Row, 1961), p. 6.
4. F. F. Bruce, *The Epistle of Paul to the Romans* (London: The Tyndale Press, 1966), p. 194.
5. Donald Grey Barnhouse, *God's Covenants, God's Discipline, God's Glory*, Volume 4 (Fincastle, VA: Scripture Truth Book Co., n.d.), p. 28.

CHAPTER TWENTY: *GOD'S SOVEREIGNTY – MAN'S RESPONSIBILITY*

1. Ray Stedman, *From Guilt to Glory*, Volume 2 (Waco, TX: Word, 1979), p. 38.
2. C. E. B. Cranfield, *A Critical and Exegetical Commentary on the Epistle to the Romans*, Volume 2 (Edinburgh: T. & T. Clark Limited, 1975), p. 529.

CHAPTER TWENTY-ONE: *ISRAEL'S FUTURE*

1. W. H. Lewis, ed., *Letters of C. S. Lewis* (New York: Harcourt, Brace & World, 1966), p. 58.

2. *Ibid.*, p. 64.
3. *Ibid.*, p. 188.
4. *Ibid.*, p. 265.
5. Richard E. Gade, *A Historical Survey of Anti-Semitism* (Grand Rapids, MI: Baker, 1981), p. 51.
6. *Ibid.*, p. 51.
7. Frank E. Gaebelein, *The Expositor's Bible Commentary*, Volume 10, *Romans — Galatians* (Grand Rapids, MI: Zondervan, 1976), p. 118.
8. Ray C. Stedman, *From Guilt to Glory*, Volume 2 (Waco, TX: Word, 1981), p. 68.
9. Alan F. Johnson, *The Freedom Letter* (Chicago: Moody Press. 1975), p. 165.
10. *Ibid.*, p. 170.
11. Personal correspondence from Susan Perlman, January 25, 1983.

CHAPTER TWENTY-TWO: FROM THEOLOGY TO DOXOLOGY

1. John Albert Bengel, *Bengel's New Testament Commentary*, Volume 2 (Grand Rapids, MI: Kregel, 1981), p. 134.
2. C. S. Lewis, *Miracles* (New York: Macmillan, 1955), p. 108.
3. Charles Swindoll, *Mind Under Matter*, a publication of the First Evangelical Free Church of Fullerton, California.
4. A. W. Tozer, *The Knowledge of the Holy* (New York: Harper & Row, 1961), p. 39.
5. C. S. Lewis, *Surprised by Joy* (New York: Harcourt, Brace & World, n.d.), p. 227.
6. C. H. Spurgeon, *Metropolitan Tabernacle Pulpit*, Volume 10 (Pasadena, TX: Pilgrim Publications, 1973), p. 306.

CHAPTER TWENTY-THREE: ELEMENTS OF COMMITMENT

1. C. E. B. Cranfield, *A Critical and Exegetical Commentary on the Epistle to the Romans*, Volume 2 (Edinburgh: T. & T. Clark, 1979), pp. 603-605.
2. *Ibid.*, p. 605.
3. Alan F. Johnson, *The Freedom Letter* (Chicago: Moody Press, 1974), p. 196.
4. Harry Blamires, *The Christian Mind* (Ann Arbor, MI: Servant Books, 1978), p. 94.
5. Alexander Maclaren, *Expositions of Holy Scripture*, Volume 12, *Romans* (Grand Rapids, MI: Baker, 1974), p. 239.

CHAPTER TWENTY-FOUR: RENEWED THINKING

1. C. E. B. Cranfield, *A Critical and Exegetical Commentary on the Epistle to the Romans,* Volume 2 (Edinburgh: T. & T. Clark Limited, 1979), p. 615.
2. *Ibid.*, p. 616.
3. F. F. Bruce, *The Epistle of Paul to the Romans* (London: The Tyndale Press, 1966), p. 227.
4. Donald Grey Barnhouse, *God's Covenants, God's Discipline, God's Glory*, Volume 4 (Fincastle, VA: Scripture Truth Book Co., n.d.), p. 49.

CHAPTER TWENTY-FIVE: LOVE IN ACTION

1. J. Dwight Pentecost, *The Joy of Living* (Grand Rapids, MI: Zondervan, 1973), p. 55.
2. C. E. B. Cranfield, *A Critical and Exegetical Commentary on the Epistle to the Romans*, Volume 2 (Edinburgh: T. & T. Clark Limited, 1979), p. 640.
3. Charles R. Swindoll, *Think It Over . . . Indifference*, a publication of the First Evangelical Free Church of Fullerton, California.

4. James Hastings, ed., *The Speakers Bible*, Volume 13 (Grand Rapids, MI: Baker, 1971), p. 42.
5. Donald Grey Barnhouse, *God's Covenants, God's Discipline, God's Glory*, Volume 4 (Fincastle, VA: Scripture Truth Book Company, n.d.), p. 54.

CHAPTER TWENTY-SIX: HEAVEN'S CITIZENS AND HUMAN GOVERNMENT

1. Tacitus, *Life of Claudius*, Tacitus 25:2.
2. Richard Halvorsen, *Prologue to Prison* (Los Angeles: Cowman Publishers, 1964), p. 223.
3. Michael Bourdeaux, *The Evidence That Convicted Aida Skripnikova* (Elgin, IL: David C. Cook, 1973), pp. 34-43.
4. Donald Grey Barnhouse, *God's Covenants, God's Discipline, God's Glory*, Volume 4, (Fincastle, VA: Scripture Truth Book Co., n.d.), p. 114.
5. Col. Alan Shine, *Command* (Spring 1980), pp. 9, 10.
6. C. E. B. Cranfield, *A Critical and Exegetical Commentary on the Epistle to the Romans*, Volume 2, (Edinburgh: T. & T. Clark Limited, 1970), p. 648.
7. *Ibid.*, p. 668 where the writer says:

   Syneidesis is responsible awareness that the ultimate foundations both of one's own being and also of the state are in God. Members of the community are to have neither a higher nor lower estimation of the state than as a specific servant of God.

8. Ray C. Stedman, *From Guilt to Glory*, Volume 2 (Waco, TX: Word, 1979), pp. 126, 127.
9. William Barclay, *The Letter to the Romans* (Philadelphia: Westminster Press, 1957), pp. 186, 187.
10. *Ibid.*, p. 186.
11. *Ibid.*
12. Kirsopp Lake, trans., *The Apostolic Fathers*, Volume 1 in the Loeb Classical Library, *I Clement*, LXI:1, 2 (Cambridge, MA: Harvard University Press, 1970), pp. 114-117.
13. Dietmar Schmidt, *Pastor Niemoller*, trans. Lawrence Wilson (London: Odhams Press Limited, 1959), pp. 106,107 records that

   The flagrant injustice remained, fanning his impatience until one day when the prison chaplain came to see him, he finally boiled over. "But Brother! What brings you here?" "Why are you in prison?" asked the chaplain somewhat foolishly. To which Niemoller replied angrily: "And Brother, why are you not in prison?"

CHAPTER TWENTY-SEVEN: LOVING ON THE LEVEL

1. Alexander Maclaren, *Expositions of Holy Scripture*, Volume 10 (Grand Rapids, MI: Baker, 1974), pp. 227, 228.
2. *Ibid.*, p. 228.
3. C. E. B. Cranfield, *A Critical and Exegetical Commentary on the Epistle to the Romans*, Volume 2 (Edinburgh: T. & T. Clark Limited, 1979), p. 674.
4. Ray C. Stedman, *From Guilt to Glory*, Volume 2 (Waco, TX: Word, 1978), p. 136.
5. *Daily Bread*, n.d.

CHAPTER TWENTY-EIGHT: UNITY AND DIVERSITY (I)

1. C. E. B. Cranfield, *A Critical and Exegetical Commentary on the Epistle to the Romans*, Volume 2 (Edinburgh: T. & T. Clark Limited, 1979), pp. 696, 697.
2. Leslie Flynn, *Great Church Fights* (Wheaton, IL: Victor Books, 1976), p. 46.
3. A. T. Robertson, *Word Pictures in the New Testament*, Volume 4 (Nashville: Broadman Press, 1931), p. 412.

4. Fritz Ridenour, *How to be a Christian Without Being Religious* (Glendale, CA: Regal Books, 1967), p. 122, who quotes Judi Culbertson and Patti Bard, *Games Christians Play* (New York: Harper and Row, 1967).
5. Warren Wiersbe, *Be Right, An Expository Study of Romans* (Wheaton, IL: Victor Books, 1977), p. 156.
6. Samuel Macauley Jackson, ed., *The New Schaff-Herzog Encyclopedia of Religious Knowledge*, Volume 7 (Grand Rapids, MI: Baker, 1977), p. 287, *"In necessariis unitas, in non necessariis libertas, in utrisque* (or, *in omnibus) caritas."*

CHAPTER TWENTY-NINE: *UNITY AND DIVERSITY (II)*

1. F. F. Bruce, *The Epistle of Paul to the Romans* (London: The Tyndale Press, 1966), p. 246.
2. Donald Grey Barnhouse, *God's Covenants, God's Discipline, God's Glory*, Volume 4 (Fincastle, VA: Scripture Truth Book Co., n.d.), p. 4.
3. John Phillips, *Exploring Romans* (Chicago, IL: Moody Press, 1969), pp. 242, 243.
4. C. E. B. Cranfield, *A Critical and Exegetical Commentary on the Epistle to the Romans*, Volume 2 (Edinburgh: T. & T. Clark Limited, 1979), p. 712.

CHAPTER THIRTY: *CHRIST OUR EXAMPLE*

1. Oscar Cullmann, *Peter, Disciple-Apostle-Martyr* (London: SCM Press Ltd., 1953), pp. 106, 107.
2. F. F. Bruce, *The Epistle of Paul to the Romans* (London: The Tyndale Press, 1966), p. 254.

CHAPTER THIRTY-ONE: *PAUL'S MISSIONARY HEART (I)*

1. John McCook Roots, *Chou: An Informal Biography of China's Legendary Chou En-Lai* (New York:Doubleday, 1978), p. 34.
2. James Hastings, *The Speakers Bible*, Volume 13 (Grand Rapids, MI: Baker, 1971), p. 143.
3. William Barclay, *The Letter to the Romans* (Philadelphia: Westminster Press, 1957), p. 223.
4. Phrase attributed to John Masefield.

CHAPTER THIRTY-TWO: *PAUL'S MISSIONARY HEART (II)*

1. John Albert Bengel, *Bengel's New Testament Commentary*, Volume 2 (Grand Rapids, MI: Kregel, 1981), p. 161.
2. William Barclay, *The Letter to the Romans* (Philadelphia: Westminster Press, 1957), p.235.
3. Charles Reich, *The Greening of America* (New York: Random House, 1970), pp. 8, 9, 182.

CHAPTER THIRTY-THREE: *THE END IS PRAISE*

1. F. F. Bruce, *The Epistle of Paul to the Romans* (London: The Tyndale Press, 1966), p. 9.
2. W. E. Vine, *Expository Dictionary of New Testament Words* (Old Tappan, NJ: Revell, 1966), p. 41.
3. I. M. Anderson, "When Sankey Sang the Shepherd Song," *Moody Monthly* (February 1986), pp. 77, 78.
4. Donald Grey Barnhouse, *God's Covenants, God's Discipline, God's Glory*, Volume 4 (Fincastle, VA: Scripture Truth Book Co., n. d.), p. 180.
5. Logan Pearsall Smith, *Donne's Sermons* (Oxford: The Clarendon Press, 1916, 1968), p. 228.

Scripture Index

* Not all specific verse references from Romans are included in this index. For example, 1:3 is covered under the subhead citing 1:2-4 in the portion of this book which discusses those verses, as well being specifically cited when referred to individually elsewhere in this book.

General Index

Index of Sermon Illustrations

Origen: love is a debt we must pay and yet
always owe, 250

Sing Sing prison warden's wife was so loved
that the prisoners were let out, uncounted, to
visit her wake, and all returned!, 255

Ancient critic: "Promiscuously they call one
another brother and sister, etc., 255

Blake's poem which begins, "Love seeketh not
itself to please," 281

Paul's heart was like the "tracking board" of
the New York Yacht Club, 296

The love of God
H. Taylor gave his life to the Chinese, not
because he loved the Chinese, but because
he loved God, 26

Mistake
Guinness Book states that the oldest woman to
give birth was fifty-seven; wrong!, 97

Mortality
C. Baker's description of E. Hemingway the
year before he died, 153

Motivation
Snoopy: "I want people to have more to say
about me than . . . he chased sticks," 24
H. Taylor gave his life to the Chinese, not
because he loved the Chinese, but because
he loved God, 26

Obedience
Freedom which comes from obedience demonstrated in the liberating obedience of a shepherd collie, 131

Bonhoeffer's quotation regarding "cheap
grace," 133

Family dog which never enjoys freedom of
being unleashed, because he always runs
away, 133, 134

Chesterton: "Obedience is but the other side of
the creative will," 135

Omnipotence
Dr. R. D. Wilson's question, "Are we 'little-
godders' or 'big-godders'?," 99

God's miraculous protection of Ira Sankey
from a sniper, 307

God's miraculous protection of missionaries
from arrows by a great gust of wind, 307,
308

Omniscience
Since God created everything, the first idea
had to come from him, 205, 206

Passion
W. Booth: "Some people's passion is money
. . . but my passion has been men," 25

Positiveness
Second grader's essay, "My Face," which concludes, "I like my face," 16

John Stott: we should be the most positive people in the world, 111

Potential
Aquinas: Man is positioned somewhere
between the angels above and the beasts
below, and can move upward or downward,
48

Power
Conversion of Mel Trotter, who had just stolen
the shoes from his daughter's corpse, 118

Power of the gospel
Radical conversion of Joseph S. Olzewski S.K.
2/c U.S.C. through the witness of Allan
Emery, 23

Prayer
Tertullian's prayer for government, 245
Clement of Alexandria's prayer for govern-
ment, 246

Presumption
C. S. Lewis's fanciful conversation between a
resident of Hell (who does not know he is
there) and an old friend visiting from
Heaven, 61, 62

Little boy: "I'm drawing God"; teacher: "But
no one knows what he looks like"; boy:
"They will when I'm through," 312

Pride
W. Whitman: "I find no sweeter fat than sticks
to my own bones," 220

Pride seen in the self-deprecation of Uriah
Heeps, 220

Little leaguer who took credit for a "home run"
which, in reality, occurred because nobody
could field on the opposing team, 289

Protection
God's miraculous protection of Ira Sankey
from a sniper, 307

God's miraculous protection of missionaries
from arrows by a great gust of wind, 307,
308

Reason
Faith without reason is fideism; reason without
faith is rationalism, 101

Reductionism
Einstein: "We should make things simple, but
not simpler than they are," 113

Responsibility
W. Rogers on the two eras in American history: the passing of the buffalo and the passing of the buck, 184

About the Book Jacket

Ths design of the book jacket brings together the talents of several Christian artists. The design centers around the beautiful banner created by artist Marge Gieser. The banner is more than eight feet tall and was displayed in College Church throughout Pastor Hughes' series of semons on Romans. It is photographed here on the jacket at about one twentieth of its original size

Concerning the sybolism used in the banner for Romans Marge Gieser writes:

> Emerging from the Reformation of the sixteenth century are three slogans which summarize the return to the essentials of Christianity as set forth so eloquently by Paul in the Epistle to the Romans. *Sola scriptura* — by Scripture alone — affirms that only the Bible is the final authority for faith and life. *Sola gratia* — by grace alone — affirms that God's salvation comes as his free gift, not by human merit. *Sola fide* — by faith alone—affirms that God's gift is received by humans by faith and not by works. The design at the top of the banner was John Calvin's personal seal.

Other artists contributing their talents to the creation of the jacket include: Bill Koechling, photography, and Mark Schramm, overall design and art direction.